Peter Biddlecombe is a b over the world. His first described his travels (agai as his companion) through French-speaking Africa, and was popularly and critically acclaimed.

PETER BIDDLECOMBE

Travels with my Briefcase
Around the World – on Expenses

LITTLE, BROWN AND COMPANY
Boston New York Toronto London

ISBN 0–316–07664–3

10 9 8 7 6 5 4 3 2 1

Printed in England

Contents

Introduction

Travel for the sake of travel is the ultimate extravagance: it ruins the environment, destroys our heritage and consumes valuable resources.

Most travel writing is the ultimate prostitution. I'll go anywhere; I'll go with anyone; I'll do anything, so long as I get paid for it. There is no purpose, no objective.

The only true traveller is the business traveller. Like Marco Polo, he travels with a purpose. He is not destroying the environment; he is often protecting and improving it. He is not observing a country; he is immediately part of it. More important, his experiences are authentic.

Most travel writing is bogus, unreal and superficial. It is bogus because it pretends adventure which, as Amundsen said, is simply bad organisation. Wandering around the Hindu Kush is nothing to fighting your way around the Tokyo underground in the rush hour. Rafting down the Brahma Putra is a piece of cake compared with trying to sign a deal with a government minister on his knees in the middle of a mosque during Tabaski. Even shuffling along the Silk Road is nothing to the thrill of trying to make a telephone call to the office from a brand new hotel in Abuja, the brand new capital of Nigeria, at 2 o'clock in the afternoon when the electricity has been cut, all the 'phones have been stolen before they've even been installed and there are 253 other people in front of you waiting to use the only radio link the city has with the outside world.

Travel writing is unreal. How many people do you know who can travel the world waving at customs officers heavy parchment letters of introduction from the Fellows of Trinity College, Cambridge, expressing in advance 'gratitude for whatever assistance you may be able to afford'; paddle a kayak around the Pacific moaning about their wife and catching VD off hotel blankets, let alone hang around the Waibaidyu Bridge in Shanghai waiting for the barges to pass below?

And it's superficial. Who wants to know about Indian beggars defecating at the side of the road, the condition of the Gleam newspaper in the public library in Marshall County, or the joys of having long leisurely breakfasts on hotel balconies studying open drains?

Before visiting a country some travel writers boast that they learn the language, read a book a day about it for a whole month and then when they get there head for the nearest campsite because there, they believe, is where they will discover the truth.

Business travellers have no such luck. They hit the ground staggering. But immediately they hit the ground, they are part of the history and culture of the country. As soon as he arrives, the business traveller is absorbing and mastering the customs of the country, because if he doesn't he won't do any business. He also has to learn how to survive riots, curfews, coup attempts and management reshuffles back home.

For those who think business travel is a freebie trough for travel junkies, this book is proof of the long hours wasted at airports and railway stations, the boring meetings we have to attend and the occasional glimpses we catch of a country as the taxi chugs its weary way from dreary hotel to lousy restaurant. For everybody else, I hope it is proof that horse-herding on the steppes of Asia, strolling across the Empty

Quarter of the Arabian desert or pushing a wheelbarrow across the Sahara, broadens the muscles but narrows the mind. The only true travellers today are business travellers.

Peter Biddlecombe
Departure Lounge
Gatwick Airport

Brussels

'Have you heard the one about the Belgian?'
'You'd better be careful. I'm a Belgian.'
'Okay. I'll tell it twice.'

'Bloody Eurocrats. Got it all bloody wrong again. If we have to implement this we might as well all pack up now and go bloody home.'

I was in London. We'd just finished an heroic three-course lunch at Simpson's washed down by three bottles of claret and a bottle of port which would have made Jorrocks himself give up a day's hunting – well, almost. We had talked about nothing but his plans to ditch his wife and run off with the managing director's new secretary, who I thought looked like a clergyman in drag. I hadn't fancied the port, but he had insisted. On the basis that you should always feed the hand that bites you, I agreed.

Now we were back in his office. He riffled through a pile of papers on his desk and threw me a page torn out of the *Evening Standard*.

'Can't you do something about that?' he gasped.

'My eyes were beginning to develop separate heartbeats of their own and my head felt like the end of another six-day debate on the Maastricht Treaty. But I could make out the drift.

It was a run-of-the-mill Euro-scare story. A proposal. A possible directive. The promise of extensive consultation. The need to reach an agreed Euro-solution. But he made every mini-drama into a maxi-crisis so that he could run around panicking.

'Chairman will be hopping mad unless he gets some action.'

I explained the Brussels approach. The Commission was not the *monstre sacré* everybody imagined. They were interested only in a purely European view. They wanted to establish agreed Euro-standards; the level Euro-playing field. They wanted to carry as many people with them as possible. There was already an extensive network of consultation on every subject under *le soleil* stretching out from the Commission to Euro-trade and -industry associations, even down to your local branch of Toc H.

'That's all very well,' he slurped into his chair. 'But the chairman wants some action. He wants to feel we're talking to the key people.'

The best approach, I said, was the most straightforward. We should first check the facts, see if what was in the *Standard* was true or not. If it was, find the directorate and division responsible, then put together a paper on the subject using all the correct Euro-terms such as credit institutions instead of banks, quantitative restrictions instead of quotas, derogations instead of exceptions, compartmentalisation instead of sectors, and sprinkle the whole thing with subsidiarity this and subsidiarity that and send it in to them. They studied everything, analysed, researched everything in order to develop the best policy.

'Not good enough,' he blustered around his office like an overweight pigeon. 'All that paper. What we want is action. Go and talk to the people. Tell them direct what we think. Get them to change their minds. Fix it.'

He slumped into his chair again. His head and shoulders

slipped gently forward onto the desk and rested softly in the middle of the pile he had labelled 'Action this day'. The Jeffrey Barnard of the executive floor was fast asleep. I crept quietly out of his office.

An Englishman and a Belgian jump off a bridge together. Who hits the ground first?

The Englishman. The Belgian had to stop for directions.

Brussels is obviously the hotbed of lobbying in Europe. It sprouts with lobbyists of every type, size and plumage you can imagine: ex-army colonels; old-fashioned PR consultants; works managers whose turn it is, after twenty-three years of dedicated waiting, to be chairman of their trade association; and debs straight out of *Vile Bodies*, filling in time having some super fun at mummy's suggestion before making their debut on page one of *Country Life*.

'I say, who do you represent?' a typical *Vile Body* asked me one morning as I drifted into DG VIII on the rue de Geneva. I mumbled something vaguely African.

'Sounds frightfully exciting,' she gushed. 'Do tell me, what do they do?'

'It's the association for African white slave traders,' I whispered.

'Oh really,' she whispered. 'How awfully exciting.'

You see them all marching through Zaventem airport as if they had come to bury the Commission not persuade it; filling in time munching, appropriately enough, giant waffles and wandering aimlessly around the Grande Place, which after a million visits I still feel is one of the nicest squares in the world; or sitting in expensive restaurants playing with their *pâté de poisson tiède à la Guillaume Tirel* and watching the Margaux '49 boil over, waiting for Commissioners who are never going to arrive because, like Leon Brittan, they are sitting round the corner in tiny bistros by themselves reading *The Times*.

Talk to them in the Hotel Amigo while they're agonising over which type of kir to risk drinking, or when they are waiting to be served in the Comme Chez Soi, where I was told a glass of Courvoisier costs over £60, and they will tell you what a hard life they have; what a struggle it is finding the right man to talk to; how impossible it is to make anyone understand what they are saying; how much more time they are going to have to spend traipsing backwards and forwards to this godforsaken city.

'The Duke of Wellington was right, y'know,' an old colonel who was chairman of a nondescript trade association told me over drinks in the wonderful *fin-de-siècle* Hotel Metropole. 'They've ruined his battlefield.'

Don't listen to them. Lobbying in Brussels is the most straightforward, efficient system anyone could possibly imagine. Because the Commission wants to be lobbied. It wants to hear as many views and opinions as it can. Lobbying here is far more direct than in Westminster or Whitehall.

In London, the old boy network still reigns supreme. I was once involved with a group of companies when we were all given forty-eight hours by the government to come up with a solution to a highly complex and technical financial problem. We gathered at the trade association's offices for a council of war. The director general asked their legal adviser to speak first.

'Not to worry, old boy,' he grunted. 'Know the Permanent Secretary very well. Eton. Guards. That kind of thing. I'll pop up to Kings. Have dinner with him. Do it some time next week. Sort it all out.'

'Next week,' the DG spluttered. 'We've got to come up with a solution in two days.'

'Pheasant won't be marinated by then,' said the legal adviser.

In Brussels it's much easier to establish contact and find your way around than in, certainly, Paris or even The Hague. In Paris I once spent days trying to find the official in the ministry of finance responsible for African development. In The Hague it took dozens of calls before I found the right man in the ministry of economic affairs to discuss an offset agreement on behalf of a British electronics company which had just won a big order from the Dutch Air Force. Under Dutch law any foreign company which lands a major contract has to find a Dutch company as a partner and split the work with them. But my telephone calls were not in vain.

'Just ask the Air Force to split the contract in two. That way you come under the limit. They do it all the time. But you've got to ask them. It's against the law if they suggest it,' I was told.

Brussels is also far, far easier than Washington, where the law is such that nobody nowadays dare pick up the 'phone to talk to anybody about anything unless they first declare all their possible interests and register themselves and their whole family including the dog. Then nobody dare answer the 'phone in case the guy calling has not registered himself, his family and his dog. Even then there is the risk that thirty years down the road they're going to find themselves blown up all over the press as an accomplice in some banking or stock exchange scandal. So nobody answers the 'phone if they can avoid it.

It's gone so far now that on one visit to the State Department, the desk officer I was meeting in the African section kept insisting he pay for his own cups of instant coffee from the machine, even though it meant he spent most of the meeting looking for change.

In parts of Africa, of course, it's different again. Years ago I saw French businessmen and officials turning up for meetings with ministers carrying all kinds of briefcases and plastic bags. Though why they should think a plastic bag would influence anyone I don't know. In recent years, as more people have learnt to count carrier bags, they have become a little more subtle. So many times I've known African government officials invited to France for meetings, visits to factories, banquets at Le Crillon with all its marble, gilt, silver and crystal. And so many times I've known them to have their cars stolen, their luggage taken or their pockets picked. To avoid diplomatic incidents that would embarrass both sides, the French promptly pay for the loss out of their insurance, plus a little extra for the inconvenience. Everybody's happy; the French, the insurance companies and the Africans – doubly so, as they can then say how going to Paris is so dangerous because something is always stolen or damaged, but if they have to go, they will, for the sake of their country.

Brussels is a million times easier, providing you know how. Like getting a taxi at the airport. Everybody queues at Arrivals. Real professionals go upstairs to Departures and get a taxi there. Brussels is not Heathrow; in Brussels there are no rules forbidding taxis from collecting passengers at Departures. And there are no queues. Alternatively I hang around the end of the queue downstairs for a Moroccan driver. They're always prepared to break the rules and do deals. Trouble is you've got to know where you're going and how much the fare should be.

One so-called professional lobbyist told me he was writing to his European Member of Parliament to complain. He had given a Moroccan taxi driver the address of one of the Commission's out-buildings, 'all written out neatly on the back of my business card,' he said. The driver took him to the first nondescript office block on the boulevard de Woluwe, about ten minutes from the airport. He handed over the full fare, plus a generous tip, he said, of BF50. As soon as he got inside the building he realised he'd been taken for a ride. 'Can't trust the Belgians,' he kept saying. 'You just can't trust them.'

In Brussels if I want to talk to anybody I get on the 'phone. I speak to the main Commission switchboard and get put through to the correct directorate general. Within seconds I am speaking to the director general. He says he is interested in our views. He promises to send me the relevant 'draft decision concerning the establishment at Community level of a policy and a plan of priority actions'. Within two days it arrives. Who needs professional lobbyists?

How do you make a Belgian laugh at the weekend?
Tell him a joke on Thursday.

Pace the Euro-sceptics, I'm convinced one of the major reasons for the success of the EC is that it is based in Brussels. Because in Brussels there are no distractions. Every night is like Monday night anywhere in the world. Everybody gets on with their job; making waffles, boiling up another bucket of *moules*, frying another three tons of *pommes frites*, brewing another 10,000 litres of Trappiste, or just running Europe. It is the only city in the world where I've spent an evening in the hotel reading a book of essays on Belgian stamps 1840–1914. And enjoying it.

I mean, can you imagine the mess the EC would be in if the Commission was based in Paris, with all those distractions? Or in Venice? Or even in Madrid?

But why Brussels is so successful I cannot make up my mind. Somebody – not a lobbyist – once told me it was because the Belgians have the moral courage of the French, the fighting spirit of the Italians, the work ethic of the British and the sense of humour of the Germans. Maybe it's because of their dynamism, their single-mindedness, their drive and determination to succeed. But somehow I don't feel it is.

To me, Brussels sometimes has that certain East European feel about it. All those cobblestones which stop anyone from rushing around. The drab buildings. The trains. The railway stations. Sabena – you know what it stands for? Such A Bloody Experience Never Again – the sandwiches they serve at the airport. The uniforms. Even the ferry from Ostend boasts 'Any luxury items; tee-shirts'. Admittedly the Brussels *vie urbaine* is dedicated to munching chocolates and devouring cholesterol-rich cakes and cream with weak filtered coffee. But why do they queue outside on the cold street to buy the cakes which are inside in the warm?

'We're not really interested in politics,' a Belgian ambassa-dor once told me. 'We're only interested in doing a job. And doing it the best we can while we're at work. After that we forget work. Not like the Germans or the Dutch. But at least we do the job. The French. They are crazy.' He waved his hands helplessly. 'They'll shout and scream and take to the streets for any reason. Politics. They're crazy. The Belgians – add one franc to the housing tax, they'll go mad. But politics? They're not interested.' Maybe that's why they have suc-ceeded. Because they are not interested – in business; in trade; in politics; in success – in anything, really.

Son Excellence then told me that the late I'll-abdicate-for-a-day-if-I-want-to King Baudouin once visited a major trade exhibition in Brussels. He strolled up to a Belgian who was running a stand for a big French company and started asking him about the company, its products, how they were tackling the European market. The Belgian explained everything to the King, who thanked him and went away happy. The French president director general of the company then went *ananas complètement*. He fired the Belgian because he had not introduced the King to him. It was a serious misdemeanour, he said, an affront to *la gloire de la France*. The ambassador waved his hands in the air *encore*.

It caused a dull little Belgian uproar. The Belgian went to an industrial tribunal, which ruled in his favour. It was not for Belgians to introduce their King to anyone, they said. It was for the King to decide whom he spoke to, nobody else. They gave him his job back, damages and back-pay.

Belgians always seem to me slightly dull, slightly drab. Belgian offices are the only offices I've been in anywhere where all the working wives and mothers actually look like working wives and mothers. Can you imagine a rip-roaring night out on the town with a bunch of Belgians? Even on Friday night when all the French have flooded back to Paris for their instructions for the following week. No way. I've had more laughs being measured up by my undertaker.

The French, if you can add *deux* and *deux* together, you can easily wind up. Not the Belgians. Ask a group of Belgians if there have been any famous Belgians since Carausis, Emperor of Britain 287–293AD, and they'll shrug their shoulders. Ask a group of French the same sort of question and they'll tear the place apart in front of *vos yeux*.

In fact, don't tell anyone, but I always feel guilty teasing the Belgians. 'No, there really have been some famous Belgians,' I insist on telling them. 'I was only joking.' They just look at me. 'Simenon, Magritte, Jacques Brel, Monsieur Gramme, Monsieur Mercato . . .'

But they're not interested. They're concerned about Bruges football club; how much interest they are getting on their illegal bank accounts in Luxembourg; whether arm wrestling will ever become a national sport and where to buy the cheapest Damart underwear. Maybe that's why everyone tells jokes about Belgians.

If the Belgians are dull, Brussels is undeniably an accurate reflection of their personality. The Royal Windsor, the Hotel du Lac, the Amigo – they are all great hotels. For Brussels. Yet I somehow feel they should be grander, more spectacular. Similarly the restaurants. People always say that Brussels has a gastronomic reputation to rival Paris. I can't see it. All I know is that Brussels prices rival Paris, if not beat them into the ground.

I've never been able to get away from even a fairly good

Brussels restaurant where they say 'Une excellente appetite' instead of 'Have a good taste' without paying around £100 per head for an ordinary three-course expense-account meal, including, of course, champagne beforehand, two decent bottles of first growth clarets and a couple of large cognacs afterwards. The prices at the really good restaurants I still daren't think about. But the service, the ambience, the sheer *joie de vivre* is nothing like Paris.

In spite of that, the one hotel I've stayed in longer than any other is the big, impersonal, slightly run-down Sheraton in Brussels. I once stayed there day and night for two weeks.

Years ago there was a big printing strike in the UK. All the City printers were brought to a standstill. Suddenly the flood of prospectuses, offer documents, annual and interim reports that comes pouring out of the City every day came to a stop. Suddenly it seemed that bankers, brokers, accountants would have even more time for lunches and dinners.

This was in the days when very few people had contacts in Europe, and printers none at all. At the time I was working with a number of Dutch printers. As soon as I heard the strike was going ahead I contacted them and we decided to take the City into Europe or, at least, as much of its printing as we could get our hands on. I quickly offered all the big City printers printing facilities in Holland and Belgium. Immediately they agreed. By six o'clock on the first day of the strike I'd taken over a suite in the Brussels Sheraton and turned it into a production centre. Text, proofs and even films we were switching out of City printers into Brussels. Dutch and Belgian printers were working around the clock producing everything from two-page interim statements to complicated 120-page offer documents. The hotel assigned us our own staff who kept us supplied day and night with coffee, cognac and whatever else.

We also started handling annual reports. If you've never been involved in producing an annual report for a small private company, let alone a four-language edition for a multinational, you've never lived. An annual report is a guaranteed shortcut to ulcers. Accountants, lawyers, auditors, the company secretary, the finance director, the chairman's wife, the tea lady – everybody gets involved in producing an annual report. Everybody has an opinion, nobody is prepared to take a decision. The text is always too long or too short. If it's the right length, everybody thinks it should be rewritten. The photographs are either the wrong colour, or out of focus, or feature a junior office manager's assistant who is thinking of leaving and whom we don't want to include because it will upset old Harry in maintenance who has been with us for thirty-three years and decided to stay on for another three weeks.

At first, all the British companies were adamant that their annual reports couldn't possibly be produced as far away as Brussels. Out of the question. They don't even speak English – how can they print it? Then, of course, they began to realise that not printing in faraway Holland or Belgium meant postponing the annual meeting; postponing the annual meeting meant not getting shareholders' approval for new loans; not getting new loans meant problems with the banks, more negotiations, higher rates . . .

'Look, you've got us over a barrel,' the finance director of a big pharmaceutical company told me as I was trying to tell him how we could solve his problems. 'I'll agree on one condition.'

'Sure,' I said.

'That I don't let the copy out of my sight.'

Within two days we were occupying I can't remember how many floors in the Sheraton. Finance directors and company secretaries and, I'm certain, one or two secretaries as well had moved in with their scribbled backs of envelopes, memos from managing directors and rewrites of previous reports. We somehow turned everything into beautiful, glossy annual reports. Were they pleased? Not on your life.

'Now, you will make certain there's nothing in the report to show it was printed in wherever,' they all kept stressing.

'The chairman says he will only agree if you give him a categoric assurance that it will look exactly the same as last year's,' said the head of communications of one of the oil majors.

'It must be strictly understood that next year it will be printed by our usual printer,' said the company secretary of an enormous paper and packaging group.

I even got a call one morning at about three o'clock, while we were still proof-reading the German version of an oil company report, from the company secretary of a paper-making group. 'The senior partner of our auditors has just called our chairman, who has just called me. They want to know that the paper you are using is also available in Britain.'

'Sure,' I said. 'We all buy it from the same paper merchant.'

'In London?'

'No. In Brussels.'

Back I went to my German proof-reading. Ten minutes later the 'phone rang again. 'The senior partner has just called the chairman again, and the chairman—'

'*Jawohl.*'

'They want a categoric assurance that the typeface you are using is also available in—'

'Of course it is.'

'It's British?'

'It's European.'

'But you can't,' he screamed. 'It's impossible. I demand that you ... I shall call my chairman ... Even at this late stage ...' he shrieked.

'The typeface,' I interrupted, 'is a European typeface. It's used extensively in Britain. It's exactly the same as the one you used last—'

'Just checking,' he calmed down. 'You know how crazy other people get about their annual report.'

At the end of two weeks of hectic, crazy, non-stop panic the Belgian printers wanted to take me out to celebrate. Where did we go? To a fabulous restaurant? We went to Le Cercueil in the rue des Harengs just off la Grande Place, which is a funeral parlour turned into a bar. There we spent the night drinking glasses of Heineken on coffins instead of tables and listening to Bach's Requiem on the muzak. It could only happen in swinging Brussels.

> Belgian businessman: 'I can't find my pen.'
> Secretary: 'It's behind your ear.'
> 'Which one?'

Now, for the last time.

Flanders is the northern half. They speak Flemish. Flemish is like Dutch. But isn't Dutch, although many people think it is.

I know a Belgian who became a US citizen and, because of his languages, applied for a job at the State Department in Washington. When he was selected he was told he had to have five languages.

'Sure,' he told them. 'English, German, French, Dutch and Flemish.'

They accepted him. After a few years, he told me, he got a call from personnel. They said they had just realised Dutch and Flemish were the same. He didn't want to argue so he told them, 'I made a mistake. Instead of Flemish I should have said Afrikaans.' They accepted what he said.

Apart from making good excuses the Flemish are a northern, hardworking people like the Dutch and the Germans.

Wallonia is the southern half. They are called Walloons and speak French. Which is French French, unlike Flemish Dutch. The Walloons are southerners, relaxed, carefree, like the Spanish and Italians and, of course, the French French in the South of France.

Brussels is the centre. It is neither Flemish nor Walloon. It is neutral and indifferent. It belongs to Europe. But it speaks French. Apart from everybody else who speaks English, German, Dutch, Spanish, Portuguese, Danish, Greek, Turkish – and Flemish.

The Christian Democrats are Flemish. They believe in supporting everything Flemish. They sometimes speak French to the Walloons. And sometimes they don't, especially near election times. After elections they speak to everyone in a desperate effort to form a coalition government. The last one took 104 days of talking before it was formed.

The Socialists are Walloons and speak French. They've controlled Antwerp since Karl Marx was a little boy. They believe in supporting everything French. They never ever speak anything but French.

In between are other smaller parties like a Flemish right-wing party which believes in supporting everything Flemish, wants independence for Flanders and sometimes speaks French, and a liberal Walloon or French-speaking party which, in fact, is the least liberal and most extreme party in the country, calling for anti-immigration policies ('*stop à l'invasion*').

In Ostend, once 'one of the most fashionable and cosmopolitan watering places in Europe', the Flemish complain about having to subsidise the Walloons. In Zeebrugge, which is a little more exciting, but not much, they complain that their hard-earned taxes go on paying the dole for the Walloons. Nearby is Knockke, which on a sunny day is like Hove or Eastbourne – tidy, clean, packed with the middle-aged and middle-class wondering how much money they dare risk in the casino that evening, they complain about having to pay for Walloon pensions. On a rainy day, it's like Hove or Eastbourne in the rain, full of old people wondering how to fill in time until dinner, and still complaining about those pensions.

Once I visited a company just outside the town for a

demonstration of portable televisions powered by solar energy which they were making for developing countries. The owner spent more time complaining about the Walloons and their damn pensions than about the lack of sunshine which meant his television sets couldn't work.

But whether they are Flemish or Walloon, Flemish-speaking Christian Democrats or French-speaking Christian Democrats, French-speaking Socialists, Flemish-speaking Socialists or whatever, they all have one thing in common. They complain all the time, about everything. The only people who don't complain in Belgium are the Trappist monks making their heavenly beer. They've taken a vow of silence.

Bruges is a stunningly spectacular medieval town, especially when you see it for the first time at night, floodlit in the distance, and drive slowly towards it. Usually when I go to Bruges I stay at the Holiday Inn, a beautifully converted old manor house which must be one of the best Holiday Inns in the world. Between meetings, I try to wander around the old streets, tiny narrow canals and old buildings. I always try to visit the old convent where the sisters still make lace.

In many ways the splendour of Bruges, even after all these years, is evidence of the shortsightedness of British industry. For Bruges prospered by buying cheap English wool, turning it into a thousand items of clothing and exporting it all over the world. We became better and better farmers; Bruges, along with Gent and Ypres, became better and increasingly more profitable manufacturers, merchants and middlemen. Which, of course, is where the money is.

But even in Bruges, early morning in the middle of winter, queuing up to buy fresh bread, I've been trapped by disgruntled Flemish complaining that the Walloons had stopped a local company from exporting telephone exchange equipment to the Middle East. 'How can they expect us to pay their pensions if they won't let us earn the money?' a retired farmer kept asking me.

In Mons they don't just complain about Walloons. They complain all the time about the eternal symbol of freedom: discos. The sound of heavy guns has given way to the sounds of heavy metal. Mons is today the *nombre une* spot for dancing. From all over northern Belgium; from northern France; from Gognies Chaussé, a tiny village in northern France; from Cegnies Chaussé which is the other side of the street in northern Belgium, and even from Brussels, young people flood in for the discos. I was once at a factory not far away in Feignies on the Belgium–France border. The director's secretary kept telling me the disco was better than in Paris. Since I was virtually brought up on Henry Williamson and *The Chronicles of Ancient Sunlight*, this gave me a shock.

The Walloons complain about the decline of their once massive steel and coal industries, the rise in unemployment and the Flemish stopping them from exporting arms to the Middle East.

In Brussels everyone complains about the cost of living; about foreigners, especially Eurocrats, buying all the houses and pushing up land prices even higher; about Brussels being big enough as it is and how it shouldn't be allowed to get any bigger; and, of course, about Flemish v. French. Or do I mean French v. Flemish?

What happened when a Flemish minister from the Flemish government attended a speech ceremony in Brussels commemorating the four-day battle by Belgian revolutionaries in 1830 to free themselves from the Dutch? As soon as he began speaking in Flemish, half the crowd shouted, '*En français*'.

Belgium is a country designed by Magritte with a constitution written by Simenon. As a result they don't know what they are doing or what they want. They argue about everything you could think of concerning their own country, except Europe. When it comes to Europe they are united. Unity is vital. Shared policies are essential. The future is togetherness.

In any other country this would be a recipe for disaster; in

Belgium, it's a recipe for reconciling the irreconcilable, squaring the circle, for success; for the famous *compromis à la Belge*, which pushes every single decision taken in the country through six governments, sixty ministers, nine provincial governors and 550 communes. Of course it shouldn't work, but it does; because don't forget, this is the country that produces one diplomatic trick after another. Who thought of stopping the clock because negotiations at the EC were not going to be completed by the deadline set by the Community? The Belgians. Whose former king decided to abdicate for a day because he didn't want to sign legislation he didn't agree with? The Belgians'. I was in Brussels shortly after the abdication, waiting to see the president of a multinational. I asked his secretary what she thought.

'Wonderful,' she grinned. 'My baby was born the day the King abdicated. He is a Republican.'

Is Belgium going to split apart? After yet another agonising debate about the future I got back to my hotel, where I picked up a copy of *Les Echos*, Belgium's *Financial Times*. The first story I spotted said that more and more Belgians were buying government bonds. Which to me says more about the Belgians' long-term confidence in Belgium than anything else.

Two Belgians in a bar.
'Have you heard the latest Belgian joke?'
'No.'
'In that case I'll tell it very slowly.'

Le jour de gloire arrived. After another heroic Jorrocks lunch of roast beef, yorkshire pudding and cabbage, washed down by two bottles of Château Gruaud-Larose '78 followed by stilton, a bottle of Taylors '63 and treacle tart, I managed to mention the fact that I had the actual draft in my possession.

'The walls have ears,' he said. 'Later,' and carried on

discussing, in a voice that could have been picked up by a microphone three cases of champagne away, his plans for the managing director's secretary. 'She fancies me, I can tell,' he kept giggling.

Back in his office, I finally handed over my report. 'Now, according to the director general . . .' I began.

'Shhh,' he whispered, grabbing the draft out of my hand, throwing it in his desk drawer and locking it fast. 'We can't talk about it yet. Chairman will think it's too easy. Must make it look difficult.'

'B-but you said it was urgent. We had to get them to change their—'

'I know, I know,' he said, ushering me to the door. 'All in good time. You mustn't rush these things. Give me a call next week. We'll discuss it over lunch.'

The Hague

'You must come to my retirement party.'
  'But I'm afraid I've already . . .'
  'No, I insist. I want you to be the guest of honour.'
  'But it'll mean . . .'
  'I insist. And bring all my British friends with you.'

I've been backwards and forwards to The Hague almost as many times as I've seen a Dutchman query his hotel bill. In fact, air traffic control permitting, I can often get from home to The Hague quicker than I can to London. And I live in the middle of East Sussex, forty minutes drive from Gatwick.

The Dutch call themselves the Chinese of Europe. To me, they are more like the Taiwanese or, given their obsession with cleanliness and order and the environment – all Dutch coffins, for example, must be buried *exactly* 65cm below the surface – Singaporeans.

Flying into the ultra-modern, Singaporean Schipol – the site, would you believe, of a sea battle between the Dutch and the Spanish in 1573 – is like flying into no other country. Look out of the window and you are assaulted by right angles. Dutch fields are always perfect squares or rectangles. Dutch homes are always tucked neatly into the corners, or else line up exactly with the edge of the field. Dutch cars are always parked at right angles to the home. When Dutch farmers go to bed I swear they line their clogs up at 90° to the bed. And when they get up in the morning at six o'clock, because that's when the clock hands are vertical to the floor, they find all the chickens have laid square eggs in a straight line down the middle of the field.

When you land, Dutch efficiency takes over. You must realise that Schipol was up and running when Heathrow and Gatwick were still happy feeding grounds for cattle. In the UK the trains are late so often nobody takes any notice. In Holland, if a train is late it is front-page news. Only once I landed at Schipol and the trains from the airport station were running late, because police and airport workers were trying to catch a pit bull terrier which had escaped over the lines. It was front-page news the following day.

Passport control is a dream. I don't think it has ever taken me more than three minutes to get through. Your luggage arrives when you do, and Dutch customs automatically wave me through, whereas at Heathrow I'm stopped every time I saunter through carrying a Dutch duty-free bag. In the old days, before the rail link was built, the KLM bus for The Hague always turned up on the dot. I always arrived precisely when the timetable said I should.

The pity is that all this efficiency takes you to The Hague, which to me is like one, big fat, indolent, bland Edam cheese, whereas Amsterdam is a vast, rambling, gorgeous, smelly blue cheese. Admittedly a bit too smelly and a bit too blue in some places. At least so I am told. Talking of smells, it is the only city I know which actually calculates and publishes the amount of dog mess deposited on their pavements every day. Which, if you must know, is around 10,000 kilos. Either way, give or take a kilo, it's far more exciting than The Hague.

The Hague should be another Geneva; a calm, safe, faceless centre for boring political conferences or peace initiatives. For inside the government buildings you could be anywhere; the buildings are functional, they do the job they were designed for. The interiors are adequate; neither too grand nor too spartan; just right. The whole place has the feel of a giant Holiday Inn, designed by a committee and run during the day by Calvin and during the night by Peter Drucker. It's as if the Dutch have spent so much time trying to be international (and there are very few people as international as the Dutch) that they have lost all sense of their national identity.

In any bookshop in Holland there are more English books on sale than Dutch ones. Go into a typical Dutch restaurant. Apart from *erwtensoep*, thick green pea soup, and herrings, the Dutch don't have a national cuisine. (Neither do the British, it's just that we make a god out of our appalling food and our atrocious service with a snarl.)

Go into one of Holland's famous old business clubs. It's nothing like Boodle's or White's or even the RAC in Pall Mall. It's like a Masonic hall on a Wednesday night. Except that in a Dutch club after a committee meeting, everyone rushes into the bar to each buy themselves a drink. To the Dutch, being careful is more important than being mean.

Down in Roosendaal, the big railway junction near the Belgian border, everything from the town square to the famous Eye-Tech Park specially designed and built for ophthalmic companies, is tidy, balanced and a little dull. Even on Sunday nights, I've noticed, all the luggage racks in trains in and out of Roosendaal are full of students sleeping neatly head to toe. The French and Belgian trains are full of students sleeping in the gangway, sprawled over the floor, or even halfway out of an open window in an air-conditioned compartment.

In Maastricht, in the south west near the Belgian border and the Ardennes, with its French, German, Flemish, Dutch dialect, its rambling farmhouses and vineyards and its Dutch mountain road which rises to a staggering, for the Dutch, 1,000 feet above sea level, I swear the tables and chairs in Vrijthof Square are lined up more in the Dutch than the French way.

In the church of St Bravo in Harlem, the second oldest town in the country, you'll see that this sense of order is nothing new. Apart from the great gilded Muller organ once played by Mozart, there are special chapels for lepers, brewers and 'dog whippers'. It makes you wonder how the Dutch would organise heaven if they got the chance.

In fact, in many ways, the Netherlands is also very much like Britain; everybody speaks English, everybody watches or listens to the BBC. Doing business with the Dutch, however, is not like doing business with the British. They are organised, practical and 100% trustworthy. If a Dutchman says yes, he means yes; not *peut-être* as in some countries I won't mention.

'The Dutch like to talk,' a British lawyer working in The Hague warned me once as we were about to go into a big session. 'They like to go round and round a subject. They want to feel involved. But don't worry, they'll agree in the end.' And they did. The meeting probably took twice as long as a meeting in the UK, but in the end we all agreed and, more important, there was no going back on the agreement afterwards. Unlike in some *pays* I won't mention.

'But whatever you do, don't suggest lunch,' the same lawyer told me. The British like to discuss problems over lunch or dinner. They think that way they can soften up the opposition and get an agreement over large brandies. Not the Dutch; they want to do business first, then eat.

You can imagine what the Dutch thought of Mrs Thatcher's way of doing business. Shortly after Mr A.A.M. van Agt stepped down as Dutch prime minister I arranged a series of visits for him to the UK, during one of which I asked him what it was like trying to negotiate with Mrs Thatcher. Did she really demand her money back from the EC?

He laughed. 'We couldn't believe it,' he said. 'There is a certain formality to international negotiations, but here we had the British prime minister banging the table and saying she wanted her money back. Those were her very words.'

What did all the other heads of state do? 'They were very angry,' he grinned. 'The UK was not exactly popular at the time. Some just wanted to ignore her. But we found a solution.' The practical Dutch again.

The Dutch have also come up with a kind of solution to the – dare I mention it? – religious problem or, should I say, religious question.

'Never get far in the ministry,' a middle-aged, middle-ranking civil servant mumbled to me one evening in one of the many fantastic fish restaurants in Scheveningen, just outside The Hague.

'Why not?' I muttered, ordering another round of Jonge, the young Dutch gin you are supposed to drink either straight and chilled or slow, as a chaser with your beer.

'It's a Catholic ministry and, of course, I'm a Protestant,' he replied.

I didn't know what to say. It had never occurred to me. Why should it? Then it all came pouring out. Beneath that bland, international, efficient exterior, the Netherlands was really Northern Ireland without the violence. Until very recently, many towns and villages had Catholic shops and Protestant shops, and you always went into your own shop.

'Why do you think we have so many radio and television stations, each belonging to one religion or the other? So many newspapers? So many political parties?'

Now and then, however, you come across a Dutchman who doesn't fit the mould.

'G'day. Van Tholen's the name.'

Was I hearing correctly? I was in the bar in the Central Hotel in Bergen op Zoom, somewhere in the middle of North Brabant down near the Belgian border. He looked the typical Dutch businessman; dark suit, white shirt, striped tie. But – flaming apples – the accent was pure 100% Australian.

'Van Tholen,' he said thrusting out his hand.

'Picklehareng,' I said. I wasn't going to give my real name to a complete stranger in a bar in a place like Bergen op Zoom. Especially if he looked like a Rotterdamer and spoke Australian.

The day had started early. I was at Schipol Airport at just gone 7 o'clock to meet the first flight from Paris. An African minister was flying in for a meeting at the Dutch ministry of foreign affairs in The Hague. I had made all the arrangements. After that we had meetings with businessmen, a speech at a chamber of commerce, lunch, then radio and television interviews before a quick dash to Hilversum for more interviews with the Dutch overseas radio service.

Everything had worked like clockwork, but I had bargained without the efficiency of the Dutch motorway police. Every time we hit 103kph cars would appear from nowhere, overtake us, and their rear windows would start flashing STOP STOP STOP. I would explain who we were, show them our official invitations and diplomatic passports, then we'd be off again. 'Maybe we shouldn't go so fast,' I said to the minister as we were stopped for the fifth time just outside Utrecht.

'Nonsense,' he said. 'I am a diplomat. I have a diplomatic passport. Why shouldn't I break their law?'

The meeting at the ministry of foreign affairs was interesting because the Dutch obviously didn't expect to see me on an African official delegation. But a word from the minister and they demurred as any diplomat does. Now the minister was on his way back to Paris and I was in Bergen op Zoom after another dash across country in a much slower car ready for more mundane meetings the following day.

If The Hague is a big bland Edam and Amsterdam a large, sweaty blue cheese then Bergen op Zoom is a bowl of warm yoghurt. It was also having a terrible attack of conscience. It was the time of the early Ronald Reagan and Star Wars. The United States, or rather Nancy, wanted cruise missiles all over Europe. There were protests throughout the Netherlands. The

Dutch government was dithering. Bergen op Zoom, however, was torn in two. Naturally they didn't want missiles anywhere in Europe. Trouble was the US military had said their base just outside the town was going to be one of their big new depots. Over 2,000 new houses would have to be built, that meant lots of business and lots of jobs.

'Care for a beer?' Van Tholen still sounded more like Crocodile Dundee than a Dutch burgher. I shook my head. Early the following morning I had a meeting with the chairman of a big Dutch company who, apparently, didn't believe in drink. I was determined to have a quiet evening.

'You drink Dutch beer,' he said. 'You'll never get better.'

(The Dutch, of course, speak perfect English. It's just that sometimes we have different ideas of perfection. I once parked under a sign in Eindhoven that said Free Parking, and came back to find I'd landed a hefty fine. 'But that sign says Free Parking,' I told the policeman. 'Yes,' he said sharply. 'It means the space must be kept free of parking. You parked there. You must pay the fine.')

I downed a beer, just to be sociable. 'I don't think I'll ever get better,' I told Crocodile van Tholen.

'I knew you'd like it,' he said.

It turned out that he had just landed a big job and while he looked for a home he was staying at the Central Hotel.

'We were liberated by the Canadians. Everybody thinks I've got a Canadian accent,' he said.

'What accent?' I replied.

We had another beer. And another. And another.

'Now I tell you a Dutch joke,' he mumbled.

I nodded. My experience of Dutch jokes was not very funny. They tell lots of Belgian jokes – the Belgians have just sent a regiment to the Gulf: the Mexican Gulf – which can be quite funny. They tell jokes about Rotterdam – in Rotterdam everybody works so hard the shops sell shirts with the sleeves already rolled up. Then they tell what must be typical Dutch jokes. A man got up to speak at dinner. He said, Ladies and gentlemen. Then he saw someone shaking the pepper on his food and he said, and Dutchmen. Which I don't find funny at all, but tell a Dutchman and it brings the windmill down. The omens, therefore, were not good.

'Man on a desert island,' he began. 'Has a case of wine. Every year drinks a bottle, puts a message in the bottle and throws it in the water. After six months gets a letter back from London saying, Terribly sorry old chap. If you escape, give me a call, we must have lunch together at my club.'

I smiled weakly.

'Next year he drinks another bottle, puts another message in the bottle and throws the bottle in the water. Back comes a message from Paris saying, Chéri. Next time you are in Paris give me a call, we must spend the weekend together in the south of France.'

So the Dutch are as paranoid about the French as we are.

'Next year, he drinks another bottle, puts another message in the bottle. Three months later he gets the bottle back. There's a message inside. It's from Amsterdam. It says, It is wrong to throw bottles in the water.'

I have to admit I laughed. Not so much at the joke which is, of course, another variation on a theme; more because it was told by a Dutchman in a funny Australian accent. After that I could do no wrong.

'Today,' he said, 'is Leidens Outzet. Tonight we eat pickled herrings.' And he fell all over the bar. 'But first . . .' he stumbled against the bar. 'But first, my old shiner . . .' he slapped me on the back. 'We have another Dutch beer and—' he took a deep breath, 'and genever.'

Oh no, not genever, I prayed. I didn't want to drink because of the meeting. If I drink spirits I drink whisky or cognac. Never gin. And genever is Dutch gin.

'Two Jonges,' he shouted across the bar. And especially not Jonge, the young genever. The last time I drank Jonge was somewhere or other I can't remember.

He drank his beer and Jonge down like a true Australian, trained in the ways of the 6 o'clock swill. 'Now Picklehareng,' he slapped me on the back again. 'Now Picklehareng, we eat pickled herring.'

For the next three decades we went from bar to street stall to hotel to restaurant and back to the bars again. Everywhere everybody was eating pickled herring. 'Tonight,' he told me as we held our fifth or sixth filleted, salted herrings by their tails and swallowed them head first, 'Dutchmen all over the world eat pickled herring.'

Leidens Outzet to the Dutch is a bit like Thanksgiving to the Americans. While the Americans eat turkey the Dutch all over the world eat pickled herring. Vast mail order companies send them to Dutch expats wherever you can think of, packed into wooden barrels. When they arrive, whole colonies of Dutch gather and witness the opening. One Dutch engineer who was in Japan for twenty years told me it was the only time of year he ever shed a tear for Holland.

I picked up another herring, dangled it gently in the air like everybody else, then lowered it slowly into my mouth. It was almost meltingly soft. There was a hint maybe of sweetness; definitely a whiff of the sea. It was quite unlike the dried-up vinegary bottled herrings of home. 'So you'll never get better,' van Tholen laughed.

We staggered out of the restaurant, along the street and into a tiny courtyard, past a pile of scrap iron – or was it another Dutch sculpture? – into a tiny bar. 'This is the first time for seventeen years I can eat herrings in my own country,' he gasped as we went for number twelve, or was it thirteen? He had been summoned back because the company was in trouble. He had to pull them back from the brink.

As I swallowed one herring after another I found we were discussing them with all the seriousness people usually reserve for the finest clarets. Soft. A touch of sharpness.

Perhaps a trifle ripe. Could do with longer in the barrel. Inevitably we proceeded to the subject most businessmen talk about in Holland; the growing expense of the Dutch welfare system.

'Disabled? You know what disabled means in Holland? It means you don't want to work. If you don't want to work, the government will say you're disabled – and pay you not to work,' he growled. 'Twenty-five years. That's how long you can be disabled. And we'll pay you not to work. If I want to get rid of people I don't fire them, I say they're disabled. The government looks after them.'

We swallowed another genever and another herring. 'Do you know how many disabled people we have here?' I tried – gently – to shake my head. 'There is one disabled person for every one person who has a job.'

The last bar I can remember visiting was the best one we'd been in all evening. The herring was better than ever before – or maybe the mixture of more beer, more genever, just made it seem better than ever before. Or maybe I'd stopped worrying about what John Calvin thought of the Dutch welfare state. I'll never really know.

The following morning I was on a train shortly after 6.30. Everybody was well-dressed, serious, either reading newspapers or staring aimlessly out of the window. I'm sure that if a couple had started having sex on the compartment floor nobody would have looked up from the pages of the *Telegraf.* But had somebody started smoking in a *niet roken* compartment they would have been torn apart.

On the dot of 7 o'clock I walked into reception on the ninth floor (one over the eight?) of this very modern head office. 'Mijnheer Smulders,' I said.

'Jonkherr,' replied a rather stern receptionist who obviously couldn't take her herrings.

Oops, I thought. Not many of them left. The egalitarian Dutch abandoned titles years ago. I'd only ever come across one other Jonkherr, who told me it was similar to a knighthood. He used it, he said, only because of his wife.

'He's in his office with his chauffeur.' She pointed me across the reception area. 'Go straight in. He's expecting you.' I knocked and went in. Standing in front of the desk were two elegantly dressed elderly men. Both had white hair. Both were holding a pair of glasses. Both looked immaculate. Which was the chairman, which the chauffeur? Should I shake hands with the stocky man on the left or the taller man on the right? If I picked the chauffeur, would the Jonkherr take that as a snub? Would I lose the job?

Suddenly the phone rang. The taller man grabbed it and the stockier one backed off towards the door. He was obviously the chauffeur. Thank goodness I hadn't shaken his hand first. 'Come with me,' he said as he reached the door. 'While he's sorting out my car, I'll show you around.'

We toured the office; all very modern, clean, efficient. All humming with activity, at 7 o'clock in the morning. Nothing like most of the rambling, sprawling offices back home. We discussed the company's history, their recent dramatic growth, their expansion plans, how they had decided to raise more money to stay ahead of the competition. Things were going well. The chemistry was right. I could see the terms of the contract in front of me. We talked about the Netherlands, the work I had been doing for the Dutch government.

'Good. Good,' he kept nodding. 'Had some people here the other day. Not serious at all. Very bad.' We turned into a long corridor. 'Now,' he said, 'I'd like you to meet our new finance director. You'll get on very well with him. Speaks perfect English.' We turned into an office. There was Crocodile van Tholen.

'Hey Picklehareng,' he sang out in his ringing Australian accent, 'how's your head? Have you recovered?'

The retirement party was in one of the big ministries in The

Hague. I'd managed to rustle up about a dozen of the great man's British friends; no mean achievement, as it meant their giving up virtually two days, not to mention the cost of the flight and a night at the Babylon, the swish French-owned hotel next to the station.

It was all very organised and formal – or at least as formal as you can get in Holland. We had to queue up to shake hands and say our goodbyes to the great man. When I arrived the queue already stretched the length of a big hall in the ministry, out on to the landing and partway down the stairs.

'Dutch one-upmanship,' grunted a Prussian-looking old soldier in front of me. 'The longer the queue, the more important you are supposed to be.'

'But the longer you talk to everybody, the longer you can make the queue.'

'Precisely.'

We shuffled along, up the staircase, on to the landing, through the door, into the long hall.

'*Godverdomme,*' gasped an American accent about three ahead of me. 'No wonder these guys are the second biggest investors in the US. They deliberately keep us waiting so they don't have to spend any money on booze or food.' He had a point. At the top of the queue was a single table which was supposed to feed us all.

Practically an hour after we started queuing, we shuffled up to the great man. 'Now, you're all coming to my retirement party,' he said, tapping the side of his nose. 'Want to spend some time with all my British friends.'

Within five seconds we were shuffled off to the table so that he could gossip for five minutes with one of his enemies. The table only had beer and orange juice left. I didn't have the courage to ask if this was because the demand was so great after the ordeal of the queue or if the Dutch government had not been able to stretch to a couple of bottles for its illustrious retiring servant. We toasted each other with warm orange juice.

Minutes later, we were all shuffled back across the hall, onto the landing and back down the stairs. Outside in the street we waited while the great man spoke again to all the people he'd spoken to while we queued up for hours to see him.

Finally he came across to us. 'And now,' he said, rubbing the side of his nose and pulling his ear, 'my retirement party.' He laughed and gargled at the same time. We all looked at each other. So what exactly is a Dutch retirement party, I began to wonder. Green pea soup with candles on top?

'Follow me, all my British friends,' beamed the great man, and he led us around the corner into the first Indonesian restaurant in the street. It was like a million other Indonesian restaurants in Holland.

So this was a typical Dutch retirement party. We'd given up two days, travelled from all over Britain, spent money on airline tickets and the most expensive French hotel in Holland, to have yet another Indonesian meal. To say the meal never attained that je ne sais quoi would be an understatement. But as the hot spicy meat followed the saffron rice, the pork in soya sauce, the chicken in coconut, the shrimps and paste, the beef in peanut sauce and a thousand other combinations, and especially as one genever followed another, the party began to warm up.

'Genevers all round', the great man cried again from the top of the table and dozens of waiters appeared carrying every type of Dutch gin, from the Jonge, the younger, lighter gin, to the Oude, the older, heavier, more mature gin.

Out came another course. 'Genevers all round', the great man cried. Out came citroengenever (lemon-flavoured), bessengenever (blackcurrant), and something I vaguely remember being called Dutch drop gin, although I felt we were dropping more than the gin.

The table was now covered with its second layer of dishes. Still the food was coming. 'And more ...' the great man mumbled. Out came an orange genever; a Hollandsche genever Sweet Bill and something called an Original Starling genever, which I can remember definitely not wanting to taste let alone swallow in one go. This was certainly a party to try and remember.

Finally the table could take no more. The pile of plates in the centre was beginning to slip on to the smaller piles of plates scattered around the edge. The plates on the edge were falling on the floor. The kitchen staff were collapsing with exhaustion. The waiters were unable to walk another step. There was probably not another bottle of genever in the country. The architect was asleep with his head on a plate. The civil engineer had slipped off his chair and was sprawled all over the floor. The banker had curled up on the long bench with the lawyer. Everybody else was just gaping at the ceiling.

The restaurant manager tiptoed up to the great man. 'Your bill, sir,' he whispered.

'Oh no,' the great man thundered to the whole of The Hague. Staggering to his feet and heading for the door, he bellowed, 'This is not for me. This is for all my wonderful British friends. This is my retirement party.'

Hannover

It was 3.15am. I'd been asleep for less than four hours. I got up, shaved, dressed and dragged myself downstairs. The taxi was waiting. For the tenth morning in a row I was bursting with pumpernickel, pretzels and black coffee and being bombarded by James Last telling me 'Here Comes Summer'. But I didn't believe him. For almost an hour we drove through icy winds in the pitch black, down slippery mountain roads in the middle of the Harz mountains until we hit the autobahn. From then on it was hurtling after all the Porsche GIIs and 40-ton container lorries at nearly 200kph until, *Gott sei Dank*, we swooped around the outskirts of Hannover which, *Gotterdämmerung*, in terms of length alone must be the ultimate ring road.

From then on it was good old-fashioned British stop-start-crawl-stop-start-crawl. Except it was still only 6 o'clock in the morning. At 7 o'clock I was on our exhibition stand for yet another fourteen-hour day of the Hannover Messe, the enormous ten-day industrial trade fair, the largest in the world, which boasts no fewer than 6,000 exhibitors from forty countries and regularly attracts hundreds of thousands of visitors from literally everywhere.

At the time, I was with a big British engineering group. We were desperately trying to boost our exports. I had appointed a subsidiary of the Rank Organisation as our agents in Germany.

'If your agents we are going to be, you must take part in the Messe,' the Herr Direktor told me in no uncertain terms during our friendly discussions about increasing sales. 'If not you at the Messe are, you not serious are.'

I to be serious wanted. Herr Direktor to make all the arrangements undertook.

Two weeks before the Messe I flew over to meet him. He wanted me to double-check everything had been arranged. And of course it had. The Germans are not Klotz. They are organised, workmanlike, efficient. If they say they will do something, they do it. Unlike some *gens* I won't mention.

The stand had been paid for.

'Paid for,' I gasped in the traditional British manner. 'But we always wait at least . . .'

'In Germany always we pay on time. Immer,' Herr Direktor told me quite sharply. Obviously I was a Klotz to think otherwise.

Invitations to potential visitors had been mailed, each one listed on a massive computer print-out with headings and subheadings and sub-subheadings explaining whether they were an existing customer or not. If not: where they had obtained their name; how much they could buy within twelve months, two years, three years, even five years; their bank; a bank reference and a credit reference. If they were existing customers: their annual expenditure over five years; major products they had purchased; their payment record; estimated future sales – all valuable information. Sales literature and back-up technical sheets had been delivered. A visitors' book was ready. Sales enquiry forms were ready. Even the name badges were ready. And correct. Not like at home.

'Fantastic. Fantastic,' I kept telling Herr Direktor. 'You've thought of everything.'

'Not everything,' he said. 'Hotel now inspect you must.'

'Not at all,' I began. 'I'm sure . . .'

'In Germany everything we inspect.'

'Okay,' I said. 'Hotel inspect let us.'

We drove across to the hotel, where we inspected reception, lounge, restaurant. *Alles* was perfect.

'Fantastic, fantastic,' I kept telling him. 'Everything you've thought of. *Alles.*'

'Now bedrooms we inspect,' Herr Direktor said.

'Bedrooms,' I started. 'I don't want to—'

'In Germany we bedrooms inspect. Immer.'

For the next hour and a half we inspected practically every bedroom in the hotel, from the suites down to the humble singles. In each room Herr Direktor, in his funny green burgomaster coat, Tyrolean hat and rimless glasses, insisted on bouncing up and down on each bed to test the springs.

'Good sleep is very necessary during Messe,' he bounced. '*Sehr* important.'

He was beginning to get *mir auf den Wecker gehen*, or on my alarm clock as the Germans say when something slightly irritates them, but in the spirit of Maastricht, I went along with him. When our tour we finished had, we shook hands. 'Okay,' I said. 'I'll see you all here the day before the Messe opens.'

Herr Direktor looked at me. 'Is not for you, this hotel,' he said slowly. 'You are big boss. Here you cannot mit uns stay. At big hotel, you stay. Is important.'

'But that's crazy,' I blurted out. 'We're all supposed to be—'

'Is what has been decided.' Herr Direktor drew himself slowly to attention. I sensed this was to disagree not the time.

As Herr Direktor dropped me at the airport, I remembered to ask the name of my hotel.

'Tannerhof,' he said.

'Where's that? Next to yours?'

'*Nein. Ist in Braunlage.*'

'Braunlage,' I gasped, running for the check-in. 'That's the other side of Goslar. That's miles away.'

'Is hotel for bosses,' he smiled efficiently through his rimless spectacles.

Hannover, as a result, is the one big business town where I have spent a great deal of my life but seen very little. You don't get much chance to look around between seven in the morning when the car arrives and nine at night when it leaves. Especially during the Messe. But ask me anything about the Harz mountains, the pseudo-Alpine hotels and special skiing facilities for old-age pensioners, about the country lanes around Goslar, which boasts more old buildings than any other town in Germany, the autobahn to Hamburg, the car parks, the exhibition halls, or even the bars and restaurants. I can tell you *alles*.

As anybody knows who's ever seen Germans very early in the morning neatly spreading their towels on all the best seats around the swimming pools of this world, Germany is *sehr systematisch*.

The government machine purrs like a Mercedes in over-drive. Regional and city government work hand-in-hand. Every town has an orchestra, a ballet troupe, a Stadttheater, a choir and probably a puppet theatre as well. Every village has a band. Everything looks permanently springcleaned. Everything is ultra-modern. *Vorsprung durch Technik*.

Banks and financial institutions think and act long-term. Companies have constitutions which stress they should do more than just make money for their shareholders. The whole country behaves like a republic which wishes it was a monarchy which is probably why they have a Fatherland when everybody else has a Motherland.

They know they are the dominant economic power in Europe. They know they have the fastest growing economy. They know they are the engine if not the whole European locomotive of growth, and that if they catch a cold France, Holland and Italy will catch pneumonia while Austria, Belgium, Denmark and Switzerland will get a severe migraine.

They know they will be the *milch*-cow of a European

Community stretching eventually from the Atlantic to the Urals. They know the deutschmark will be the dominant currency in the European monetary system. They know the ecu will be the mark in European dress.

'What name do you suggest for the new European currency?' is a favourite Euro-question over Euro-dinners. 'The Bismark,' I reply immediately.

Away from the swimming pools, where the early morning towel-laying ceremony seems to antagonise everybody, all the Germans I've ever met know they are living in the best place this side of paradise. But they are still not happy. They want to be loved. Which, as Goethe said somewhere or other, *ist der Schlüssel zu allem.*

Germany is like a world champion who works day and night, not to win, but to be the best member of the relay team; or like a smart, hardworking finance director who is prepared to defer at all times to the wishes of the board instead of branching out on his own, running rings round his colleagues and making the company sing. This is partly, I think, because Germans see this as their destiny; partly also because they live coalition politics. They are used to being part of the team rather than the winner.

Europe needs unification, they say. But they need it more than anybody else – to link them inextricably to Europe; to balance their size; to stop them from getting too tight a grip. Which is probably why Helmut Schmidt always quotes Shakespeare when he writes for British publications and Voltaire when he writes in French publications, instead of his own beloved Goethe. Although I notice he has always managed so far to avoid quoting *Henry V* in either English or French. Which proves just how organised and thorough the Germans are.

Even German restaurants, or at least the ones I usually end up in, are super-efficient – for the benefit of the owners, not the customers. You go into the restaurant which looks like a vast old-fashioned English pub with all the furniture and fittings and partitions removed. Packed into the open space are as many long baretop tables as possible. Around them are as spindly a collection of chairs as you'll ever see. There's none of this, Do I want to sit with my back to the wall looking out of the window or do I want to sit in the middle and keep an eye on the clock? You are immediately ushered to the nearest table with the appropriate number of empty seats. Which is fine if you like having a quiet, relaxed, intimate dinner in the middle of a riotous crowd of beer-swilling middle-class burghers wearing soft leather jackets and expensive designer jeans. There is no escape, you are part of the group. You either spend the evening worrying about your German past participles or getting bombed out of your mind.

Food and drink are simple. You have what you're given. There is a menu but nobody takes any notice of it. You go for the dish of the day, which is chalked up on blackboards. '*Das, bitte,*' you scream through the gathering crescendo of Bavarian folk songs.

Drink is even easier. You get the beer of the night. As soon as you sit down, it arrives; as soon as you finish one glass, another arrives. No trying to catch the eye of the wine waiter. It's there before you realise you want it. If there are twenty people on the table and twelve and a half of them look as though they need another one, the waiter arrives with a twenty-glass plank with twenty glasses slotted neatly inside it. Immediately twenty hands make a grab for the glasses, empty the contents of the old ones, and plug them back in the plank. The waiter retreats for yet more refills.

Nothing like the old Schmitts restaurant years ago in Soho, where everyone went because the service was so bad and the waiters so, so, well old-fashioned German. 'Excuse me, could I . . .?' you would mumble nervously after waiting maybe two and a half hours for the menu. 'Wait. I come,' you would be barked at. The amazing thing was everybody would wait another two and a half hours.

Disputes? Labour unrest? Strikes? Modern Germans no more understand what they mean than the old waiters at Schmitts understood the meaning of service. I once asked an old German engineer about strikes and he told me about the time the staff at the famous Goethe Institut went on strike for half an hour twenty years ago. An English expat working for Deutsche Bank in Frankfurt told me the Germans never go on strike because they instinctively believe the machine is mightier than the man. In Germany, the man is servant of the machine whereas in Britain we believe the machine is servant of the man. 'Don't forget, the reason Volkswagen put the engine in the back is to protect it and not the passengers in case the car is involved in an accident,' he said. It also seems to me the reason why there are no speed limits on German autobahns.

At the same time, however, there is a balance. Germany is the only country I know where it is against the law to mow the lawn on Sundays, have a shower after 10pm or put glass in your own dustbin after 8pm. In Munich it is against the law to hoover your carpet on a Sunday. In some parts of the country your dog is forbidden to bark before 8am or after 7pm. Thankfully, there is also a law stopping Germans from making rude gestures towards slower, usually British, motorists as they speed past them on the autobahns.

'So what is a rude gesture?' I once dared to ask a German policeman in Cologne.

He put his forefinger to the side of his head and twisted his hand backwards and forwards. '*Ist krazy*,' he grinned. '*Klotz*.' An expatriate British civil servant tried the same thing against a traffic warden and was fined DM2,000.

It's precisely because Germans are systematic and thorough that they are efficient. Somehow it just seems to be in their blood. I was told by a Besserwessi German banker in Frankfurt that the day after the Berlin Wall came down in the *Wunderjahr* of 1989, the first thing many East Germans did was to take back to the libraries in West Berlin the books they had borrowed before they were cut off from the rest of the world. One man apparently took back Thomas Mann's *Death in Venice* which was nearly thirty years overdue. I can't make up my mind whether it would have been more German for the library to make him pay the fine, which must have been well over DM5,000, or to let him off, or whether the man himself would have wanted to pay or to be let off.

To watch an Englishman juggling briefcases and suitcases and newspapers as he gets on a train is like watching a juggler with sore thumbs on a bad day. See a French or Italian housewife packing her shopping bags at a downtown Printemps or Carrefour and you see where Jacques Tati got his inspiration. But a German businessman or Hausfrau seems to have an inner logic. One step, one package, proceeds logically to the next. There is a natural sequence, a regularity. It is this personal approach that, translated into offices and factories, has made Germany such a power house. I cannot imagine a German secretary losing a file or a German production engineer failing to manufacture whatever on the very minute he said it would be finished.

I've been in offices and factories in Stuttgart, the Mercedes capital of the world, which the mayor, Mannfred (son of you-know-who) Rommel has succeeded in making virtually the hi-tech city of the future. Look at Germany's plans for Europe and you see Stuttgarts stretching all the way to the Urals. The offices are bang up-to-date; soft lights in the corridors, iced water in the offices and the latest James Last muzak in the lifts. The factories are like microchip palaces. Every robot, every computer, every paperclip looks as though it has just been bought. The standard of living must be one of, if not the, highest in Europe. The quality of life must also be near the top of the pile whether you have a Mercedes, or a Porsche, from their other local car plant.

But the rules are just as strict for the workers as for the machines. In Germany you cannot just turn up, give Fritz a call and drop in and see him. *Mein Gott*, never. You must make an appointment with his secretary. Top, even not-so-top, German businessmen are booked up weeks ahead. Time is deutschmarks. Similarly lunch. There's no way you can turn up out of the blue and suggest a quick *Senatorentopf* overflowing *mit* fillets of pork, beef, turkey and vegetables followed by *Schwartzwalde Kirschtorte mit Sahne.* Most Germans prefer a bowl of soup and a sandwich at their desk, although I'm told the austere Bundesbank will occasionally come up with a boar for lunch.

Neither can you play politics – see Fritz, get him to put in a good word with Siegfried. No way. Everybody has their set area of responsibility. Everybody protects their patch. Nobody is interested in even thinking about thinking of anybody else's patch.

The other thing that always amazes me about Germany is the strict formality that exists even between people who have been working together for years. There's none of this, 'Hey, kid get me a coffee.' It's immer but immer, Herr This, Frau That, Herr Doktor The Other.

Maybe I expect it in Munich; Munich is formal and cultured. Maximillianstrasse with all its big fashion stores is like the Champs Elysées. Admittedly the Marienplatz, the shopping precinct, is always full of *Schickies* (yuppies), but somehow that seems the right thing. Even the artists around Schwäbing look as though they've qualified as management consultants.

But I don't expect it in Frankfurt, or Bankfurt as it is known because of all the banks that are moving in as it becomes the leading financial centre in Europe. Regularly I visit one company in Frankfurt where the number one *Wunderkind* is a doctor of engineering and a doctor of philosophy. *Everybody always* calls him Herr Doktor Doktor.

I was once in a meeting with the Herr Direktor of another company when we hit a point where we needed to check with the Herr Direktor of finance. When Herr Direktor of finance came into the room I actually heard the Herr Direktor ask him his first name so that he could introduce him to me. And they had worked together for nearly ten years.

It was this same Herr Direktor, however, who told me my only German joke.

'In Germany we are building three lunatic asylums, *ja?*'

'*Ja,*' I said.

'One here in Frankfurt; one in Hamburg. And one roof we are putting over Bavaria. *Sehr* funny, *ja?*'

'*Ja,*' I said, and genuinely laughed.

I once spent a blood-spattered afternoon in a slaughterhouse in West Africa set up by Franz Joseph Strauss, the hard man of Bavarian politics who at one time looked as though he was going to become chancellor. It had the same buzz, the same quiet efficiency, the same minimum of action and economy of effort. The head butcher, who was from Bavaria, was built like an ox, but he also had the same economy of movement whether he was despatching seibu cattle or sinking litre after litre of locally produced beer afterwards.

A few years ago I drove all the way from Cologne with its amazing cathedral, which took even the Germans over 600 years to build, to Stuttgart, visiting engineering and machine tool companies on the way. Whether we were in Bonn, which to me feels more like a red-brick university town than anything else, or Koblenz, the crossroads of the Rhine and the Mosel, or Heidelberg, which I'm sure invented printing just to enable it to sell picture postcards to the world, we always arrived on time. We always saw the people we had arranged to meet. We always discussed what we said we wanted to talk about. And we always left on time.

Trouble was that between each call we drove like a dragon out of *Gotterdämmerung* being hammered first by James Last and then by Wagner, non-stop at full blast. I was more than grateful when each evening we arrived at the hotels which were each, appropriately, called Silenthuis.

But don't get me wrong. The Germans are not quite as perfect as their machines. They are not, I will admit, the greatest when it comes to taking an initiative. A Frenchman, an Italian, even an Irishman will do nothing but take initiatives, often in flat contradiction of what has been laboriously agreed. But a German manager somehow feels he must first request, then be given permission, even to think of taking an initiative. A German businessman who owns his own company is even worse.

One year just before Christmas I was in Nuremburg, which I think is one of the most pleasant, relaxed, almost homely medieval German cities – it is also one of the wealthiest – negotiating to buy a local engineering company. I'd been introduced to them by a German consultant living in Gerrards Cross. He told me he acted for Robert Maxwell in Eastern Europe. When I arrived at his house in an ordinary tree-lined street near the station I was slightly taken aback; it wasn't the kind of home I was expecting. In the garden was, apart from Jodrell Bank, the biggest satellite dish I've ever seen.

'Can receive sixty-four television programmes,' he boasted. 'From all over the world.' He took a deep breath. 'And telephone calls from Mr Maxwell.'

Instead of wandering around their enormous traditional *Kitsch und Kunst Christkindl* market with its thin efficient veneer of Christmas snow in the Hauptmarket – Nuremberg is also the centre of the German toy industry – and sampling various local schnapps, I had to keep going to meetings in a tiny clump of trees near the famous racetrack because the factory owner didn't want anyone to know he was thinking of selling. All his staff had been with him for years and he felt he was letting them down by even considering such a possibility, although it was in their interests, and those of the company, that he sold out.

Trouble was, after each meeting I was so cold I couldn't decide whether to buy one of those big terrible bottle green burgomaster coats and look as though I was in the British foreign office or have another schnapps. The schnapps won. Within a few freezing days I was an expert on *glockenapfelschnapps*, raspberry schnapps, quince schnapps, orange schnapps, cherry schnapps and kirsch as well.

Over glasses of *glockenapfelschnapps*, a weak appley schnapps, and Hebkuchen, the local honey and gingerbread cake, the consultant kept explaining that the owner of the company was coming up to retirement. None of his children was interested in the business. To keep up with the competition he would have to invest a lot of money in new plant and new equipment. His best option, he thought, was to sell.

The owner was a very upright man – ramrod straight, even when sitting down. He had crewcut silver hair, his shoulders were the size of the Brandenburg Gate. His suits were always silver-grey and immaculately pressed. He also had those rimless spectacles. He talked about building up the company; how everybody felt they were part of the family; his plans for the future.

One freezing morning while we were waiting in the woods he told me he had at one time been an adviser to von Stauffenberg, who placed the bomb in the briefcase in the bunker. He said he had seen Hitler many times. 'We were military officers,' he said. 'He was our commanding officer. Naturally, we saw him.'

'What was he like at meetings?'

'Decisive. No long discussions. He knew how to take decisions. From the point of view of actions, decisions, he was very professional.'

'Did people ever contradict him?'

As far as he was concerned, he said, there was no need. The staff officers knew the options they wanted. They submitted their options to Hitler. Hitler always selected one of them. 'Just like any army or bureaucracy,' he smiled through his spectacles.

'Was there any opposition to Hitler?'

It was the same, he said, in any army. Soldiers were there to obey, not to question orders. Of course whenever any groups of people were working together there were disagreements. But German soldiers were not meant to question authority any more than British or American soldiers were.

Eventually, of course, I got round to the question: did he know? He said people suspected things. But nobody spoke openly.

'Because they were scared?'

'Because we were soldiers. We were at war. Soldiers do their duty. They don't go around questioning their commanders. German soldiers didn't. Neither did British soldiers. Soldiers have a job to do. They do their job.'

Did he have any idea that von Stauffenberg was planning to bomb Hitler?

'No,' he said emphatically. 'It would not be a secret if everybody knew beforehand. That is not what a soldier does.'

It was always fascinating talking to him, even in the freezing cold; almost like jumping into a time machine. He seemed quite happy reminiscing, like any old soldier anywhere.

I sometimes wonder if we are not obsessed with the last war. Check the *Radio Times*. Week after week you will see movies about the warmongering Germans, investigations and documentaries about the Gestapo and the SS and, heaven help us, comedies about the Nazis. Sit down with a German visiting the UK and switch on the television. Practically any evening of the year I guarantee somebody will say something about the Nazis, either in a speech to the House of Commons or in a news interview. Or on a comedy show: I once caught the end of a cartoon where Donald Duck was chasing the Nazis. After a while you begin to feel embarrassed, as if the government was using radio and television to brainwash the whole country to think that nothing has changed since 1943.

But if we are always looking back, the Germans are always

looking forward, especially as far as their health is concerned. I remember one trip to Düsseldorf, the American-Japanese capital of Germany, if not Europe, which always seems to have something *gemütlich* in the air. Whenever I walk out of the airport to a waiting taxi – in Germany taxis are always waiting – I feel as though I've just arrived in the US. In the town centre, however, with all its fashion stores, I feel as though I am in Paris or Tokyo.

I had been visiting a big engineering company outside Krefeld, a large textile town in the middle of the asparagus triangle, Europe's biggest asparagus-growing area. I had gone there planning, *mit Glück*, to go from *wurst* to *wurst*.

In Nuremberg I like the big *wurst* the size of snakes. In Frankfurt I once ate my way through a *knockwurst*, a *blutwurst* and a *mettwurst* all spiced with caraway and coriander. Somehow I couldn't then manage a *weisswurst*, a Munich specialty; but when they told me it was made of calves' brains and spleen I was not too unhappy.

This time in Düsseldorf, however, it was asparagus week. Restaurants were serving nothing but asparagus; asparagus with smoked salmon, asparagus with veal, asparagus with roast lamb. They probably even served asparagus *mit Sahne*. In the shops there was nothing but asparagus; jumbo asparagus, medium asparagus, delicate little asparagus. There was asparagus tied up with red ribbons. There was even asparagus with special asparagus greetings cards to send to asparagus friends all over the world.

The Herr Direktor told me he was looking for ways to speed up production of *Hodenschutzkäfseln*.

'Was?' I said.

He was the world's leading manufacturer of radiation-proof codpieces; for power-station workers, surgeons, doctors, dentists, anybody who came in contact with radioactivity.

'Make them all shapes and sizes,' he said. 'Make economy version for poor country. Make luxury version *mit* velvet for rich country. All sizes,' he beamed. 'For little countries, I have *kleine* ones. For England . . .'

'*Natürlich,*' I mumbled.

'And for Germany . . .'

'*Natürlich, natürlich.*'

Afterwards my mobile Wagnerian concert hall blasted its way back into Düsseldorf accompanied by a thousand Valkyries. The streets were deserted. At midday. For a second I felt as though there had been a nuclear alert and I was the only one who didn't know about it. I walked along the pavement. It was empty. Not even any Japanese off to their own shops, restaurants or schools. I came to a big traffic junction. No traffic. I waited until the lights changed. Even in the middle of what I thought was a nuclear alert, with nobody watching me, I instinctively did the German thing rather than dash across the road. That's how the German sense of order and discipline affects my soul. I came across a bar. I walked in. It was practically empty.

'So where's everybody gone?' I asked the enormous friendly Valkyrie behind the bar.

'Ozone warning,' she said, 'on television.'

'You mean if there's an ozone warning everybody stays inside?'

'*Natürlich,*' she said, serving me a large glass of the local, very malty, slightly weak Alt beer. '*Ist* dangerous. People not want to risk health.'

'The beer?'

'*Nein.* The ozone.'

No wonder Düsseldorf seems to have something *gemütlich* in the air.

Another special feature in Germany is the most comprehensive waste recycling programme I've ever come across. In the old days, company car parks were full of Mercedes. Today they are full of Mercedes – and a thousand containers. Under their 'Green' legislation, everything that can possibly be recycled has to be recycled. Paper, board, bottles, metal, plastic, strips of metal, coat hangers, white corundum, chromium corundum, sillimanite bricks, tarred magnetite stones. Even yoghurt-pot tops. Everything has its own separate container.

The government is not interested in what happens to the material once it has been collected. That's the company's problem. They must find a solution and find the money to pay for it all. In any other country this would create uproar. In Germany, industry has simply said, *jawohl, natürlich.* They are doing as they are told. They are solving their own problems. They have set up their own Duales System Deutschland which collects the waste from them, recycles it and probably makes a lot of *gelt* in the process.

They are also re-examining their whole attitude to packaging and waste collection. Buy a word processor in Germany and it will probably come in a second- or maybe third-hand cardboard box. New cardboard boxes are also getting smaller and less bulky. German Hausfraus complain if they are too big. As a result German trucks are now also becoming even more careful and more professional at handling less protected products.

Talking of waste, another thing that always amazes me about the Germans is – dare I mention it? – the way they are, like the Catalans and Noel Coward, obsessed by what polite society would describe as their bodily functions. To me a bathroom is a bathroom, a toilet is a toilet. To the Germans it's practically a research laboratory.

I once crossed the Sahara with a group of journalists from Africa, Europe and the States. Each morning we would go our separate ways and do what a man's got to do. One morning as the Land Rovers were ready to roll, we spotted way behind us in the shimmering heat, the august, serious and slightly boring representative of *Der Spiegel* on his hands and knees, peering intently at something in the sand.

'He's found an E-number,' shrieked a particularly intense American. (Ten days earlier the German had complained bitterly because none of the Arab traders in the markets around Tamanrasset were selling washing powder without bleach in it.)

'He's lighting a fire,' grunted the Ivoireans. 'He's crazy.'

'He's burying the Cokes he's been hiding,' snapped a Frenchman, and they all leapt across the sand towards him for their different reasons.

What he was trying to do, he told me later, was to see whether he was likely to develop arthritis. Somehow I felt that, for all his organised research, I'd prefer to suffer from arthritis.

It was coming up to Hannover Messe time again, so I telephoned Herr Direktor.

'This time I come to you. Is fair,' he said.

'Okay,' I said, 'let's meet in London.'

'Agreed.'

'Don't worry,' I added, 'I'll fix the hotel for you.'

'Is very kind.'

Two months to go. I got a telephone call to confirm our meeting in London. 'Hotel you have booked?' he asked.

'No problem,' I said. 'You're in the Piccadilly.'

There was a long pause. 'The Piccadilly. But that, I think, is in Manchester.'

'Sure,' I said. 'Is hotel for German agent. From London, only two and a half hours.'

Villefranche

Paris, I love. I'll go to a meeting in Paris any time. In fact I frequently do. There is nothing better than a breakfast meeting at the Crillon, although lunch round the corner at the RAC club is as exciting. Well, almost. Rheims is fabulous – a dream world; the restaurants, the cellars. The whole place bubbles with champagne. Anywhere within thirty miles of Bordeaux is *magnifique*. Lunch at Château Latour, tea at Château Rieussec, or just a stroll through the vineyards at Château d'Yquem. Even Lyon with its impossible traffic, Marseille with its dangers. They are all fantastic. So is Rouens with Madame Bovary rattling round in a closed carriage on her secret assignations, not to mention Carcassone, the astonishingly well-preserved medieval vaulted city of the Cathars and troubadours.

So where do I spend my time in France? Villefranche. *Mon dieu*. It's dull, drab, boring. It's like one vast, sprawling, old-fashioned English industrial estate. It's the kind of town that makes you think that maybe France is not the best country in the world after all.

On my first trip I arrived early. I wanted a chance to explore; to see churches and the town square; to visit the local museums and, of course, the bars and restaurants. Not any more. It's the last plane in and the first plane out. Trouble is that the last plane in is always the previous evening and the first plane out is always late the following evening. As a result, I've spent many a happy hour looking out of the window of the Hotel Plaisance on the avenue de la Libération at the traffic plodding slowly round the town square.

As the plane lands at Lyon, I find I'm wishing I was in Paris, or Nice, or Toulouse, or even Domrémy, birthplace of Joan of Arc where I once spent four gentle days studying her saintly ways of butchering the English.

As the taxi crawls along the motorway into Lyon, which must have the worst traffic problem in France, then inches through the tunnel to the motorway the other side, I'm dreaming of *langouste* in la Tour d'Argent, or *caneton au bouzy* in Rheims, or even apple dumplings in Normandy. It's about the only time I regret travelling.

Usually I stay in one of the hotels on the main square. They are small, cramped, seedy and, worst of all, terribly un-French. They are like Blackpool boarding houses exported by Lebanese middlemen. Bars are non-existent. At least I've never been able to find one. Usually when I arrive, admittedly as late as possible, the only sign I see of alcohol is the doorman with a couple of bottles of pastis on the reception desk. To say the rooms are adequate is to exaggerate. Even – shock, horror – the restaurants make your typical British tearoom a gastronomic delight. I've had meals at British Rail which are out of this world compared to those I've experienced in Villefranche. You think I'm exaggerating.

I've stayed in every type of hotel in France. I've stayed in Le Crillon in Paris where there is so much gold on the plates I swear the reason they have so many staff is to protect the china. I've stayed in seaside hotels in Calais. I've stayed in Tunisian boarding houses at the back of Lyon station.

I once spent an unforgettable night in the Hôtel de l'Armistice in the virtual kasbah of Marseille after driving ten hours from Paris, seeing Gaston Defferre, the legendary Socialist mayor, then driving to Aix-en-Provence for dinner and back to the hotel. But Villefranche . . . It's the only place in the world where I can read *Germinal* and not feel sorry for the characters.

Maybe my first visit coloured my attitude. I was then director of a machine tool company in Leeds. I'd negotiated an agreement with a company in Villefranche, which I've since discovered is the centre of French overall production. Now they were breaking the agreement.

'But you can't do that,' I can remember telling the director general in his heavily furnished, dismal office overlooking the company car park. 'That's not what we agreed, *mon vieux.*'

'But why? It's good for business. We got the order,' he said in an accent as thick as bouillabaisse, with that what-can-I-do-about-it Gallic shrug. The bags under his eyes were the size of croissants. He reeked of Gauloises.

'I know. But in the contract . . .'

'The contract! What is a contract?' Another shrug.

'What is a contract?' I collapsed over his boardroom table. 'It's what you argued about for four months. That's what the contract is.'

'But that was just the basis of our agreement. It doesn't mean we have to follow it every day.'

For four whole months we'd had meeting after meeting with *le beau salaud*, draft after draft, letter after letter, fax after fax and one long headache after another.

'But first, monsieur, the most important question of all,' their suave Parisian lawyer, an obvious product of the super-élite Ecole Nationale d'Administration, oozed at our first meeting in Leeds. 'Should the contract be in English or French?'

'French,' I said immediately. 'Next question.'

The look on their faces. You should have seen it. 'No. I don't think you understand the question, monsieur. The contract. I was saying should it be in our language or the language of . . .?'

'No problem. French,' I said.

They didn't know what had hit them. The lawyer shuffled his papers as if he was preparing to pass the death sentence. 'And now monsieur,' he oozed again across the table, 'will the contract be binding under French law or . . .'

'French law,' I said. 'No problem.' He looked as though he'd shot through the trapdoor and out the other side. 'Why not?' I smiled. 'Is there anything wrong with French law?' He grimaced. 'Or the French legal system?' He positively squirmed. 'Because if you don't have any confidence in it . . .' He went blue, white and red – in vertical stripes. He looked at me with his *yeux de crapaud*.

French law, English law, European law – I wasn't deferring to the French, I was being practical. If a situation gets so out of hand you even have to consider going to any kind of law, you've lost, whether you're right or wrong. Whatever you do, therefore, you have to avoid the law. Nobody ever wins going to court and getting tangled up with lawyers, of whatever nationality. I was determined that we should draw up a practical working agreement. If everything worked out, we wouldn't need a contract. If things didn't work out, we had to make sure either side could back off without too much fuss, without incurring too much expense and without upsetting the other partner too much. Whether the contract was in English or French, subject to French or English law, made no difference. The contract I wanted would be subject to the law of the jungle. In the most friendly terms, of course.

Could I get this Parisian lawyer to agree? *Jamais*. Every *point* and *virgule* had to be checked and doublechecked and cross-referenced with his Code Napoléon.

I said we'd supply machines at a set price. The French could then set their own market prices. But I wanted a commission on whatever price they set.

Why was I allowing the French to decide the prices? Didn't I trust them, he asked me, banging the table. It's precisely because I trusted them, I said, that I was allowing them to set the prices. If I didn't trust them I would set the prices myself.

I said we'd deliver three machines at a time: one for the customer, one for installation on approval, one for the showroom. It would cut down transport costs, ensure they never had problems with deliveries and help the sales campaign.

'Why three?' He threw his papers across the table at me. Didn't I have confidence in the machines? Did I have to supply three so that at least one would work? French machines always worked. And so on.

Not at all, I explained wearily. All the machines would work. That was why we were sure we could sell them in France. Giving them three at a time was a sign of our confidence, our wish to keep costs down and proof of the extent of our willingness to keep our French agent. I'd been studying up on my French gestures and mannerisms, so I gave him a gentle imitation of James Galway playing his flute. In other words, he was beginning to bore me.

He didn't take any notice, or if he did he didn't want to let on. Clever, these graduates of the Ecole Nationale d'Adminis-tration. 'Now monsieur,' he said, swinging his fist into his other open hand. If I had interpreted that fast enough, I'd have thrown him out there and then. Instead I simply said, 'No problem. We'll give you three months' credit on the initial order; one month on all subsequent orders and we'll take payment in French francs.'

He went beserk. For a moment, I thought I was going to be dragged to the nearest *lanterne*. 'How dare you slur the French franc,' he screamed, banging his fist in his hand again and again. 'I will not have you suggest the French franc is a weak currency. The honour of France is the honour of our currency. *C'est un scandale.*'

'I am not saying for a moment the French franc is a weak currency . . .'

'You've said it again.' He leapt up and hit the ceiling.

'What I'm saying is that from your point of view it's probably easier to pay—'

'You are suggesting we are going to find it difficult to pay.' He was now standing to attention. 'Nobody ever says that to a Frenchman, never.'

'I never said that.' I collapsed again across the table. 'What I said was . . .'

'You think you will make more money being paid in French francs than in English pounds. You are a cheat,' he spat at me in a cloud of garlic. 'Never, never have . . .' He was gone. Out of the office, across the car park, marching for all the world like Napoleon's troops on the first day of their walking tour of Russia.

The following day I received a letter from his office in Paris agreeing everything I had proposed: French language, French law, French francs. What's more, it was written in English. I picked my way through it without really bothering to read it, although I noticed it referred all the time to UK, not England. Suddenly I spotted section 33, para 14, sub-section 2a. Changes of directors they had translated into English as 'mutations in the boardroom'. Which, I thought, summed it up perfectly.

Now, less than six months later, I had discovered our beloved partners were not only selling all the machines we were supplying, even though we'd agreed one would be for loan to customers and another for the showroom, but they were selling them at a far higher price than they had told me. As a result our commission was far lower than we had agreed. On top of that, they were taking our name off the machines and putting theirs on instead.

'But. But. But,' I stammered. 'You can't. What we agreed was . . .'

'But that was just the contract.'

'Just the contract,' I spluttered. 'You made me go through life and death with some crazy lawyer . . .'

'But that is all over. That is history. Today is today,' the DG said in a voice smoothed by generations of Krug. 'We can't keep discussing the contract again and again can we? We must do business together, *n'est-ce pas?*'

'Of course.'

'We are partners, yes?'

'Yes, of course.'

He put his hand on my shoulder. Always a bad sign in any language. 'So you agree?'

'No. How can I agree?' I gave him my British version of his shrug. 'We had an agreement. You wanted the agreement, not me. I was happy to have an exchange of letters. But you wanted a contract. Now we have the contract. And what do you want to do? You want to break the contract you insisted on having.' I waved my hands in the air. 'That's not the way to do business.'

'Now, my friend,' he squeezed my shoulder. 'Tell me this. Am I suggesting we break the agreement?'

'No.'

'Am I refusing to do business with you?'

'No.'

'Am I saying we're going to do less business?'

'No.'

'Am I refusing to pay you?'

'No.'

He threw his hands up in the air. 'So where's the problem?'

'The problem is,' I began. Then I thought, I'm not going to win. It doesn't matter what I say. And if I disagree, am I going to go to court over it? Of course not. 'There is no problem. I agree. On one condition,' I said. 'That you buy lunch . . .'

'I agree.' He nodded enthusiastically. 'Let's go.'

'. . . in Paris,' I said.

He nodded even more enthusiastically.

As we climbed into his car he said, 'Where is OO-KAH? I thought you were an English company.'

We drove 250 kilometres to the most fabulous *petits blinis aux deux caviars et sauce raitfort* and *perdrix aux Perles d'Orges*. After that we did it their way. We stuck to our side of their contract. They completely ignored theirs. But in all fairness, it was a big success. Of course it meant I had to go to Villefranche regularly. I never enjoyed it. I always dreamt of Paris, of Rheims, even Lyon. But business is business.

My last visit, I remember, was on a Friday. The director of one of their banks had arrived late for the meeting. He blamed the traffic on the road from Paris, which fooled the others, but not me. I knew he was late because he was coming to Villefranche. Anywhere else he would have turned up around 11 o'clock, the meeting would have been over by 11.30, then we would have gone out for an enormous *pot-au-feu des côtes d'Armor* and three types of fish served on julienne vegetables with a delicate perfumed sauce, washed down by a couple of bottles of the vigorous Krug '87.

This meeting, however, started late. We raced through the agenda – the only positive reason I can think of for having meetings in Villefranche. By 4 o'clock it was all over and we raced for our cars. The banker's big Peugeot 504 screamed off towards Paris. The Citröens and Renaults shot off towards Mâcon, Grenoble, Geneva. My taxi had given up waiting, so I ambled through the backstreets in the company's fifty-year-old camion.

'Short-cut, monsieur,' mumbled Alphonse, the 300-year-old driver, who 200 years ago had been chauffeur to the director general until an unfortunate incident in the Bois de Boulogne which nobody had ever explained to me in detail. We trundled past dirty, miserable factories. (In most dirty, miserable French factories I've visited the code to their security locks is one-seven-eight-nine, the date of the French Revolution.)

Along the back streets we swayed. 'We'll get there on time?' I asked casually.

'*Pas de problème, monsieur*,' he grunted. 'It's a Friday evening. This is the fastest route.'

Two days, I swear, it took us to cross the Paris-Lyon road. 'But isn't that the way to Lyon?' I cried as at last we shot into second gear heading in the opposite direction to which the signpost was pointing.

'Friday night, monsieur,' he grunted. 'All the roads will be blocked.' He twirled his fingers round and round in the air.

'But isn't it still better . . .'

'The tunnel. The whole city.'

'But it's a fast road. Surely . . .'

He slammed the brakes on. We juddered to a halt.

France's third biggest city, Lyon is a nightmare for traffic at any time, let alone Friday evenings. Unfortunately they have launched a massive anti-car campaign including halving the width of many inner-city roads without waiting for all the alternatives, including a fourth metro line, to be built. The result, of course, is non-stop jams, pollution and breakdowns – both automobile and personal.

'If monsieur prefers, I can . . .' His fingers began to twist again. 'No, no, that's all right,' I grovelled. 'You're the expert.' We spluttered forward again. 'Providing of course . . .' He dropped back into first gear. 'No, no,' I jumped. 'You're right. You're the expert.'

Suddenly the van leapt forward like a bat out of hell. I grabbed the door for safety and prayed for the French government to make seatbelts compulsory. In an instant Lyon and Villefranche were behind us and we were in rolling, beautiful countryside. The grass was green and velvety, the trees elegant. We dropped down to the River Saône and meandered at the speed of sound through Ambérieu, over the bridge at Neuville-sur-Saône, along through Fleurieu-sur-Saône, Rochetaillée and Fontaines-sur-Saône.

This was a different world, the France we all know and love. This was not the France that was destroying me with

Villefranche and its blue overalls. This was the real France that didn't rate a mention in the guidebooks. I wanted to stop and explore, check into a hotel, blame the meeting going on too long, stay the weekend. But I didn't have the courage.

It was three minutes to final check-in. Alphonse was coaxing this old camion along like Fred Winter gliding Mandarin to victory in the Grand Steeplechase de Paris in 1962.

We arrived with ten seconds to go. I leapt through the van, across the terminal, straight to the check-in desk and, of course, the plane was late. It hadn't even left London yet. I collapsed on the floor. I could have taken it easy. I could have let poor old Alphonse drive at his own pace. I could have stopped off at Neuville or Fontaines-sur-Saône.

In the office on Monday there was a note on my desk. It said 'DG wants to see you again about the contract. He's thought of a way of getting round 1992. He wants to negotiate ten-year contracts with all his clients. Wants to know if you agree. He suggests a meeting next week in Vile France.'

Zurich

'54-74-62-00-91'

'What's that?'

'My new client.' He tapped the single, anonymous-looking black plastic folder in the centre of his anonymous-looking desk in his anonymous-looking office just off the Bahnhofstrasse in Zurich which, even in a recession, looks extremely opulent.

It was my first visit to a Swiss gnome's sweet home. The office was functional; Swiss functional, that is. He was wearing some kind of green Yves St Laurent suit, which struck me as odd for a Swiss banker. Not as bad as in Luxembourg, where most private bankers turn up to the office wearing jeans and running shoes. But still not quite Swiss.

Normally I meet Swiss bankers in other people's luxury homes and offices; in private apartments; in the avenue Foch in Paris; in the Negresco in Nice where they are invariably deep in conversation with Italian construction companies or Dutch dredgers and their mysterious Middle East clients; or in sweaty waiting rooms all over Africa.

'*Pas d'argent, pas de Suisses*,' as the French elegantly mutter to themselves.

Once I even met a Swiss banker on the train at Haywards Heath. He told me he had been playing golf. His partner, an eminent City lawyer, had just whispered in his ear that a chum had told him in confidence that the Bank of England were going to start investigating a big pension fund. A few months later I read in the *Financial Times* that as a result of the confidential information he had received, the Swiss banker had sued the fund's advisers and picked up a fat compensation cheque.

This time, however, I was at the very heart of Swiss banking. I'd been invited to see a gnome in his new office in one of the 900 small, very secretive, very anonymous, very discreet banks which help to make tiny Switzerland the world's largest financial centre after New York, London and Tokyo. He'd just been put in charge of a special department, for what he called high net worth individuals. He was supposed to ferret out the super-super rich, promise them the earth, then sign them up with the bank. A special individual service. Terribly discreet. But with big, big promises – anything up to 30% growth a year, guaranteed. And absolute secrecy, even more guaranteed.

Most Swiss bankers look like, well, gnomes who have been used as target practice by William Tell. Some, however, are as switched on as a Swiss watch. He used a Swiss swatch. We'd first met in Nairobi during a big African stock exchange conference I helped to organise for the African Development Bank. 'It will be difficult to make the function fulfil,' he kept saying.

We swapped stories about Africa; I told him what little I knew, he told me what the Aga Khan does every afternoon at 2.30 whenever he's at his European headquarters just outside Paris. After that we seemed to bump into each other on the international conference circuit – in Paris, in Brussels, in Abidjan, once even in Niamey when he was going on safari and I was on one of my regular African trips. Two weeks later I saw him again in Niamey. He was white. He certainly didn't look as though he had been on safari. 'Got caught when I arrived. Spent the whole two weeks with you-know-who.' He tapped his nose. 'He wanted to make certain arrangements just in case. I never set foot outside the door,' he said.

He was about fifty, and had been in and around banks all his life. He'd worked in London, New York and Paris. Originally he had been a project banker; you had a big project, he would come up with the finance – textile mills, bakeries, port extensions. As a result his contacts were superb. He also knew the fixers, the middlemen who put the deals together and take the big commissions. He was as far removed from your usual Wall Street banker as a Nat West branch manager is from a professional banker. He was the obvious man for a big, discreet, serious Swiss bank to select to set up a special department for the seriously super-rich. Now he spent all his time travelling, drifting through cocktail parties, making contacts, picking up leads and being discreet.

'If you see a Swiss banker fling himself out of a window, follow him. He must have discovered a new way of making money,' I was once told by an American wheeler dealer. This Swiss banker was a man to follow through an open window.

It might sound crazy, but it is this softly, softly, open window approach that has given the Swiss over 50% of the world's booming private banking market. That and the fact that everyone instinctively seems to believe a Swiss banker. Especially very discreet Swiss bankers.

They might now be the richest, most egalitarian, most democratic people in Europe – they can hardly tell you the time on their cuckoo clocks without having a referendum – but the Swiss are not exactly a bundle of laughs. Some people say Switzerland is a prison without walls where everyone is their own gaoler. I can see what they mean. But instead, to me it's like a fondue; okay to dip into, but too much of it is hard work and not very satisfying.

All the time I am travelling in Switzerland, I feel that the Swiss are like strangers you meet in a lift; mildly polite, but very, very quiet, and definitely no sense of humour. It's as if they are living in Puritania instead of Ruritania and are embarrassed to blow their Alpenhorns about having had fifty years of high economic growth and ever-increasing income.

Switzerland, maker of watches to the world, has no natural resources, no raw materials, no natural borders, no language of its own. Over 150 years ago Switzerland was already Europe's biggest exporter per capita with earnings twice as high as the British. Now they want to export even more. They are joining the EC. To shift the extra goods they are also planning to build more tunnels through the Gotthard massif and the Loetschberg mountains which makes the Channel Tunnel seem like cutting through butter.

All Switzerland does, some people say, is sit on the fence and pick up the pieces afterwards. 'Trades on the misfortunes of others,' they say.

Others, however, would give anything to be like Switzerland. All over Africa governments claim they are trying to turn themselves into 'the Switzerland of Africa': safe, neutral, financially stable. The Swiss, however, are continually worried in case they say something that will offend you and make you take your money to another country the other side of the Alps or, perhaps, further south.

I was in a hotel once in Zurich overlooking the beautiful, glittering, long, thin, blue lake. Normally hotel rooms are full of glossy brochures assuring you that you have just arrived in the best place in the whole world, plus Gideon's Bible. Inside the Bible was a card which said, 'If you've decided to sin no more, congratulations. If not, telephone St Paul's Bar.' Instead of the glossy magazines there was a 650-page book entitled, *Switzerland: Breakout from Behind*, a collection of seventy-five papers each giving the author's proposals for the future of Switzerland and published by the Foundation for Philosophical Sciences.

Maybe it's because they have been isolated for so long. They have virtually cut themselves off from the history of

Europe since the Congress of Vienna in 1815 and seem determined to preserve what is theirs and not to buy what is somebody else's. The Swiss Alps, like some giant Gruyère cheese are, as a result, pitted with nuclear shelters. The skies are full of jet fighters. The mountains are crawling with part-time soldiers who – typical Swiss – have to buy their own rifles, which they are allowed to take home and use for hunting the rest of the year. 'I suppose you keep it in your nuclear shelter under the floorboards,' I once said jokingly to another banker in Zurich. 'Yes, of course, where else?' he replied, all serious.

Another banker in Bern told me he kept his rifle with the iodine tablets the Swiss government have started distributing free to protect people from radiation in the event of another nuclear accident like Chernobyl.

'Why iodine?' I asked.

'It protects you against thyroid cancer.'

'And what happens if a Swiss nuclear power station explodes?'

He stared at me. The thought had obviously not occurred to him. 'We are a *Willensnation*,' he said eventually. 'It is what we have decided.'

We are all, of course, *Willensnations* in the West; at least in theory. But in Switzerland it's become unbelievably compli-cated. The country has six million inhabitants, four national languages and a religious divide between Catholics and Protestants (and every other belief under the sun). It is divided into twenty-three cantons which are, in fact, mini-sovereign states. Each has its own mini-government with its own batch of mini-ministers, mini-assemblies, mini-police forces and mini-housing, educational and social services. Below them are over 3,000 communes even more mini.

Some communes even have an annual open air *Lands-gemeinde*, like the Maoris' marae, where everybody can stand up and have their say. Everybody then votes, and if there's a majority, that's it, no more debate, they get on and do it.

Whether you have a *Landsgemeinde* or not, however, everything is subject to a vote, whether it be a small-scale show of hands or a full-scale mini-referendum. If you're not satisfied with the vote then you go for a referendum. Just another 49,999 signatures and you've got yourself a referendum. Recent referenda have been on vital subjects such as: 'forty firing ranges, that's enough' and 'For a public holiday April 1st, Switzerland's National Day.' You still don't feel you're being consulted enough? Get 99,999 other people to agree and you have your own initiative.

Up until 1971 it was only the men who spent their lives trudging backwards and forwards to vote. Even in 1971 eight cantons refused to enfranchise women, but they have since given in. The last, Appenzell Innerrhoden, only agreed in 1990 and then only after it was ordered to do so by the suddenly decisive Swiss Supreme Court.

For big issues, joining the EC for example, the government itself has to call a national referendum. In order to win, it not only has to win in most of the twenty-six cantons, it also has to have a majority of all the voters. The result is a weak, non-professional, federal parliament which meets for just sixteen three-day weeks a year and a very strong business sector, because nobody with any sense wants to get involved in running the country.

The parliament is dominated by the grand coalition of the three bourgeois parties: Christian Democrats, Radicals and the People's Party, which has 80% of the 200 seats in the National Council and a near monopoly of seats in the forty-six-seat upper Council of States. The People's Party together with the Social Democrats have been in power since 1959.

At the top somewhere is the president who is known only by his postman and possibly the other six members of the Federal Council who take it in turns to be president for one year at a time. If a Swiss is lecturing you about what should be done to solve the world's problems, ask them who is the president of Switzerland. They never know.

'So who actually runs the country?' I asked the banker in Zurich. This time he was wearing an Armani suit, two-tone shirt and what looked like a Hermès tie. His office had become a department of the bank which, he told me, was now so efficient they had more photocopiers in the office than people.

He tapped the small pile of anonymous-looking smooth, black leather folders on his desk. 'The Swiss priviligenzia,' he murmured. 'They are a close-knit group of around 100 people who actually run the country.'

'So all these referenda . . .'

'Shall we have lunch?' he said.

They're slumped under trees. They're sprawling all over the grass. The bandstand is splattered with blood. A stone's throw from the quiet, discreet, anonymous banks and glittering shopping centre, near the Landsmuseum is Platzspitz Park or Needleplatz, home to 5,000 drug addicts.

I've seen drug addicts all over the world; in Amsterdam in the old days, when you could hardly walk through the Central Station without stepping over them; in Casablanca; in Washington at receptions given by the State Department. But I've never seen anything like Needleplatz. I was frightened to breathe in case I became addicted.

Drive past there in the early morning when they are distributing their free clean syringes and you will see addicts from all over the world injecting themselves all over the place. I once saw a girl injecting herself in the tip of her finger. All around are Swiss, Turkish, Italian, Yugoslav dealers openly selling heroin, Polish soup – a highly concentrated and particularly lethal variation developed in Eastern Europe – cocaine, methadone, rohypnol, cannabis. You name it, they're selling it. They even provide spoons and syringes for free samples.

Switzerland has 20,000 registered addicts each with their own identity card – up 80% in four years – out of a population of 6.5 million. They have drug advice schemes, special syringe centres, free syringes – Zurich alone distributes over 10,000 every day to heroin addicts – social workers by the thousand and an apparently bottomless source of funds to try to contain the problem.

With typical Swiss efficiency, registered addicts both Swiss and non-Swiss – there is no discrimination in Switzerland – have at their disposal hostels, surgeries, halfway houses, special doctors, free meals, blankets, syringes. No charge; all courtesy of the God-fearing Calvinists. They even go around every morning and clear up after them.

'To look at them you would never believe this is a £200 million-a-year business,' one driver told me. 'Police reckon over 5 tons of heroin come into Switzerland every year. A kilo costs around US$150,000, ten times as much as cocaine. Most of it changes hands here.'

Drug smugglers, or mules, many of them from desperately poor South American countries, turn up at Zurich Airport with their pockets overflowing with drugs. While I was on one trip a Brazilian arrived at Zurich, his suit completely impregnated with 14 kilograms of cocaine. Bulach, the district close to the airport, is home to an army of overseas drug smugglers.

Most people in Zurich are convinced that while it is right to control the use of the car – the centre of the city is virtually car free – it is wrong to try to control the use of drugs. 'It is the Swiss policy of openness, treating drugs as a social instead of a criminal problem and desperately trying to limit the spread of AIDS among drug users, that's what is important,' the secretary of a Zurich businessman told me. 'It is important we give them, how do you say, a shot in the arm.'

In a country where wearing white socks to the office is virtually an offence to the dignity of the state, one or two people think things have gone too far. 'Most of the addicts are poor. *Das ist richtig, ja?*' said an elderly taxi driver outside Zurich station. 'Swiss jails are like luxury hotel, *ja*?'

'*Ja*,' I said.

'Zo. Zay come for hotel, *ja*.'

Maybe he had a point. Of all the police forces in the world, the Swiss police have the highest rate of success for capturing escaped prisoners, including even Lebanese Muslim extremists. Some people, however, say that after a taste of life on the outside, prisoners are only too pleased to give themselves up. Some even beg to be taken back. The minimum jail sentence for drug smuggling is thirty-eight months. With prisoners entitled to earn up to £7-£8 a day, in thirty-eight months you could stash away around £10,000 – tax free, rent free, freely transferable to any part of the world afterwards; by courtesy of your friendly local bank, of course.

In spite of Needleplatz, I find that in my own way I am also addicted to Zurich. It is a safe, friendly, pleasant, cautious town full of beautiful bookshops, antique shops, jewellers and art galleries. If the whole world is in recession, hovering on the brink of economic collapse, you'd never guess it wandering the streets of Zurich. Maybe it's just because they're Swiss. They're safe and cautious. They're the kind of driver who insists on making certain there's no train coming before they go over a level crossing.

Take William, or rather Wilhelm, Tell, the rough, tough mountain farmer. The Swiss still look upon him as a folk hero, when in fact he is a glorious joke created by a German and set to music by an Italian. I mean, if you were so confident of your ability to shoot that damn apple off that kid's head, would you have taken two arrows? Of course not. I mean, damn it, St George only took one lance when he went off to kill the dragon. The cautious Swiss would have taken two.

It's the same with Swiss banks. The Swiss like to gamble. But they don't like to lose their *gutes Geld*. Swiss banks as a result are the only banks anywhere with special accounts which enable investors to invest without any risk of losing their money. If you want a high rate of interest, you risk getting a low return on the success of the investment. On the other hand if you opt for a low rate of interest you stand to make a lot of money on the success of the investment. When the scheme was first launched, one bank had so many takers they were forced to pull down the shutters after taking over SF150 million in SF5,000 blocks in a matter of minutes.

To me Geneva is caution personified. It exists for caution. It is also hospitality, conferences, dinners, restaurants; tables groaning under the finest tableware, heavy cream brocade cloths, George Jensen cutlery and damask napkins. It is chefs in stainless-steel rimless spectacles. It is the hum of Swiss efficiency.

Geneva is spotless, almost blameless – probably the most blameless city in the world. It is clean, it is green. It must have more grass per head of population than any other city. It is sparkling. By day Lake Geneva sparkles in the sun; by night it sparkles in the glow of a million multi-coloured light bulbs. The people are all *bien passant*, as the right-thinking French never tire of saying. The biggest problem it has to face is probably the threat of diplomatic double parking outside the Palais Wilson, the original home of the old League of Nations, on the lake. You can see why it's home to practically every international organisation you can think of. If I was an international civil servant looking for something to do, I would not be unhappy to be living in Eaux-Vives, the fashionable part of the city, shopping in *les grands hôtels particuliers* along the rue Faubourg St Honore and locked into endless committee meetings in Geneva. And yet it seems to lack that certain something. Why Byron and Shelley met up with the two Godwin sisters in Geneva when they had the rest of Europe to choose from I don't know.

Lucerne is even more Geneva than Geneva. A trip by train from Geneva to Lucerne on a sunny spring afternoon is as unlike a trip on British Rail as you can imagine. When counting all the private schools around the lake – there are fifty-seven – you are constantly interrupted by people cleaning the train.

Basel is fantastic if you have a pocket full of Russian roubles and kopeks. It's about the only place in the world where they are useful, because they fit the 'phone boxes and parking meters throughout the city, just as the Swaziland pound, worth a fraction of the pound sterling, will fit slot machines in the UK.

But wherever you go in Switzerland the neutral, tolerant Swiss will have one thing in common; they all look down on everybody else. The people in Geneva look down on the people in Zurich as uncultured and uncivilised. Especially since they agreed to let Citizen, Japan's biggest watchmaker, grab the advertising space over the eight-foot-square Swiss-made clock in the main railway station. The people in Zurich think the people in Geneva are only concerned about style and image and hosting international conferences. Everybody looks down on the people from Bern.

The Swiss German, or *Schweizerdeutsch*, who make up two thirds of the population, think the Swiss French a bit too quiet, and the Swiss Romans dull. On the other side of the 'rosti curtain', the Swiss French, who account for 20% of the population, think the Swiss Germans are dull and stolid. French Swiss are worried about the threat of 'Germanification'. They tell you *entre nous* that more German speakers are now using the *Schwyzerdutsch* dialect rather than the High German taught in schools in French-speaking areas.

But the Swiss Germans and the Swiss French think the Swiss Italians around Lugano, with its clean mountain air, its sweeping green fields and its lazy cattle still with bells around their necks, are crazy. Especially their banks. Neither the Swiss Germans nor the Swiss French would lend them as much as a cuckoo clock. 'If they want to be different, they should go to Italy,' I am always being told. 'If not, they should be like us.' The *cittadini* (citizens) of Lugano just sneer at talk about Zurich as Svizzerna interna, inner Switzerland.

All three, the Swiss German, the Swiss French and the Swiss Italians, hardly know what to think of the Swiss Romans, let alone their three dialects, Ladin, Surmitan and Sursilvan, which are based on a mixture of Latin, Rhaetian and Celtic dialects dating back to the first century AD.

The Swiss Germans, it is said, are the only people who understand *Schwyzerdutsch*. When Luther translated his Bible he put it into *Sachsische Kanzleisprache*, the language of Saxony. The areas which did not accept the translation stuck with their own *Mittelhochdeutsch*, today's *Schwyzerdutsch*.

How James Joyce spent so much time in Zurich I can't imagine. I can only suppose that it was while he was trying to survive without wearing glasses, so he didn't see a thing. Instead he concentrated on listening to their unique mix of *Hoch Deutsch*, *Schwyzerdutsch*, French, Italian and English and came up with *Finnegan's Wake*.

I was at dinner at the Schweitzerhof with a group of sparkling, lively English businessmen and dull Swiss business-men. We'd chosen the Schweitzerhof because it serves nouvelle cuisine quality in *ancienne cuisine* quantities. It also serves a somewhat unusual Swiss red wine, Sang de Lenfer. We were between the cheesecake and cheese.

One of the English businessmen was convinced the Zurich dialect of *Schwyzerdutsch* was as near as damn it fourteenth-century English. His son, he said, had had problems with his Early English studies, and couldn't tell the difference between an octosyllabic couplet and the 'Legend of Good Women'. He had packed him off to an aunt living outside Zurich. Within a few weeks he'd cracked it. He was reading the *Canterbury Tales* in the original and creating his own legend with the not-so-good women of Zurich.

* * *

'The weather? What do you mean, the weather?'

The Zurich banker had now moved into a bigger office actually overlooking the lake. He had swopped his Yves St Laurent outfit for, would you believe, a Gieves and Hawkes pin-stripe suit. He was wearing one of those regimental-looking ties. The pile of anonymous-looking black folders, I noticed, had grown a little higher. He was now on the 'phone to a correspondent bank in London.

'The weather is all right,' he said carefully, and gave me that helpless look foreigners assume when they listen to the British talking about the weather. He pretended to look out at the lake as if to confirm the weather was still there. 'Yes. It's all right,' he mumbled.

If the Swiss are sometimes unable to understand each other, apart from private bankers in search of super-super rich clients, they don't exactly find it easy to get on with other people either. Wherever they are they tend to be about as flexible as a Swiss Army knife; the bow, the limp handshake and the endless glasses of water.

They find it hard to understand the British, and have even worse problems in other parts of the world. They desperately want to get into Eastern Europe but cannot understand the East Europeans. 'They are incredible,' they whisper. 'They say it's because they can't telephone and say they are going to be late. But if they know the telephones don't work they would make certain they didn't have to telephone in the first place.'

We gossiped about Africa, where he'd been travelling, people he had met, where Mrs Babangida was doing her shopping nowadays, why President Bongo had sent his private jet to Paris the previous week, and what the Aga Khan now got up to at 2.30 every afternoon at his headquarters outside Paris.

He was also picking up the jargon. He kept referring to the adviser to one African president as the Milkman.

'The Milkman?'

'He creams 10% off the top of everything,' he smiled.

African politicians, he said, had three homes; their home, the grave and prison. He was there to look after them between one and two.

He'd picked up a lot of private banking business in Africa, much of it, he said, from British banks. 'You mean the British are not prepared to be so flexible?' I smiled. Not at all, he said, in many cases the British could be even more flexible. It was just that Africans did not like bankers who sat rolling their own cigarettes while the Dom Perignon was being passed around.

So who was his biggest client, I asked.

'54.' He tapped the smooth black leather folder in the centre of his polished Louis Quatorze table tucked in the corner of his new elegantly furnished suite of offices.

'54. That's not 54-74-62-00-91, your first client?' I hesitated.

'Except now he is one of my oldest and largest clients,' he smiled pulling down his shirt cuffs below his pin-striped jacket. 'Which is why he allows me to call him by his first name, 54.'

It was my first Swiss gnome joke.

Addis Ababa

It was my first day in Addis, as we old Africa hands say. I came out of the hotel, saw a line of taxis, threw my briefcase and jacket in the one at the head of the queue and climbed in alongside the driver. 'I'd like to go to the Organisation for African Unity,' I said, shaking hands with him. 'I've got a big meeting about plans for the future economic development of Africa.'

'Sorry,' he smiled. 'Can't take you.'

'But why? What's wrong?' I stuttered.

'You haven't got a voucher. I need a voucher before I can take you anywhere.'

I clambered out, grabbed briefcase and jacket and went off to discover the joys of Marxist-Leninism in action in a continent that is always dreaming dreams.

I had always wanted to visit Addis Ababa (which means 'new flower', and is pronounced A-bar-bar not Abba-ba. At least that's what the old Africa hands say). My chance came during the last days of the civil war. The rebels had taken the road between Addis and Dessie, the main highway to Assab in Tigray. Other units were now fifty miles west of the city.

I had to visit the Organisation for African Unity. I was commissioned to prepare a report on their plans for an African Economic Community, which would stretch from Cairo to the

77

Cape and from Nouakchott to Nairobi. Was it a practical possibility? How far had the OAU got in drawing up their proposals? Would they get the necessary backing?

As I was getting ready to leave London I had a call from one of the leading members of the fast-growing Ex-African Presidents' Club. He had heard I was going to Addis. He had had a call from one of his contacts there, a colonel. He had some interesting proposals. We met at the Reform Club to discuss them. Would I call and see this colonel, while I was there? I agreed.

'As soon as you get to Addis, telephone this number.' He gave me an airline ticket. On the back, etched out with a thick blunt pencil, was a number. 'He's sent me a fax. He says he wants to talk about some big military deal. You could talk to him for us.'

I tried to book Ethiopian Airlines which, amazingly when you think of the country and what it has been through, is one of the most efficient, pleasant and reliable airlines in Africa. But of course it was fully booked. Instead I had to take Air France.

If Tamanrasset was the biggest disappointment of my life, Addis Ababa, the world's third highest capital city, was the second. In terms of cities, that is. Thousands of years of history; a kingdom that has flourished since biblical times; Coptic Christians who have lived side by side with Muslims since the fourth century; an alphabet with forty characters and three versions of each letter.

So what was it like? Terrible. It's a modern, characterless city that could be the capital of a dozen different countries. There's no atmosphere, no feeling, no sense of history or culture. I thought Addis would be like Cairo, or Algiers or even, heaven help us, Lagos. Not on your life. It's less than 100 years old.

I expected cloud-capped towers, gorgeous palaces, solemn temples, spectacular views and a million tiny mysterious side streets and alleyways where the world had stood still for thousands of years. Instead I found an ordinary nondescript town that looked like a dress rehearsal for any ordinary nondescript town anywhere.

I had imagined a world of towering, impressive nomads, melancholy monks and warriors; gnarled, sculptured, Amharic faces; characters straight out of the book of Kings. Instead it was virtually a ghost town decorated with pictures of Marx and Lenin and posters proclaiming 'Long Live International Proletarianism'. Maybe a car would trundle along Africa Avenue every ten or fifteen minutes. Apart from that, nothing.

I had thought everywhere would be examples of their fabulous culture, the Solomonic dynasty: libraries, schools, universities dating back three thousand years. Instead I saw a shepherd leading his tiny flock the wrong way up the once fashionable Winston Churchill Avenue – and it didn't matter a bit; what little traffic there was simply drove around him.

I had read about the Amharas, the people of Addis, and had imagined they would be proud, civilised, aristocratic; the type of people who have no hang-ups or pretensions because they know they are born to rule. Instead I came across a once-proud people, dishevelled, listless, desperately poor, desperately hungry. But also desperately polite, everywhere – in the hotels; fighting your way through the tiny boys offering to clean your shoes; in offices; even walking along the street. It was as if they were hoping you hadn't noticed the pitiful position they were in.

But worse than the poverty, if that's possible, was the all-pervading Marxist-Leninism. There were slogans in Revolution Square, inside the hotels, outside the office buildings, in shops. There were giant portraits of Marx and Lenin outside the Wabi Shebele Hotel, on government buildings, inside all the offices.

In fact Ethiopia was a back-to-front country. While the rest of the world was busy rejecting the whole idea of people's democracies, they were busy trying to build the last Marxist-

Leninist state, and the last (I hope) people's democracy to make the people suffer. At least Haile Hariam Mengistu was.

Everybody says Mengistu overthrew Haile Selassie. Not true. A slim, slightly built man with a steely gaze, he was one of the secret group of soldiers who seized power from the emperor in 1974. Trained largely in the West, they wanted to introduce not communism but democracy. They hated the corruption, the waste and the inefficiency that were destroying the country. Their first leader, General Aman Andom, was mysteriously shot. Next they were led by General Teferi Benti, until two years later he was shot. Then they were led by General Atnafu Abate. Nine months later he was shot. Nobody knew who the other members of the group were. They had all virtually imprisoned themselves in Asmara, which they turned into a military town. Nobody was allowed in without special permission. Few people seemed to come out.

Then Mengistu appeared. On February 3rd, 1977 he seized absolute power – because all his opponents had somehow disappeared. Out went all talk of democracy and devolving power to the regions. In came Marxist-Leninism and all the trappings of a full-blooded Stalinist state: terrorist squads, secret police, arbitrary executions, public lynchings, street massacres. Then the Workers' Party of Ethiopia was formed, collective villages were set up, huge resettlement programmes were put in hand. State economic controls were clamped on trade and industry, ensuring that if the hammer didn't get them the sickle would.

People told me it was so dangerous in those days, nobody went out. If you had to go out at night, you drove with the lights on inside your car. 'That way you made certain people could see you. You were not shot by accident.'

The Russians then took over. 'We could tell the Russians were taking over,' I was told. 'Their ambassador started driving around with the lights inside his car switched off.'

As if that wasn't enough, there was the civil war. Originally an Italian colony, Eritrea never accepted integration into Ethiopia. First they fought Haile Selassie, then Mengistu. By 1985 it looked at last as though they were going to win. By 1988 they were walking all over Mengistu's conscript army. The Tigrayans joined in. The Russians provided an estimated US$12 billion in arms and weaponry. But it was all in vain. Inevitably things got worse. The whole social, economic and political structure of the country disintegrated. Coffee, once responsible for 60% of Ethiopia's budget, just disappeared. Over 6 million people were facing starvation. The country, once almost self-sufficient, breeding cattle and producing abundant crops of barley, cotton, maize, potatoes, wheat and tobacco, was now one of the poorest in the world, if not the poorest.

By the time I visited Addis the party – the Marxist-Leninist Party – was virtually over.

The official taxi authorisation office was tucked behind the hotel lobby next to the travel agents. To get my bit of paper, I had to queue up behind a million other would-be travellers.

'Where you go?' a completely uninterested girl who would have been happy in a VAT office growled at me.

'All over,' I replied. 'I want to go to the Economic Commission, the OAU ...'

'You only authorise for one place only. Which one?'

'But I want to go to lots of different places.'

'No problem,' she grunted. 'I give you authorise for one place. You come back here and get another authorise for another place.'

'But that's no good,' I began. 'I haven't got time to keep coming back ...'

'They are rules,' she said. 'You want taxi or not?'

'Okay,' I grunted, 'I'll take it.'

'Where to?'

'OAU.' I grabbed my authorisation and ran. All the taxis had gone. 'How long until I get another taxi?' I asked the doorman, who looked more like the dustman.

'Maybe lunchtime. Maybe tomorrow.'

'But that's crazy,' I said. 'I've got a million things to do. I can't—'

He came and stood alongside me. 'My brother has a car,' he whispered.

'You mean for hire?' I whispered back.

'Sh.' He jabbed me in the ribs. 'That is against the law.'

'Of course. Of course.'

'He drive you around, if you want. Go anywhere. As friend, of course.'

'Of course,' I said.

Five minutes later I was sitting in a battered Fiat, chugging our good old free enterprise way through Mengistu's Marxist-Leninist State.

My first meeting was not with the OAU but with the mysterious colonel. Somehow I felt it might not have been prudent to give his name to the authorisation office. I had telephoned the number on the airline ticket the previous evening, and the voice that answered gave me an address in Patriots' Square, the other side of town, on the edge of the Mercato – the Italian for market – which calls itself the biggest market in Africa. I imagined an enormous open-air market similar to those you come across all over Africa, a heaving, thriving, throbbing mass of humanity arguing and yelling for days about the price of a cup of rice. Instead it was street after street of tiny, dusty, yellow sand-and-brick shops, jammed with food, inner wheels, sandals made out of car tyres, baskets, everything. It looked a bit like Pompeii before the earthquake.

Hanging around the street corners (in the Mercato there are lots of street corners) were small groups of ragged soldiers dripping with AK47s, automatic rifles and bandoliers stuffed with bullets. But everyone looked decidedly unmilitary.

We found the office and parked outside. Inside it was like a bank that had ceased being a bank three hundred years before Addis was founded. There was a long marble counter down the far end. Small doors lined the walls behind it. I asked for the Colonel. Two tiny, very polite men wearing dusty white suits who could have been aged anything from sixteen to sixty disappeared through different doors behind the counter. Before I'd finished reading the revolutionary slogans dripping around the wall, they had returned. 'I'm sorry,' they said together. 'The Colonel, he say he is very busy. You are to call back, please.'

The Economic Commission for Africa, which turned out to be near the hotel, was in a different world altogether; the twentieth-century world of international bureaucracies. It was big. It was modern. It had a huge reception area, tower blocks, chauffeured limousines. It was completely at odds with the world surrounding it. The air-conditioning was so efficient I felt chilly with my jacket on.

I wanted to meet Mary Tadesse, one of the few Ethiopians left in the Commission, who was fighting her own kind of battle.

'All the others have left,' she told me. Her family had also left. But she had decided to stay, for the sake of her battle. Which was on behalf of all the women in Africa.

Officially she is Chief of the Trading and Research Centre for Women at the Commission. Unofficially she is the power house behind seminars, conferences, research studies, projects and a whole string of publications designed to liberate African women from their traditional role, tear down the barriers and allow them to develop their full potential. In other words, she is the unofficial leader of the African women's liberation movement.

Which is obviously why she is based in Addis, which was founded by Africa's first liberated woman after Cleopatra. The Emperor Menelik wanted to build his capital high in the

Entoto Mountains. His wife, Taitu, wanted it built down on the plains where it was warmer. So where was it built?

'It is the right thing for women. It is the right thing for business, industry, commerce, government, everything. It is the right thing for Africa,' Mary Tadesse told me. 'Africa needs more business skills. Africa needs more managers. The women must be allowed to contribute.'

She even forecasts an African woman prime minister by 1995. 'Why not? Today we have women ministers, women ambassadors, women judges. Five years ago people said it wasn't possible. Maybe in five years' time we'll have our first African woman prime minister,' she said.

When she first established the Research Centre, women's issues were seen as a marginal subject. 'They put us in a corner and thought that was it,' she said. But today, throughout the ECA, the role women can play in developing Africa is seen as an integral part of every department and every issue tackled by the Commission.

'In agriculture, industry, commerce, banking – every department now accepts that women are a vital part of every activity. In the past they used to put us under Social Affairs. Now we are everywhere,' she said.

The same, to a degree, is happening all over Africa. Nigeria, Cameroon, Uganda and Rwanda all have women ministers. Some, like Uganda and Côte d'Ivoire, have ministries for women's affairs. More women are standing for parliament. In Tanzania, for example, at the last general election twenty-five out of 244 seats were taken by women; similarly in Madagascar, in both elected and legislative positions. In Angola, Ethiopia, Mozambique, Seychelles and Zambia, women's organisations play a leading role in government.

'Women are equal partners with men. Their participation in politics and in economic decision-making is crucial to development. They are an economic asset whose contribution must be acknowledged and utilised,' she says.

In business also, women, the traditional traders of Africa, have made enormous gains. At the top of the league I've met women like Mrs Evelyn Mungai, president of Kenya's Evikar International, and Mrs Cathy Mwanamwambwa, managing director of Zambia's Whitbi Enterprises. Both run big companies they've built up themselves. In Gambia there is a special Women's Finance Company; in Kenya a Women's Finance Trust, and in Uganda a Women's Finance and Credit Trust. There are organisations like Women's World Banking which every day throughout Africa is helping women like Mrs N.M. Glickman in Botswana, who over fourteen years has built up her company specialising in knitwear, school uniforms and dresses until now she is employing 100 people, mostly women.

'We organise seminars for women in business,' Mrs Tadesse told me. 'They come, and they bring their goods with them. They say they are not interested in talking, only in making business. Throughout the seminars they are buying and selling. They are making money, not just talking.'

But there is still a long way to go. Women for example, still have big problems getting credit. 'Although women produce more than half the food in Africa, all the loans go to men because the banks are more prepared to accept a male signature than a female one,' Mrs Tadesse told me. 'What could be more absurd? It's got to be changed.'

When a woman wants a loan – even a woman running a big company of her own – she has to get her husband's signature, although in many cases he knows less about business than she does. 'And in some countries,' she said, 'even if a woman wants to put her own money in a bank they still require her husband's signature.'

But I have come across exceptions. The Mraru Women's Group, a community self-help organisation in the Taita Hills of Kenya, runs their own public transport system to get goats, maize and cassava roots to the local market as well as their own foodstores. They started in 1970 with forty-seven members. Today they have over 200 members. Yet again and again they faced problems with banks. First, they needed finance to get started. The banks turned them down. It took them three years to save up enough money to start. Next, they lost the chance of purchasing a bus at a good price because the post office insisted on two weeks' notice before they allowed them to withdraw their own money, by which time the bus had been sold. They had to buy a bus at a higher price, and because they had to borrow more to buy the bus, it had to be worked much harder. As a result they needed a replacement sooner than they should have done and, of course, they didn't have enough money. They were only saved when somebody – not a bank – offered to make up the difference.

The Duterimbere, another non-profit women's organisation in Rwanda, has to date helped over 600 women go into business by organising training sessions, producing market studies and working alongside individual entrepreneurs. They want to expand and raise more money for their increased activities. The local bank is sympathetic but says the organisation must meet their credit guarantee requirements. Which, of course, is beyond their means.

'There are women all over Africa who could succeed in business if only they had the resources to get started,' says Mrs Tadesse. 'They don't need much. We must find a way of helping them.'

Many women were already involved in informal credit systems such as credit unions, borrowing from moneylenders or from relatives. They did not know anything about the formal borrowing system, the approach, the terms and conditions.

'In market places all over Africa you find men collecting the money the women have made and taking it to the bank for them. The women are grateful, they think the men are being helpful. What they don't know is the men are keeping all the interest on the women's money for themselves and not telling them,' Mrs Jennifer Kargbo, a successful Sierra Leone businesswoman who is helping Mrs Tadesse put together the campaign, told me.

'When a woman goes into a bank, the officials will probably be prejudiced against her. She will not be treated the same way as a man,' adds Mrs Tadesse, 'although she has probably broken out of that vicious circle of poverty, is ambitious, an achiever and has access to other resources, human material, technology, and the skills to use them effectively.'

Banks thought women did not save, did not repay loans and were a poor credit risk. But survey after survey proved the contrary.

The Research Centre report, 'Accessing Women to Credit', called for a three-stage packaged approach: giving women information and confidence to apply for credit; helping them develop their know-how and financial and technical resources; and assisting them to be better at the technical and financial aspects of running and developing a business.

'We want women to be seen as low-risk clients, capable of meeting credit requirements and obligations and being able to repay on a regular basis,' Mrs Tadesse told me as we walked back to my free enterprise car.

'And in spite of all the problems,' I said, 'you still think we'll have an African woman prime minister in five years?'

'Why not?' she grinned. 'They couldn't make a worse job of it than the men.'

We drove back to Patriots' Square. As we passed Menelik Palace, troops were massing outside. They didn't seem as weary and dishevelled as the soldiers I'd seen earlier. They were obviously some of the 3,000 presidential troops who, towards the end, were said to be guarding Mengistu and the skull of Haile Selassie which he kept in his office. Tanks were rolling along outside. That night I heard guns firing in the distance.

The following morning I had decided private enterprise was one thing but when in a Marxist-Leninist state, even one in its dying moments, it was best to do as the Marxist-Leninists do. I queued up at the voucher office for my official bit of paper. It took twenty minutes. Outside the hotel, all the taxis had gone except one. It was the driver who had turned me down. I threw my briefcase and jacket in the back and climbed in beside him. 'Okay,' I said, 'I've got my voucher.'

'You needn't have worried,' he grunted. 'Two days you don't need voucher. Only for one day.'

'Well why the hell . . .?' I thought. But I just grinned weakly. 'Okay,' I said, 'Patriots' Square.' I wanted to see the Colonel.

There seemed to be even more soldiers outside the Menelik Palace than on the previous day. There also seemed to be more military trucks and convoys.

The message at the mysterious Colonel's very mysterious office was, however, the same. He was busy. He was in a meeting. He would call me.

Now for the OAU, which I always think is a cross between a trade association and a trade union for 650 million people. It consists of three old-fashioned, dilapidated buildings. It's like a block of council flats converted into offices and run by the housing committee of Camden Council.

The great hall that played host to conference after conference, that witnessed some of Africa's greatest statesmen, is now home to a table-tennis table. The Secretary General's office is like a sixties' Blackpool boarding house. It has a dark red carpet consumed with holes. The furniture looks as though it was rejected by Oxfam. Other offices are worse. In the Economic Department the carpet is so thin everyone is working on bare concrete. In one office all the fittings have fallen away exposing the bare pipes. And everywhere there are mountains, veritable Kilimanjaros, of dusty reports, analyses and political papers for solving the continent's problems.

The glorious thing is that none of the staff believe there is anything wrong – partly because, from their point of view, there isn't. Compared to government offices in Ouagadougou or Cotonou, the OAU offices are the height of luxury. And also partly because no way are they going to let you see that they believe they've got it wrong. Except, of course, the Ghanaians. Because the OAU was Nkrumah's idea, and Ghanaians believe that had Nkrumah got his way the OAU would be based in Ghana, and a billion times better than it is now.

I once spent an evening with a very international group of Ghanaians who talked about nothing but how different the OAU would have been if it had been based in Accra. 'So have you been to Accra lately?' I asked. They hadn't. They had all been too busy battling to solve the problems of Africa surrounded by the inefficiencies of Addis. I hadn't the heart to tell them what Accra was like nowadays.

With the OAU and the Economic Commission for Africa, Addis is an international city. It should be a hard-nosed political city like New York with its United Nations, Brussels with the EC or even Abidjan with the African Development Bank. Its bars and dining rooms should echo with politics and bargaining. But the bars and dining rooms are nonexistent. Instead of wrestling with the problems of today the few African diplomats and bureaucrats who are left dream dreams. In the Economic Department they told me their greatest dream; Africa one day should be a single political whole. In the meantime, it should be a single economic community.

'But there are no roads, no infrastructure, no common links. Only 5% of all African trade is within Africa.'

'You can do it in Europe. Why shouldn't we do it in Africa?'

They quoted me the fourth out of over 106 articles, divided into twenty-two chapters, that make up their Economic Treaty. Socio-economic development and integration will 'increase economic self-reliance and promote an indigenous and self-sustained development.'

'Yes, but . . .'

'It says so in the Treaty.'

They went on to wax lyrical about the 'development, mobilisation and utilisation of Africa's resources in pursuit of the goal of self-reliance, the promotion of all-round co-operation among African countries so as to raise living standards and ...' A framed photograph of Nkrumah, I noticed, lay shattered in the gaping hole of what used to be the office carpet '... and enhance stability, peace and the co-ordination and harmonisation of policy among existing and future regional economic communities so as to foster the gradual establishment of the continental economic community.'

'But will it happen?'

'Of course,' they chorused. 'We are all brothers. We are all Africans.'

They didn't tell me, but I later discovered that the treaty will only come into operation a month after two-thirds of the OAU agree to it. When will that be? Even if it does come into effect it will be phased in gradually over thirty-four years.

'Why thirty-four years?' I asked another OAU official later, while we tucked into a traditional Ethiopian wat, a red-hot sauce made of chicken, beans and lentils; slices of injera, the local bread which tastes like foam rubber and is made with millet and yeast and left to go sour for three days before being cooked; and a bottle of local Duka red wine.

'Because of the experience we have gained looking at the way the European Community has been established. We know,' he smiled a smile that looked more like a sneer, 'that not all countries can be rushed.'

There would have to be secretariats, secretary-generals, officials of ministers and assemblies of heads of state; even courts of justice and, wait for it, a pan-African parliament. 'But Africa's not like that,' I said. He asked for another bottle of Duka.

We got back to the hotel late. 'Thanks,' I said to the driver. 'So how much?'

'You'll have to go back to the office,' he grinned. 'They'll tell you.'

'But you must know.'

'It's the system,' he shrugged.

I ran into the hotel. He came running after me. 'Don't forget your authorisation,' he shouted. 'You'll need it.'

'But you said . . .'

'Not for getting a taxi. But for paying, yes.'

I spent I don't know how long, first queuing up to have my authorisation authorised. 'But if I hadn't completed my journey, I wouldn't be here,' I protested weakly. 'We know that sir,' said the girl. 'We're not stupid, you know.'

Then I had to queue up to pay. 'It says here the Economic Commission. That's only two minutes. But now it's nearly ten o'clock.' The pay girl looked at me. 'I'll have to charge you a supplement of 500%,' she said.

'That's outrageous,' I exclaimed. 'No way does it cost that much.'

'I know,' she said. 'It's because while you are in the taxi nobody is able to use it.'

'But there's nobody else here who wants to use it.'

'That doesn't matter,' she insisted. 'We are a Socialist country.' I gulped, and paid their capitalist prices.

The driver was waiting for me outside. 'Something for the driver, sir,' he whispered.

I reckon the whole trip cost me more than if I had bought a Russian tank and driven myself around Addis.

I rang my ex-president in London, which was surprisingly easy compared to the problems I've faced getting calls through from other parts of the world. I explained the situation.

'I'll call you back,' he said, and did so within ten minutes. 'The Colonel says he is very busy, but he must talk to you. You are to keep trying.' Click. The 'phone went dead. That night the guns were louder.

The following day I ignored the taxis at the hotel and borrowed a Ghanaian driver from the OAU who was looking for some extra money. That's African capitalism.

I made my regular call at the Colonel's office in Patriots' Square. I was beginning to feel part of the dusty furniture. I saw his two minders. 'He's not here. He said he had to leave. You are to call him tomorrow at 10.30,' said Rosencrantz. 'He's not here. He waited until 10 o'clock for you to ring, then he had to go out,' said Guildenstern.

I spent the rest of the day going from government office to government office, from ministry to ministry. First I went to the ministry of industry, which looked like a building site – or at least a site where building used to take place. By comparison the OAU was unbelievable luxury. The ground floor was open to the world – no walls, no front, no back. Talk about open government. Everybody was walking on bare concrete. My first meeting was on the fourth floor. The stairs were still concrete. There were no handrails. As I climbed the floor seemed to get more even; walls and corridors began to appear; people began wandering around aimlessly like they do in all government offices.

And it was worth the climb, for I discovered that in spite of Mengistu's call to abandon the current five-year plan and put the nation on a war footing, the first cracks were already appearing in Ethiopia's implacable Marxist economy. Buried deep down in paragraph three of part two of the Council of State Special Decree No. 9/1989 which had just been issued I read: 'Co-operative business organisations and individual entrepreneurs may establish small-scale industries in accordance with this Special Decree.'

'This is revolutionary,' an official told me in his cubby hole of an office. 'Two or three years ago this would have been unthinkable.'

Since the revolution the only way to do business had been to establish a general partnership with five partners with unlimited liability. What happened? Nothing. Business ground to a standstill. Factories were operating at less than 50% capacity, offices gathering dust. The shops along by Revolution Square were practically empty. There were desperate shortages of cooking oil, flour, wheat and even coffee beans which were once the pride of Ethiopia. There was virtually no sugar, rationed or unrationed, in spite of there being two enormous, high-yielding sugar estates at Wonji and Methara, south of the capital. Not one car in Addis had four good tyres.

'But this will all change. You watch,' the official whispered.

A special division had already been set up in the ministry under Mrs Masaret Shafaraw – Mary Tadesse was obviously a prophet honoured in her own country – to manage the return to the private sector. Already it was being inundated by people eager to go into business.

'So far we've had over 900 applications from people in Addis alone,' another official told me in his office overlooking the Hilton, the only luxury hotel in the capital. 'We tell them they can go ahead and start without waiting for the government to issue all the rules and regulations.'

Some rich Ethiopians who left the country years ago had come back and were already considering projects.

'Everybody is looking for feasibility studies,' a businessman in the shoe industry told me later. 'We still have to submit them to the government for permission to go ahead because obviously it's no good if everybody is building a brick works. We need a wide range of projects. But at least we've started.'

There had even been enquiries from foreign investors. 'Literally every embassy and foreign trade representative in Ethiopia has been knocking at the door,' the minister for foreign economic relations, Mr Aklilu Afeworle, told me. 'The response has been very positive.'

But it was only the first step. 'We've still got to look at the whole range of company legislation, joint ventures, foreign participation, foreign investment. There is a long way to go.

There will be many problems – foreign exchange, for example. But we've reached the point of no return. We've realised we must encourage the private sector,' a ministry official promised.

What made them change? Some people say it was perestroika. The more old President Gorbachev turned his attention to solving his problems at home, the less inclined he was to support Ethiopia.

International pressure, say others, while others put it down to unemployment, and the amount of foreign goods being smuggled into the country. 'Something has to be done about unemployment. People are saying they have to work, they want to work. The only way to fix that is to stimulate the private sector. They've tried everything else and failed. On top of that the government can see that they are losing revenue because of so much smuggling,' an official at the Commercial Bank of Ethiopia told me.

But not everybody is in favour of the new policy. Officials in the ministry of domestic trade complained to me that they were losing control of the private sector. They would be unable to plan and regulate its development.

'But it's because they've done nothing over the last fifteen years we've had to introduce these new regulations,' an official told me.

As I stumbled back down the concrete stairs, I was swamped by a group of fragile matchstick men with Old Testament beards and long, flowing white robes. 'Falashas,' an official with a pile of papers under his arm whispered at me. The famous Jews of Ethiopia are the direct descendants of King Solomon and the Queen of Sheba, although the Chief Rabbinate in Jerusalem didn't get round to accepting them until 1975.

The reason there are not many left in the country, I discovered over dinner with a ministry official, is thanks to Mossad, the Israeli secret service, which in 1984 turned itself into a travel company and airlifted over 15,000 Falashas out of Addis in what many people believe was part of a secret arms-for-refugees deal with Mengistu.

In the late seventies, early eighties, the Falashas were suffering the effects of drought, famine and war, although whether they were suffering more than the ordinary non-Jew in the street nobody can say. But they were Jews, and if Jews are in trouble Israel is prepared to do its utmost to bring them home. The problem was handed over to Mossad. Then things become hazy.

Everybody in Addis told me that suddenly all the Falashas' problems disappeared. Internal travel documents which had been like gold suddenly appeared out of the blue. Rented vehicles were two a penny. Safe houses were all over the place. The authorities in the Sudan, who had previously done nothing to help them escape from Ethiopia, were suddenly co-operative, willing to open up secret routes, turn blind eyes and forget to ask for every piece of paper to be verified five times. Israeli missile ships were suddenly cruising off the Sudanese coast ferrying heavy-set Israeli tourists wearing dark glasses who liked nothing better than to disappear into the desert for weeks on end.

Hercules transport planes began losing their way and being forced to make emergency landings in the middle of the desert, though somehow they managed to become airborne again in the time it would take 300–400 people to scramble on board. Then suddenly in January 1985 it was all over. Sudan started checking the documents again.

'Were they glad they got out?' I asked.

'I don't know,' the ministry man replied. 'The Falashas think a light bulb is hi-tech. How they are adjusting to a country which can produce a nuclear bomb is something else.'

I got back to the hotel. It was beginning to get dark. The rich and young of Addis were gathering for the nightclub. As soon as I got to my room the telephone rang. It was my contact in

London. 'The Colonel's just telephoned,' he said. 'He has a lot of scrap from the war; tanks, guns, even planes – fighter planes and bombers. He wants to sell them all. I said we could help him.'

Help him! I knew a Jordanian once, years ago, who made a fortune buying up all the scrap left behind in the desert after the Six Day War, cleaning it up, repairing it, then selling it on to all and sundry. The sundry paid the highest prices. Apart from that, I knew nothing. He gave me an address which was not the one in Patriots' Square.

'Okay,' I said, 'I'll go and see him.'

It was quickly getting darker and darker. I collected all my authorisations, grabbed my usual taxi and gave the driver the address. 'No problem,' he grunted nervously.

We were out of Addis in seconds; military unrest has its civilising side, in a city. About ten minutes to the airport we swung off the highway on to the sand and bumped and crashed our way along winding tracks, alternately between shacks and pleasant home-counties-style bungalows. It was now pitch black. Before I had begun to wonder whether this was a sensible thing to do in a strange car with an unknown driver in a city on the verge of civil war, we came to a halt before a pleasant, small, one-storey bungalow.

'This is where he lives,' said the driver. I strolled as casually as I could up the path to the front door. It opened almost immediately.

'You've come to see the Colonel,' said an elderly woman, who could have been his wife, mother or cleaning lady. I nodded. 'He's been arrested,' she said. 'The police have just taken him away.'

Gee, I thought. On top of everything, I'm visiting a colonel who's just been arrested. I drove straight back to the hotel, trying not to keep looking behind me to see if we were being followed. Somehow that night the guns seemed even louder.

The following morning around six, the phone rang. It was

the Colonel. 'We must speak,' he said.

'But I thought you were in gaol. I went to your house . . .'

'I arranged it all,' he replied. 'Had to show the rebels I was on their side.'

'But I thought you were supposed to be . . .'

'I am,' he said. 'But the rebels are going to win. We've got to show we're on their side if we're going to get the scrap.'

'Which is why you got yourself arrested.'

'Exactly. Now, when can we meet?'

'I will get my car.'

Somewhere behind the post office I was ushered into a dusty waiting room in a two-storey building. Government slogans were on the wall. I was taken to see the director. I crossed a vast area like another banking hall with hundreds of clerks working their way through mountains of paper. Not a typewriter, let alone an adding machine, was in sight. The director, a small, busy man, was wearing a scruffy open-necked white shirt. We shook hands. He opened his desk drawer and brought out a thick file. 'Please sign here and here and here,' he said, pointing to a form. I signed. 'You are among friends,' he said. We shook hands again.

'So where is the Colonel?' I asked.

'He will telephone you.'

We spoke briefly and guardedly about the future. 'What are you most looking forward to?' I asked as we shook hands yet again.

'To wearing my suit to the office,' he said.

Algiers, Casablanca, Tunis

Prayer mats.

Al Hamdulillah. I've been all over North Africa. I've crossed the Sahara two and a half times. I reckon I've been to Morocco, Algeria and Tunisia more times than you've had hot couscous. And the one thing I remember more than anything is prayer mats. According to my own personal Prayer Mat Futures Index, North Africa is at the start of their Islamic Reformation. Luther or his Imam equivalent is shuffling up to the door with a scrap of paper in his hands.

Morocco is Geneva before the arrival of Jean Calvin, the last Frenchman who believed in working for a living. Tunisia is keeping its fingers crossed, praying he'll give up the whole crazy idea of working for a living, and go back to Picardy and live off EC subsidies for the rest of his life. Algeria is Luther actually standing before the church door, hammer in hand, picking the nails out of his teeth. Libya is, well, Libya. The Great Jamahiriya is the Great Jamahiriya.

To me it seems they are about to abolish the harsh, corrupting regime of indulgences and replace it with the liberalism and understanding and kindness of the Orange Lodges and Ian Paisley. It's a bit like putting the earth at the centre of the universe and making the sun go around it.

At the start of the Reformation the traditionalists were in power, the modernists in opposition. Today, throughout

North Africa, the modernists are in power. It is the traditional-ists, or the fundamentalists, or maybe the true believers, who are in opposition, for it is they who are flaying the modernists and trying to build Orange Lodges, so to speak, in their sandy and pleasant land.

Although the fundamentalists are no fun, they are still more fun than a bunch of masons standing around during their first degree ceremony with their trousers rolled up. Don't tell a Christian, but in many ways I admire them for wanting to turn the clock back to the time when we not only believed in our principles but also practised them. For although I'm pretty certain that there is no way Allah wants me to become a Muslim moonbeam, I can appreciate what they are doing.

The fundamentalists are simply saying, if we believe so-and-so we believe so-and-so. If this is right for the individual it is also right for the state. The Shari'a, the sayings and doings of the Prophet Mohammed, apply to both. The individual and the state cannot be separated. If it is wrong for the individual, it is wrong for the state. *Din wa dawla*, faith and the state, the credo of Islam. Shari'a is Islamic law that binds the two together. Unreconstructed, born-again, funda-mental Christian moonbeams would find the logic difficult to disagree with.

The problem, of course, is that the non-fundamentalists disagree. They yearn for that lost world when everybody agreed with everybody and debate was unheard of. They, like Christian non-fundamentalists, prefer the chocolate-box image of their faith to the raw, uncomplicated principles upon which their faith is based.

With the Koran banning the portrayal of living creatures, Islam is in many ways still pre-Michelangelo and most definitely pre-Andrew Lloyd Webber and Tim Rice. It only has the essentials to believe in. It only believes in the essentials. Which is probably why I was not surprised on one visit to Algiers to find the duty-free leaflet on the plane saying: 'Trust us your wishes. Execute us if your favourite brands are not available.'

Once I arrived at the airport just outside Algiers, the capital of a country which regards alcohol as Mrs Thatcher regards socialism, to be greeted by a drunken customs officer who looked as if his contact lenses had slipped down the inside of his cheeks. He had so many problems trying to get his rubber stamp to hit the open page of my passport that he started to tear the page out to conceal his mistakes.

'Hey, hey,' I shouted at both his swirling eyes, 'you can't do—' Immediately I was seized by six Shari'a-abiding soldiers who obviously scrupulously followed the rules and principles in the Koran and the Sunna. I got the impression I had broken at least twenty of them.

Having on one happy occasion been bounced by Algerian customs and forced to spend a night under a Land Rover in no-man's-land between Tunisia and Algeria in spite of having all the right documentation, all the correct authorisations, not to mention six-six-six engraved on the top of my head, I immediately gave in, muttered a thousand apologies and told him, Al Hamdulillah, he could do whatever he liked with the property of HM Government of Royaume-Uni de Grande Bretagne et d'Irlande du Nord.

It is not only the present development of Islam and Islamic fundamentalism that is affecting my Prayer Mat Futures Index, it is also the effect it is having on the people, the cities, the towns, the culture and, of course, the Sahara, although I will admit events are changing rapidly, in many different directions. It's a bit like watching *The Ring* in a thunderstorm. The flashes of lightning only give you a quick unconnected idea of what's going on, and what the characters themselves think is going on.

When I started visiting the Magreb it had a lazy kind of natural sophistication, like those fabulous Arab horses which seemed to be grazing everywhere. In Morocco the hotels were fabulous; the waiters all wore long white robes, service was impeccable, the atmosphere was light and relaxed and very efficient. In Casablanca, in Rabat, in Fez – the oldest Royal city – the hotels always seemed to be buried in bougainvillaeas, smothered in hibiscus, surrounded by waist-high geraniums. Every souk you went into was like a walking, talking, pushing, shouting, sweating, smelling *Sheherazade*.

The countryside was practically manicured. Cattle, mules, donkeys, sheep, goats grazed contentedly. Men with mules and ancient ploughs tilled the soil. Women washed clothes in the streams. Mud houses, complete with television aerials, somehow always reflected the colour of the fertile soil. In the red sandstone valleys they were red; in the limestone valleys they were grey. Whole towns of traditional Moorist architecture were painted nothing but white, the only colour permitted. Royal palaces littered the countryside. Palace number 13, I noticed, was lucky enough to be near the airport at Agadir.

Casablanca was a million times better than the film. It was like Harry's Bar in the sunshine; relaxed, a whiff of excitement, the slightest hint of danger, but terribly, terribly fashionable. Wander across Place Mohammed V after the rush hour is over. Most people are wearing the full *jellaba*, even the *keffiyeh*. Turn into Boulevard Mohammed V. You feel that you are on the fringes of the arms trade or are trying to break in. The bars look as though they are full of people associated with people associated with people in the drugs business. In the bar opposite the stock exchange, I overheard one obviously very Westernised Arab banging his cup on the table and shouting, 'Allah Akbar. Of course you know I'm a Muslin for Christ's sake.'

Fez, which is full of magnificent Arab-Berber buildings, boasts one of the largest souks in the world: the craftsmen, the spices, the aromas; the winding, twisting, turning alleys; the donkeys stubbornly standing still in the middle of yet another minor major traffic jam. I once landed at Casablanca, jumped in a taxi and, like Charles Ryder, drove for five hours through the night to be in Fez for breakfast. There are not many cities I would do that for. I was in Fez once when so many people packed into the mosque, which is capable of holding 2,000 people, to watch their sons being circumcised that ten people were crushed to death and dozens more injured.

Rabat on the other hand is a gracious, Cheltenham type of city. The Palais Royal broods over it, keeping it in check. Once through the fantastic Bab et Rouah, Gateway of the Winds, I can spend – I have spent – hours between meetings just wandering all over the old Islamic city.

Moroccans seem to have the elegance of the French, the cunning of the casbah, the professionalism of the Swiss banker and the ambitions of a Moroccan. They might be interested in the fundamentalists and what they have to say but it doesn't show. Instead they give me the impression that they are back home for a rest from running vast financial conglomerates in Geneva, or sewing up another arms deal.

Wander into the Stock Exchange on Boulevard Mohammed V; I swear everybody ambling around looking up at the prices has already made millions in Paris or Tokyo or New York. Collapse on the ground just outside Fez, the Atlas Mountains in the distance, with a group of Berbers who, thousands of years ago, controlled virtually the whole of North Africa from Morocco to Egypt. Immediately you are part of the family. You will be offered stew from a *tajine*, their traditional earthenware pots, lamb grilled on the coals, or maybe just mint tea brewed on a primus stove. Perhaps it is this courtesy and unfailing politeness which has enabled Morocco to survive the Romans, Christianity, the Arab armies, not to mention the arrival of Islam in the seventh century.

One Moroccan I know, who lives in Marrakesh and owns a big hotel along Cromwell Road in London, dreams of a tunnel under the Mediterranean between Tangiers and Gibraltar to give them direct access to Europe. 'Why not?' he keeps asking. 'We are Europeans.'

It would also, of course, open up the Moroccan economy far more than establishing a Greater Maghreb or a North Africa Common Market with Algeria, Libya, Tunisia and Mauritania.

I once asked him who ran his hotel, and he told me his son-in-law did. Unfortunately, his son-in-law had trained as a surgeon and knew nothing about hotels. It was costing my friend a fortune. 'Why don't you get a European to run it?' I asked him. 'Can't trust them,' he said. 'You can only trust your family.'

I never complain about being Morocco bound. To me Morocco has a style, a panache that you don't find anywhere else in North Africa. Its Prayer Mat Index is also pretty low. Or at least it used to be.

Tunisia is different. In Morocco I look out for prayer mats, but I don't bother to take my worry beads. In Tunisia I count the prayer mats and I take my worry beads, just in case.

I was in Tunis just after the old President Bourguiba was overthrown. It was like party time. It was the first time I had felt at home there. Avenue Bourguiba still ran through the middle of Tunis, but all the pictures had gone. The statues were slowly disappearing throughout the country. Security had been relaxed. Thousands of political prisoners had been freed, the state security court had been abolished, police rights to detain suspects had been curtailed. Democracy was being slowly encouraged; opposition parties were being given a platform and encouraged to speak out. The age of parliamentary candidates was cut to twenty-five. The power of the president and his term of office were being strictly defined.

Islam, however, was taking a step forward. Prayers were being broadcast five times a day on television – plus 10 on the Index. An Islamic university was being re-opened – plus 20. Perhaps more significant, the life sentence passed on Mr

Rashid Ghannoushi, leader of the Radical Islamic Tendency, had been squashed and he had been freed – plus 100, and suspension of trading pending an investigation.

More surprisingly, and probably more significantly, while Carthage nearby was full of Germans inspecting the glory that once belonged to another empire, every hour Tunis was filling up with more and more Libyans. The good Colonel, the Great Jamahiriya, had just dispensed with all formalities at the border at Ras Djedit on the main Tripoli-Tunis road. He had even dynamited the frontier post. As a result, hundreds of coal-burning trucks, lorries and cars were pouring into Tunis in search not only of food, spare parts and basic necessities, but of all the luxuries that Libyans had been denied for so long. Tunis was a boom town.

All around the Place de l'Indépendance, all along the Avenue de la Liberté, around the railway station, Libyans had thrown away their Little Green Books and were staggering back to their ancient vehicles with armfuls of Western, or rather Far Eastern, goodies they could not find in the bleak souk al-Jumaa supermarkets on the outskirts of Tripoli, around Green Square or even in the bigger stores tucked under the Italianate arches in Tripoli centre. Stalls near the bus station were cleared out in minutes. Shops along the Avenue de la Liberté were emptied in a matter of hours. It was like being attacked by a swarm of deprived consumerist locusts.

'We are becoming an entrepôt for Libya,' Abdelwaheb Ben Ayed, a leading Tunisian banker, told me at the tiny stock exchange on Rue Kamal Ataturk. 'They are taking everything they can lay their hands on – consumer goods, radios, electronic goods. We've never seen anything like it.' Everything was so hectic I forgot to count the prayer mats.

I've never been to Libya. Well, I may have strayed across the border somewhere in the middle of the Sahara a number of times. But if I did, I didn't mean to, O Great Jamahiriya, honest.

While the Moroccans, the Tunisians and the Algerians are worldly-wise and a touch weary, the Libyans seem to have no knowledge of the real world at all. Maybe it's because they're just not interested in the rest of the world. Maybe it's because they feel that the more they know about the world the more they'll have to make up their minds and take decisions. Maybe they just think it's safer that way.

An Egyptian trader I met in the stock exchange in Tunis was frantically buying everything in sight to ship back to Tripoli. All over the country, he said, the shops were run not by Libyans but by Egyptians. And all the Egyptian shops and stores were selling Egyptian-made bulbs and soap and basic household requirements.

'But I thought the Colonel was against—'

'It's business,' he said as he dived out to buy more for the 'wage workers' of Tripoli.

Which, of course, is good news for the Tunisian economy, which is already improving faster than the IMF anticipated. With reserves of US$500 million, a thriving financial sector, booming exports and a dynamic privatisation programme to cut the state sector, suddenly Tunisia, North Africa's smallest country, looks as though it has the most to gain.

The only good thing about doing business with the Algerians is that you don't have to eat sheep's eyes. Well, I say you don't have to. On the other hand, if you want the business, it's still better to close your eyes and think of Milton Keynes.

Algeria has a thirty-year legacy of extreme socialism which crippled business every step of the way but provided subsidised food, free health care, guaranteed jobs and housing. Everywhere there was the dead hand of bureaucracy. You couldn't even appoint an agent, it had to be a government department. But inevitably, come the mid-eighties, the money ran out. The coffers are now empty, debts are high and getting higher. Management which before was trying to manage has given up and emigrated. Corruption which before was manageable is now totally out of control.

As a result they have high population growth, a crumbling education system, pitiful housing, growing unemployment and ever-growing discontent and disaffection among the young, the poor, the small shopkeepers. And an ever-increasing spread of prayer mats.

I've been all over Algeria. I've waited as long as anybody for meetings in Algiers. I've been to El Golea, the beautiful oasis town. I've driven I can't remember how many times to Ghardaia, the home of the Mozabites, a devout Muslim sect which broke away from the mainstream about 1,000 years ago and is still going strong in its own small, privileged way. A little like the Church of England. I was once arrested in In Saleh by an Algerian secret policeman for driving the wrong way up an unmarked one-way street. I've even visited for me one of the most memorable vineyards in the world, with the irresistible name of La Clappe. 'Would sir be having La Clappe again this evening?' How can you just not have it in a crowded restaurant?

I've been down to Tamanrasset which, as I have mentioned, was one of the biggest disappointments of my life, and across the Sahara (as I may also have mentioned) two and a half times. But the things that stick in my mind are the prayer mats.

Most Algerians are surprisingly relaxed about it. Partly because they don't think the Index will go any higher; they just can't see a red raw full-blooded Muslim state being imposed in any one country. Partly also, I must admit, because they feel that if such a state became a reality there is precious little they could do about it. 'Let it flourish. It will perish of its own accord in the oxygen of publicity,' one banker told me.

Then there are the subtleties. 'Ban it. But let it survive.' This is the approach in Egypt, where in theory the Islamic fundamentalists are illegal, but where in practice they operate virtually unhindered by the authorities unless they step over a constantly shifting, yet undefined, political line. If they do, its off to a semester in the Tora Istigbal prison, which I'm told is the largest Islamic university in the world after the 1,000-year-old Azhar University in Cairo.

Then there is the mixed view: 'Vote for them if you want to,' the King of Morocco seems to say, 'but first of all ask them what their policy is on the economy, on foreign policy, on . . .'

A few even want to admit the fundamentalists to government. 'Let them see the squabbles and compromises we have to make every day of the week. They'll soon lose all their idealising,' a young civil servant told me. 'When the voters see they can't work miracles they'll soon lose interest in them as well.'

So what started it all in the first place? Everybody blames the French, especially the Algerians, who blame them first for the war of independence. It began on November 1st, 1954 in the Auvers Mountains, spread to the cities, provoked a vicious counterattack by the French who threw everything into the fight including torture until the battle of Algiers in 1957, the year after Suez. Although it was won by the French, politically they had lost. In July 1962, against all the odds, General de Gaulle granted Algeria independence.

As the French fled, Iraqis, Egyptians and Palestinians came flooding in to replace them as schoolteachers and university lecturers. At first they had problems. Classical Arabic did not mix easily with the Algerians' less cultivated dialect. But eventually everything sorted itself out. Trouble was, the newcomers brought new ideas.

'It is not about religion, it is about jobs,' the civil servant continued. 'A third of the population is aged between fifteen and thirty. Over three million of them are unemployed. They live eight, nine, ten to a room. They want jobs, money, they want to settle down, to start a family. How can they do that without a job? Is Northern Ireland about religion? Of course not. The FIS [Front Islamique du Salut] is not about religion either.'

One of the first things the FIS did was to set up Islamic markets for food and consumer goods. 'Brilliant. People like it. They can buy food cheaper in the market than anywhere else. At first the traders didn't like the competition, but they couldn't complain otherwise they would have been against the revolution and their customers and for the government. Now they like it because even though the markets have forced them to lower their prices they have got the volume they didn't have before,' he said.

People are dissatisfied; they want a change. It is natural they will turn to religion. It happens all over the world when people are in trouble. What the FIS have done is to use religion as the cement to bind everyone together, just as the IRA are using religion to bind their supporters together.'

For the same reason the FIS is against the World Bank. They say they are not going to pay back any of the loans because everybody sees the World Bank as creating the financial problems in the first place. If you are against the World Bank you are for the people. You can't go wrong.

Women seem to take the same attitude, which surprised me as I imagined they had more to lose. Western clothes would be barred. Everyone would have to wear the *hegab*, head-scarf. Only women who were orphaned, divorced or widowed would be allowed to work. 'So they won't let me drive a car,' the civil servant's wife shrugged. 'So I haven't got a car. What difference?'

Algerian men were as objective as men always are. 'Why should women go out to work? They should leave the work to the men. They should stay at home, look after the house and the children.' 'If they go out to work all they do is spend their money on clothes and make-up. Is that serious?'

Apart from the more important question of alcohol being barred, businessmen seemed to be split in their opinions.

Bigger businessmen seemed to think they could operate with or without women, under any regime that came along. 'If the ulema or the authorities say that toilets must not face Mecca, it's okay by me,' one big Algerian trader grunted.

The present situation was nowhere near perfect. In spite of that they had made money; many had made a lot of money. A Muslim state would still need food and drink, if not alcohol. Maybe it wouldn't need as many luxury hotels. There would still be plenty of scope to make money.

Smaller traders and businessmen just shrugged. They had suffered and survived long enough. What was another problem? 'If I can put up with the government I can put up with the Mufawaiin [religious police],' I was told again and again.

'How about banking and finance? The Koran forbids moneylending,' I ventured.

'Instead of charging interest they will charge a service fee. What's the difference?'

My Prayer Mat Futures Index was beginning to hit record levels. Along the Haussman-like boulevards of the old town, down bumpy roads edged with stinking drains and littered with battered cars, throughout the decaying old city, which is rotting away like a French industrial town amid the faded elegance of high ceilings, broken-tiled floors and green-and-yellow paintwork, they were appearing all the time. On one visit I noticed people seemed to be carrying prayer mats instead of briefcases. One morning at the post office I counted more of the former than the latter.

The next time I noted that the people carrying the prayer mats, especially in Algiers, had begun to grow big black beards, wear white caps and those funny short trousers, the unofficial uniform of the FIS. Then slowly through 1989 I could see that people were sporting the *bourmon*, the rough, long woollen cloak with the elfin hood which, Allah be praised, has also kept me warm on many bitterly cold long nights in the desert. Next came the black turban, the sign of a *sayyid*, a descendent of the prophet Mohammed, although I was told this was also the uniform of the mujaheddin guerrillas who went to fight for their Sunni brothers in Afghanistan.

Next, instead of playing cassettes of Lotfi Attar, Algeria's own rock stars which mix Western rock with Arab rhythms, taxi drivers began playing religious music. Popular music was out, and there were fewer boys on the streets selling cassettes. Cinemas began closing down or switching to safe religious or historic films. One cinema had been forced to close because it showed a film about a faith healer. Singing, I was told, was no longer acceptable at weddings. Whether that was because the fundamentalists thought that weddings were not an occasion for rejoicing or because they did not like the singing, I never found out.

The streets began filling up with *hitistes*, people who prop up walls, the unemployed.

Alcohol was virtually barred. Even my evening La Clappe. Eating special foods on special days and after funerals was made compulsory. The way of burying and praying for the dead was changed.

More and more women, the size of pillar boxes and draped from head to toe in black, began to block up the streets, although one banker told me they were all secret service men. 'If you're quick you can see their beards behind the veil,' he laughed. 'We have bets among ourselves. For every one we spot we get $100.'

I then had to wait longer and longer for breakfast. First the fat, balding, middle-aged American businessmen at the hotel suddenly gave up jogging. They had been chased through the streets in their running gear by more than the usual number of boys screaming at them for being 'naked'. Then they gave up coming altogether. But even though there were fewer people in the hotel I still had to wait longer and longer for breakfast.

The modernist government started building spectacular modern buildings – maybe even post-modern buildings. The Ministry of Foreign Affairs looks like a deflated flying saucer. The traditionalists started building spectacular unfinished traditional buildings: mosques. They were deliberately left unfinished because as soon as a mosque is finished it is considered under government control. Unfinished mosques are outside government control. If there is no facing on the concrete it is still unfinished.

Imams of completed mosques are government Imams. They have to pass government examinations, and the mosques are financed from government funds. The Imam, therefore, is unlikely to stray very far from the government line. Imams of unfinished mosques are not under any government control at all. The *majlis ashura*, the Muslim equivalent of parish church councils, can do what they want, though they tend to be more interested in politics than organising jumble sales. As a result, out of nearly 10,000 mosques in Algeria, more than 5,500 are unfinished. Clever guys, the FIS, at reading the small print.

One evening I was in Algiers for the big fair. I had spent most of the day trying to explain yet again to the policeman at the entrance who, for a Muslim, had a particular interest in alcohol, that a Beefeater was a soldier but not really a soldier; that he was guarding a castle which was not really a castle; and that it was quite normal in London for men to walk around wearing fifteenth-century clothes. In the catalogue for the fair, all the thirty-five countries taking part had glossy advertisements featuring their kings and queens meeting prominent Arab dignitaries, their latest technology, the modern machinery they are making which would be perfect for solving Algeria's problems. The British advertisement featured a Beefeater. No caption. No explanation. Just a picture of a Beefeater. Hence, I suppose, his interest.

In the evening, I felt like a break. Algiers, especially during an Islamic revolution, is not exactly the kind of town that lends itself to a bar crawl. Instead I decided to do a mosque crawl.

I was driving through the back streets of Bab El Oued, the poor working-class huddle of narrow streets next to the Casbah, the old Spanish quarter of the city, looking for the great unfinished Al Sunna mosque. Algerians returning from the Afghan civil war, where they learnt their guerrilla techniques the hard way, had made it their local parish church, virtually turned it into the Kabul mosque and made it the Front's church militant.

I parked the car, walked round a corner near the mosque and was suddenly surrounded by a group of fundamentalists. Allah help me, I thought. The tyres of a Christian car – the tread has been leaving obscene messages about Allah in the dust.

The biggest of the group stood right in front of me. He tapped me on the shoulder. 'Please to show us the way to the mosque,' he said in an impeccable Church of England accent. 'We are lost.'

Why me, of all people to ask? In Algiers? In the middle of an Islamic revolution? I mean, do I honestly look as though I've just got back from Afghanistan? 'First left. Second right. Al Hamdulillah,' I gasped. And ran for my car. My Prayer Mat Futures Index missed a beat.

The fair was over; I wanted to leave on Sunday; but still I hadn't got the exit stamp in my passport. The passport office was the usual Algerian chaos. I sat around biting my prayer mat in frustration. Algiers was covered in a blanket of high cloud. There was the occasional flash of sunshine. It was hot. And it was getting pretty muggy.

I strolled up and down in front of the desks. I sat on tables. I queued up. I let the whole world and their camels push in front of me. Eventually I found myself in front of Saddam Hussein's elder brother. After all the traditional Arab courtesies on my part, including the 100-franc note inside my passport, I mentioned the small matter of an exit stamp. Saddam Hussein's brother continued to look as though he was planning another massacre.

'*Peut-être,*' I hesitated.

'*Non,*' he grunted.

'*S'il vous plaît.*'

'*Non.*'

Allah help me. Of course. He was the leader of the group who had asked me the way to the mosque. The mosque wasn't first left, second right. He's realised. They're going to –

'*Attendez,*' he grunted. Suddenly the local muezzin was in the background, calling everyone to prayer. '*Attendez,*' Saddam's big brother grunted again. He dragged himself up from his desk, adjusted his tie, grabbed his prayer mat and lumbered off to do his duty to Allah and the revolution.

'Hamdulillah,' I mumbled. I leant across his desk, scooped up all the rubber stamps, and one by one stamped them all over my passport. Within five seconds I was back at the hotel. Inside my room. Locked. I didn't leave it until the taxi to the airport was outside, engine running.

For the first time in my life Algerian customs were friendly. Well, they were not difficult. They waved me through. They didn't even ask to see my passport. As I got into the departure lounge, I turned round. They were all unrolling their prayer mats. The Index hit an all-time high.

Cairo

Travel anywhere on business and you quickly become an expert on taxi drivers: those friendly, courteous New Yorkers; those laughing and joking Germans and those sober Parisians. I once took a cab (after lunch) from Charles de Gaulle airport to the Champs Elysées, and every time we stopped, at lights or an intersection, I had to lean across and wake up the driver.

My best-ever cab driver was one in Newcastle-upon-Tyne. The British economy, he announced, was booming.

'Booming?' I was amazed. 'What about all these factories closing, all the—'

'We can't be doing that bad,' he said. 'Just look at these BMWs.'

'BMWs,' I gasped. 'But they're all—'

'Good old British Motor Works, beating all those foreign cars,' he said, banging the wheel. 'You can't beat the British.'

In Cairo, now, they have the best educated, most civilised taxi drivers in the world. Get a cab at the airport to the King David Hotel and you're more likely to get a rational lecture on economics or philosophy in any one of three or four languages than a heated discussion about last night's match. For they are almost always accountants, engineers, even professors of economics and philosophy at Cairo University, trying to earn a little extra, to survive.

But taxi drivers are not the main reason why, for me, Cairo

114

is a wonderful place. Nor is it the stock exchange, the dusty old French colonial-style building in Kasr el-Nil Street, once one of the busiest stock exchanges in the world and the only one ever quoting shares in four different currencies. Nor is it the Khan el Khalily bazaar, one of the oldest, largest, most crowded and noisiest I have ever been in.

And it's not because, as Ibn Khaldun, the fourteenth-century Arab historian, says Cairo is 'the metropolis of the universe, the garden of the world, the nest of the human species, the gateway to Islam, the throne of royalty: a city embellished with castles and palaces and adorned with monasteries of dervishes with colleges lit by the moons and the stars of erudition.'

To me Cairo is wonderful because – but don't tell anyone – it is the cheapest place to buy airline tickets.

Because of the exchange rate, the desperate competition between airlines, and the wonderful flexibility of the Egyptians, Cairo at the moment is the cheapest place to buy airline tickets – providing wherever you go it's via Cairo. Buy tickets anywhere else, perhaps with the exception of Poland, and it costs you an arm and a leg. In Cairo it costs you maybe two fingers and a thumb.

I first discovered this on a trip to Addis Ababa, Nairobi and Harare. I had to change planes and ended up in Cairo. Half of me was glad I was in Cairo again. The other half was hopping mad because it ruined my schedules – until I saw, everywhere, the possibility of cheap tickets.

I was with a group of Egyptian businessmen, on our way to Suez to have lunch with Osman Ahmed Osman who had built up Arab Contractors into one of the biggest construction companies in the Middle East. We were practically halfway there when we got a message that the lunch was cancelled. A relative had died. He had to go to the funeral. The Egyptians being big on funerals, we didn't argue, but promptly turned round and made for the new Meridien Hotel for lunch.

We began, naturally, by talking about the world economy, the role of the Bundesbank, the state of the pound. After about five seconds we started talking about travel. Naturally I thought a typical Egyptian businessman struggling to survive on less than US$250 a month would have problems taking a taxi, let alone a 747. Not on your life. Most of them had just come back from the States via three days in Rome, two days in Paris and a weekend in London. The following week they were off to Canada, Hong Kong and on to Tokyo. Next year they all wanted to take their wives – or somebody else's – on round-the-world trips. You could have knocked me off a camel. 'But I thought . . .' I stuttered.

Then it all came out. Plus the fact that the sister of the wife of the leader of our group ran a travel agency in Mohandessih, a fairly well-to-do suburb of Cairo.

It was the weekend: Thursday. So I said I would like to meet her at the beginning of the week: Saturday. 'No, no,' he insisted. The weekend was not Thursday and Friday any more. It was now Friday and Saturday.

'Okay,' I said, 'I'll go on Sunday.'

'Not possible,' he said. Their weekend was Saturday and Sunday.

'Okay,' I said. 'No problem. I'll go on Monday.'

At the time Egypt was playing games with their weekend. Nobody knew where anybody was, or was supposed to be. And if it was the right day. Or if it wasn't. The prime minister's office had decided that banks and offices should close on Thursdays and Fridays to bring them into line with the rest of the Muslim world. The president's office then said that it was not for the prime minister's office to decide such things. They should be decided by the president. As the president hadn't decided, banks and offices should remain open.

Banks were against the idea. A Thursday/Friday weekend meant they were out of touch with the world for four days a week. Unless, of course, they were strict Muslims. If they were strict Muslims they were having Friday and Saturday off whoever said what. Businessmen were against the Friday/Saturday weekend because, again, it cut their working week, especially if they were trying to do business with the rest of the world. Unless, of course, they were strict Muslims. Finally, strict Muslims were against the Saturday/Sunday weekend – because they were strict Muslims.

Then came the variations. Relaxed Muslims working for strict Muslim companies suddenly found they had Thursday and Friday at home while their children were attending relaxed schools that had Saturday and Sunday as their weekends. The Coptic Christians were sticking to Saturday and Sunday, apart from those working for strict Muslims who were having Thursday and Friday off as well. The ordinary Christians were just keeping their heads down.

'So what's going to happen?' I wondered.

'The prime minister will set up a committee.'

'And it will never report.'

'But for you,' our leader said, 'the weekend is not important. We go now. Business is business.'

We drove along high streets, took short-cuts down back streets. We did U-turn after U-turn because buildings had collapsed into the road and were blocking the weekend or non-weekend traffic. 'Always buildings are collapsing. Always,' he said. I was not surprised. To me, most of the old buildings in Cairo look ready to collapse. Since Nasser's day, nobody has been able to charge a fair rent for anything, so that landlords have either walked away, spent the absolute minimum on repairs, or even pulled the buildings down themselves. We drove past street markets that were either busy for a weekday. Or not. Or empty for a weekend. Or not.

The wife's sister, Wafaa, was brisk, organised, efficient. She looked like Nana Mouskouri's younger sister. 'You telephone. You say what tickets you want. We order the tickets. No problem.'

'Okay,' I said. 'One thing. How do I pay?'

'American Express. You leave your card here. Every time you order ticket, we make out receipt for . . .' Mrs Wafaa was definitely very brisk.

'I've got a better idea,' I said. 'You give me the American Express card receipts. Every time I order a ticket, you give me the price, I make out the receipt and send it to you.'

'No problem.' Mrs Wafaa gave me an efficient smile.

Immediately I switched my travel account. Flying east was no problem: I'd fly Air Egypt to Cairo, catch a connection right away or stay a few days. Flying west and, obviously, down to West and Central Africa was more of a problem time-wise. Money-wise it was no problem at all. I could fly everywhere first class cheaper via Cairo than by buying a regular tourist ticket and flying direct. After a while Mrs Wafaa even managed to arrange things so that I didn't have to travel via Cairo. I could catch a plane anywhere, go wherever I liked first class and not pay a penny more than the cheapest tourist ticket.

When I first went to Egypt, a gentle little old lady in the village warned me, 'Whatever you do, don't tell them you're British. They'll spit in your soup.'

Far from spitting in my soup, I found Egypt and the Egyptians absolutely super. Since then, thanks to Mrs Wafaa, I've been back many times.

Cairo, once the centre of Islam, is still virtually the capital of the Arab world – in commerce, in culture, in politics – certainly in history. It is a marvellously rich jumble of history: 6,000-year-old pyramids a taxi-ride from your hotel; Roman ruins; Coptic churches for the largest Christian community in the Middle East; brilliant multi-coloured mosques; broad French-style boulevards created by Baron Haussmann himself and a thousand narrow, winding alleyways, made for old-fashioned spying, selling everything you can imagine and no doubt many things one would prefer not to imagine. And everything is bathed in a glorious, riotous aroma of coffee, sweets, spices, incense, diesel fumes, grease, sweat, drains and, in quarters not cultivated by Baron Haussmann, a certain *je ne sais quoi*.

I've spent mornings between meetings rushing to the pyramids and dashing around the gloomy, dusty halls of the Egyptian Museum with the world's greatest collection of antiquities. Some rooms, an attendant told me, had not been opened for years. Afternoons I've devoted to visiting mosques and Coptic churches. Evenings, especially the day after the crescent of a new moon, I've spent watching Muslim clerics in their white cassocks and thick black belts with their long sticks leading processions to mark the start of Ramadan.

For me Cairo puts everything into perspective. The pyramids are unforgettable, awe-inspiring, almost unbelievable, especially glowing in the soft early morning sunshine – the sheer size; the unbelievable dimensions; the sense of enormous power and dynamism.

An American once told me that whenever he was in Cairo he just had to go to the pyramids on Sunday mornings, for the pyramid races.

'The pyramid races?'

'Sure. We get the kids to run up and down them and bet on which one will come first.'

Alexandria, on the other hand, is a big disappointment. A bit like reading Durrell after lapping up the reviews. Admittedly it's yet to be discovered by the package tour operators, which is its big plus point. But its once legendary louche sophistication has gone. The villas have either crumbled away or been turned into flats. The nineteenth-century apartments are virtually no more.

How it could once have been a meeting point of east and west, a seat of learning, Mohammed only knows. The famous Cornice is still there, but that's about it. Even Mohammed Ali Square, doner kebabs the size of an elephant's leg and lunch of ground sheep's testicles failed to knock me out. Today it's an architectural Zsa Zsa Gabor, and about as exciting.

Funerals permitting, the Suez Canal is staggering. Not for its beauty, but for the imagination and muscle that produced it. Over 100 kilometres in length, it can take all but supertankers at the rate of a maximum eighty a day in alternating north and south convoys although, in fact, the most it has ever handled to date is sixty-three, way back in 1981.

At present the supertankers go around the Cape, and the oil is then pumped through the Suez-Mediterranean pipeline which links the Red Sea and the Med. But soon, if the Suez Canal Authority has its way, the Canal will be deepened from 52 feet to 56, 62, 68 or even 72 feet, which would enable it to accommodate even the biggest 350,000-ton supertankers.

Aswan is fabulous: a blue river, date palms swaying in the breeze. It's small, compact, it has all the hustle and bustle and decaying donkeys of any Egyptian town. But somehow it seems more serene, more at peace with itself, probably because it's under the perpetual gaze of the old Aga Khan who lies in his tomb high on the west bank opposite. Even the graceful, swallow-like feluccas which skim up and down the Nile from the Philae Temple to the long narrow Elephantine Island seem to nod deferentially in his direction as they sail past on to Kitchener Island, the property of Lord Kitchener when he was governor-general and now decidedly unmilitary with vines and creepers growing haphazardly all over it.

I can't help it. Whenever I think of Luxor I think of Limpy, a nice little restaurant near the railway station which serves fabulous stuffed pigeon. I first came across Luxor on the back page of the *Financial Times* where in Worldwide Weather it always appeared with the highest possible temperatures. Today I notice somebody has realised it's not a major business city and replaced it with Luxembourg. When I first went there I was stunned. I knew it was built on the site of Thebes, the southern capital of the pharaohs, but I never appreciated the sheer size and dimension of the city, nor its tourist attractions. Most *son et lumières* are a bit kitsch. The *son et lumière* at the Great Temple of Karnak on the banks of the Nile opposite the Valley of the Kings, and set against its long avenue of ram-headed sphinxes, the Hypostyle Hall with its 134 columns and the obelisk of Queen Hatshepant, is fabulous.

Though horsedrawn *calèches* with their shining brasses and polished leathers are no longer available, even the drive by coach across the desert to the Valley of the Kings is out of this world. The sheer size of the tombs – their scale – the workmanship – it is stunning.

Abu Simbel, further down the Nile, is equally stunning. The temples of Rameses II with their massive statues of the pharaoh are unbelievable. Equally unbelievable is the fact that they were taken apart piece by piece, moved from their original location and reassembled on their present site. I mean, surely something must have got lost?

And however many times I go back, I always remember the first time, flying along the Nile. The immortal Nile, stretching like a blue ribbon edged on both sides by a thick strand of green squeezed between the enveloping sands.

'If the Nile is high, we shall have no problems. If the Nile is low ... well,' everyone tells you. The fact is, something has gone wrong. Today the Nile is undoubtedly high. But Egypt has more and more problems.

The population, currently 55 million – one third of the entire Arab world – is growing at the staggering rate of over one million every nine months. In other words, within four years they will have created a population the size of Switzerland.

Already they are having problems financing their US$5 billion-a-year bill for food imports. What will happen over the next few years, nobody is yet prepared even to contemplate.

Unemployment, currently estimated at no less than 20%, is

climbing. In spite of the government's demands in its current five-year development plan that the private sector create nearly half a million new jobs - just like that, no argument – everybody knows the situation is likely to get worse rather than better. Which is also a major factor stopping the government from pursuing any plans to privatise its over-blown public sector, which guarantees every graduate a job within four years of leaving university.

'Nobody in government will admit it,' an official with the Arab African Bank told me, 'but everybody knows that privatisation means more unemployment. And the government is just not prepared to consider any increase. Any more unemployment and they think the country will explode.'

In spite of this, however, Egyptian industry and workers together have been pleading with the government to relax their tight grip on the private sector in order to allow them to increase production and stimulate desperately needed foreign investment. But so far in vain. 'Both sides agree that the future could be even worse with fewer jobs for hundreds of thousands. Then the problem will not be how to raise wages but how to find wages for all those people without jobs,' an official of the Egyptian Businessmen's Association told me, in a whisper in case he was overheard.

The result is the Egyptian equivalent of a Mexican stand-off. On the one hand is the International Monetary Fund and the US government pleading with them to at least start repaying some of their US$45 billion of foreign debt. On the other hand is the Egyptian people, many desperately trying to survive on average salaries of less than Ef100 or US$30 a month and, in spite of government controls and rent freezes, facing ever-rising prices. Most civil servants as well as teachers, account-ants and even university professors are forced to find a second job.

'How people survive I don't know,' Hosni El-Sonbaty, an engineer, told me. 'The average house in Cairo costs E£50,000 or US$15,000. I am supposed to be relatively well paid, but even I cannot afford that.' The answer, of course, is that many people are not surviving.

The pharaohs, or their modern equivalents, are still living at the top of the pyramid. They were educated in Paris or London, trained at the Gezira Sporting Club, play polo all round the world and take advantage of Mrs Wafaa's cheap tickets. Sure, Nasser's socialist revolution in 1952 upset things a bit, but they still live in luxury apartments, holiday in Gstaad or St Tropez, own land in the centre of Cairo which costs US$5,000 a square metre, wear Armani suits and think nothing of spending US$400,000 on a sports car.

At Ramadan, the holy month-long Muslim fast which commemorates God revealing the Koran to Mohammed on the mountain, they dodge the fasting by sleeping and watching videos by day and eating TV meals by night. Instead of losing weight, many put it on. 'If you're going to get a house boy,' one Egyptian yuppie advised me, 'don't get a Muslim. You'll never get any sleep. He'll always be up before dawn saying his prayers.'

Their slaves – sorry, I mean employees – earn just US$50 a month. But that still puts them near the top of the pyramid. Below them are the families crowding together into smaller and smaller rooms. In one block of flats between Ghamra Railway Station and one of Cairo's unfinished flyovers, most rooms are lived in by at least four people. And below them are the thousands packed into the grim, squalid, crowded slums of Imbabe; the families huddled inside the northern gate of Bab al-Nasr, one of the only three remaining of the original sixty gates that protected medieval Cairo; and all the old men and children all over the city collecting rubbish in carts drawn by ponies and donkeys even more starved than they are.

Even the cemeteries, especially El Kafier, the City of the Dead, near the airport, a favourite spot for Cairo's homeless, are becoming seriously overcrowded. With both the living and dead.

I stayed several times at the Heliopolis Sheraton near the airport and regularly picked up the same driver – Dr Abdul Rahman, an economics professor at Cairo University. He had lost his life savings when the El-Rayan Bank collapsed in Egypt's big banking scandal. To survive he was buying his own taxi on credit.

'We are virtually insulated from the rest of the world. Most basic foods are subsidised. The subsidy on bread is about 40%. Rents haven't increased for over ten years. Salaries are frozen. But all other prices are increasing. The population is growing. Unemployment is growing. Inflation is about 30–35%. The government is running out of money, and time. Something has got to give,' he would tell me as we stopped and started and stalled our way into Cairo every morning.

One of the reasons for their survival, he would shout above the roar of the traffic, was, oddly enough, their recent gentle drift towards becoming more and more of a Muslim society. Mubarak's whole policy seems to be to move ever so slightly forward by standing absolutely, rigidly still. Given the enormous range of competing interests he is presiding over, and the success of his policy so far, who can blame him. On the one hand, he is trying to build a modern country. On the other, the Muslim Brotherhood, which seems to be the most unbanned banned organisation in the country, would willingly set up an Islamic state tomorrow if not this afternoon. Providing it wasn't a Friday or a Saturday.

One afternoon I had a meeting at the Cairo stock exchange. On the way there, like Charles Ryder, I wanted to talk about Etruscan notions of immortality. Instead Abdul Rahman gave me a lecture on constitutional law, Egyptian style.

The Muslim Brotherhood, Egypt's mainstream Islamic organisation, was first outlawed by Nasser in 1954 when he thought it was planning to overthrow him. It had remained banned – but not 100% banned. Under an Egyptian law banning all political organisations based on race or religion, it was banned. But it was still allowed to canvass for political as opposed to religious support and to run its own schools. It even had seats in parliament. Not in its own name, because it was banned. But in the name of the tiny Liberal and Socialist Liberal Parties, which were not banned. 'You understand?' he said.

'No,' I said.

'You are not paying attention. You are like my students. Now listen carefully . . .'

The Cairo stock exchange was once one of the leading stock exchanges in the world. It was a centre of power, prestige and influence. Today it is about as relevant to Egypt's economy as Queen Nefertiti's mummy. If that. For at least Queen Nefertiti's mummy attracts tourists and, therefore, more foreign exchange into the country than the stock exchange does. Around fifty-odd companies are listed on the exchange but trading is practically nonexistent.

The building, which is like a vast municipal library, is as empty as the safe at the Bank of Cairo. People straggle in and out. The big circular trading floor at least looks like a stock exchange. The occasional dealer sits hunched around the circular bench desperately praying to Allah that somebody wants to trade. But the odds are against it. Weekly turnover is rarely above US$5–10 million.

First, because nobody trusts the exchange. Nobody really believes that it has a long-term future, that it will be a key mechanism in building the new economy and that it would be allowed to survive untouched in a rip-roaring bull market. It's like trying to run a casino where everybody keeps their hands tightly on their wallets.

Second, because there is no market. Shareholders want to hold on to their shares. They don't want to sell, let alone trade them. One day, they dream, they will be worth a fortune. But sell a percentage of their shares today and take a profit? Never.

Third, there is precious little market-making. Partly because nobody wants a market, partly because there are no incentives to make a market; brokers – and there are fewer than twenty – can only charge a set commission regardless of the size of the deal. Most deals are made by the banks, who say they are more interested in serving their clients than serving the market, which everybody knows is code for saying they prefer to keep their clients' funds safely tucked up in their vaults than risk them in the market.

Fourth, taxation. Put your money on deposit with a bank and you don't pay a penny in tax. Put it into shares and you attract as many taxes as there are fleas on a camel's hump.

Everybody at the stock market complains that the Capital Markets Authority, their government supervisor, doesn't understand them. The Capital Markets Authority, which is squeezed into tiny, upstairs, almost derelict offices along Algom Horea Street, says the stock market does not understand the aspirations of the government. 'It's self-evident,' my economics lecturer told me on the way back to the Sheraton. 'The capitalist/socialists at the stock exchange don't understand the socialist/capitalists at the Capital Markets Authority and probably never will. At least until Egypt's state-dominated economy itself decides what type of economy it really wants.'

'Precisely,' I said. 'Now, about the Etruscans . . .'

Another day, I wanted to see the thousand-year-old al-Azhar University, the theological institute which is virtually the heart and conscience as well as the final arbiter of conservative Sunni Islamic orthodoxy, Egypt's religious establishment.

'Our problem is simple,' Dr Rahman began as we pulled out into the traffic. 'We have US$35 billion in foreign debt yet US$50 billion of private savings earned by three million Egyptians, scattered throughout the world. We have an all-embracing but completely useless, over-staffed, ineffective, debt-ridden public sector which is supposed to guarantee everyone jobs, cheap food, housing, schools and hospitals. On the other hand we have an affluent private sector awash with funds.'

'So what did you think of the television last night?' I mumbled.

Each time I went back I met Dr Rahman. He was not only my personal private driver, he was also my personal private economics lecturer. Each time, however, as he revealed more and more economic horrors, he seemed to grow happier. His taxi business was booming. He had started working regularly for a group of Americans led by Robert.

'He keeps telling me to call him Robert. But I can't,' he said. 'It's not possible.'

'Why not, if he says so?'

'Because in Egypt Robert is a talcum powder for babies' bottoms,' he grinned.

He was also building up his business at the Heliopolis, getting bigger jobs. He'd even been taking groups of Israeli tourists around the city and out to the pyramids. How did he have the chutzpah to do that? 'They're like us,' he said, perhaps a little nervously. 'They want peace. We want peace.' He paused. 'Also they have money.' Thanks to the Israelis he was even within sight of paying off his taxi.

Each time I went back I also noticed more and more women wearing the *hegab*. One morning we drove through an enormous sandstorm which was smothering the whole city in a yellow smog. I've been through sandstorms in the Sahara. This was not so bad, because it only cut visibility to a few hundred yards, but here it seemed much worse because it was in town and not in the desert. The secretary of the director I was meeting was wearing the *hegab*.

'In other countries Muslims are seen as extremists. In Egypt we're extremists also. Except that we believe in extreme moderation,' she told me. 'Girls used to wear mini-skirts and bikinis. But now we are more serious. We think this is the better way.' She had just returned to the Muslim faith, she said. She had subscribed to the five pillars of Islam. She had declared her faith. She was reciting the *salat* five times a day. She was fasting during Ramadan. She was giving around 5% of her income after necessities (*zakat*) to charity. She was even wondering about a pilgrimage to Mecca.

Another sign of extreme moderation, Dr Rahman told me, was the appearance of Walkmen. Not your ordinary Walkmen, but Walkmen Walkmen, the traditional storytellers and poets who used to wander from village to village in rural Egypt reciting famous epic poems. Except that they too have given in to the Walkman.

Instead of sitting in cafés smoking *shesha* and listening hour after hour to their most famous epic poem, about the adventures of Abu Zeyal, the tenth-century warrior who led his tribe, the Beni Hilal, from the Arabian Peninsula across Egypt to conquer Tunisia, Egyptians are now adjusting their headphones and hearing the same stories while going to work, waiting for the new Cairo metro or lazing in the sun at Alexandria. Contrary to expectation, the electronic revolution has actually made the epic more popular than ever.

'I heard of *Abu Zeyal* when I was at school. Then I studied it at University. But I haven't bothered with it for thirty years. Now it's on cassette I listen to it often,' Mohamed Hamel Mohamed, a manager in one of Cairo's international banks told me. 'So do my children, although I admit they still prefer Michael Jackson.'

M. Jackson notwithstanding, such words are music to the ears of Abdel Hamid Hawvas, director of research at the Egyptian Folklore Institute. Far from decrying the commercialisation of their epic poetry, he welcomes it. He even believes that it could save it from oblivion. In the old days no wedding, religious festival or social event was complete without its oral poet who would sing the adventures of Abu Zeyal, which could take anything between five and seven hours to complete.

'Everything that is in Egyptian life is in *Abu Zeyal*,' Ekram Elsafty, a librarian at the Folklore Institute, told me. Even today, if somebody is getting too big for his boots, Egyptians will ask him if he thinks he is Abu Zeyal.

But for the purists the electronic Walkman apparently has one big disadvantage over the old human version. It freezes the story and establishes a set edition of the poem which for generations underwent endless variations and embellishments by the different storytellers. 'If this is the price we have to pay for its survival, it's worth it,' Mr Mohamed said.

Abdel Rahman el-Abnoudi, a modern Egyptian poet who is very popular on radio and television, disagrees. He prefers the individual versions and constant additions. These, he feels, are what make what could be an old, lifeless poem into a living, ever-changing and developing story. Nevertheless, el-Abnoudi is responsible for probably the most popular electronic version because, as he says, the old storytellers are gradually dying, and since nobody is taking their place it is vital to have one definitive edition. Sung by a fellow poet, Jaber Abu Hussein, it stretches to twenty cassettes, and is already a popular success among Egyptians eager to preserve their extreme moderation and introduce their children to their greatest poet. 'If you understand *Abu Zeyal* you speak the very best Arabic,' Mr Mohammed told me. 'It is good for children to study. It will help them when they grow up.'

This unlikely popular success has led to three further developments worthy of the epic itself. First, pirates. With the Egyptians' relaxed attitude to piracy, there is an extensive network of re-recording studios turning out copies at a fraction of the original price with many, no doubt, ending up being sold to unsuspecting tourists in the Kahn El Khalily bazaar. Second, the publication of a number of texts of *Abu*

Zeyal, something which is anathema to the traditional oral poets. Again, the most important is by el-Abnoudi. Third, a dramatic increase in the number of recordings of other extremely moderate epic poems by extremely moderate modern poets.

'In the old days people would hire a poet to entertain them. Today they switch on their cassettes. They are the new patrons of our poetic heritage,' Dr Rahman told me. It is doubtful, however, whether all the epic poems combined will ever prove as popular as Oom Khalthoum, the legendary Egyptian singer whose records, fifteen years after her death, are still played for five hours every day on Cairo radio.

On my next trip, Dr Rahman wasn't around; his young brother was driving his taxi. Dr Rahman was chasing the police. The Americans he had been working for had disappeared. He had thought that by working for them he would make enough money to pay off the loan on his taxi, but when Mr Robert and co. left they paid him in counterfeit US$100 bills. He was desperately trying to get compensation. 'This would not happen if the Brotherhood was in power,' his little brother told me.

The Muslim Brotherhood was going to take over. Everything was going to change. People would have homes, jobs, plenty to eat. Americans, especially those called Mr Talcum Powder, would not be allowed to cheat Egyptian professors of economics and get away with it.

'But how will you pay for everything you say you are going to do?' I asked him.

'From the money we save abolishing the police,' he said. 'The police will not be needed in a genuine Muslim society.'

The next time I went back, I was with an African Development Bank delegation. We were checked into the big new Sheraton in the centre of Cairo, not the one at the airport. On our second night the Sheraton Heliopolis, the one at the airport, burnt down. Sixteen people were killed and another thirty were injured. There was chaos. Suddenly everyone wanted to doublecheck whether everybody had been booked into the right Sheraton. I skipped the morning's programme and took a cab to the burnt-down Heliopolis. Standing on the road outside was Dr Rahman.

'We Egyptians always say if the Nile is high we shall have no problems. But something's gone wrong,' he sighed looking at the burnt-out shell of the hotel. He was back to square one. He was wondering how he was going to survive. '*Ibn ilwisxa,*' he swore. 'The last two years is not my day.' For the first time he sounded like an ordinary taxi driver.

Freetown

'You're the last person I'm going to talk to in the whole world . . .'

I had just got back to London from Freetown in West Africa. I was in a meeting in the City. Negotiations had reached a critical stage. Should the company go public, or stay private? We were about to take the decision when the phone rang.

'Can you hold on?' I gabbled. Suicide notes, even delivered by telephone, are not something I get every day. 'I'm in a meeting. Can I ring—'

The line went dead.

I don't think I've ever been to a city so depressingly poor and destitute as Freetown. I was in Mali, Niger and Burkina Faso after the famines in the early seventies, and I can still see the children almost like matchsticks lying starving in the dust, the men and women slumped helpless as if they were just waiting for life to drain out of them, and the cattle, covered in flies, also just waiting . . . In Addis Ababa towards the end of the civil war, and all over Ghana as the IMF's structural adjustment programme began to bite, there was dire, abject, heart-breaking misery. But Freetown always seems worse, almost as if their poverty is a special poverty of their own.

Everywhere, along Liverpool Street, on the Parade Ground conveniently close to the Circular Road Cemetery, there are people begging for food, eating, sleeping in doorways, under buildings, slumped against walls and just dying in the streets.

Whole families can't even find a doorway. They live what lives they can, sleep wherever they can and die under the burnt-out wrecks of cars. If they eat, they eat palm cabbages, roots, grain. The lucky ones eat goatskin. Beggars lie in holes in the road without the energy even to beg. Every baby looks as if it is already being eaten away by worms. Outside the National Development Bank a tiny pencil-thin woman with a baby strapped to her back collapses under a sign saying 'Don't be an enemy of progress'. Lepers sit outside the post office in Westmoreland Street hoping against hope that they will get enough money for at least one halfway decent bowl of rice a week.

Along Fourah Bay Road, where they say all the stalls are owned by Lebanese, I once spotted a leper with those white and reddish patches on his skin, slumped against an old red British telephone box, reading a newspaper. The headline said, 'To be a man is not easy'. I wouldn't have thought for one second to be a man, woman or child in Freetown is exactly easy.

Children, the lucky ones who can at least walk, roam the streets. Schools are closed. Teachers are on strike because they insist on being paid. They have taken lessons from their pupils and also roam the streets begging, looking for money, food, anything to survive.

In Sierra Leone it's not unusual for salaries not to be paid. In fact, it is unusual for salaries to be paid. Most salaries are two to four months in arrears at least. Not that they're worth much. Even if you're lucky enough to get a monthly salary, it's not enough to feed one person, let alone an extended family, for a week, never mind a month.

To make it easier not to pay people, the government and the one or two companies left switched to daily salaries. If you work one day and are not paid you are virtually forced to work the second day unpaid otherwise you won't get paid for the day before. If you're going to be paid. And so on until you're working unpaid for months in case you're not not going to be not paid at some vague time in the future.

When I first went to Freetown in the early eighties I was getting three leones to the pound. On my last trip in 1988 I was getting anything from 700 to 900 leones depending on who the taxi driver's brother knew.

Then there is the smell. On a bad day the whole place smells like an open sewer. On a good day it smells like an open cess pit. What drainage there is blocked up years ago. Septic tanks have been overflowing for as long as I can remember. There are fewer places to dig pit latrines. Rat droppings are the size of billiard balls. It is amazing that the whole place has not been obliterated by the plague.

Everywhere, and I'm no doctor, you hear and see signs of whooping cough, measles, polio, diphtheria. You name it, they've got it. Over 90% of the population have TB. Cholera must be in the air. Freetown has one of the highest infant, child and maternal death rates anywhere in the world. A newborn baby is called a visitor, and has to survive three months before it is given a name.

On one visit, Dinkay, a lawyer I met at the hotel, took me to Kissy Hospital. Three years ago, if you had to go to hospital it was fine. Two years ago government money ran out. To survive themselves, the few doctors still left in the hospital began charging for their services. For a visit they decided to charge 60 leones, 20 leones less than a bottle of beer. Few people could even afford that. Today, because money is worthless and the doctors are finding it even more difficult to survive, if you want to see a doctor it's anything from 100 to 1,000 leones. Hardly anybody goes to see them anymore. The hospital, of course, barely has two 100 leones to rub together.

'If I see a doctor it will cost me at least 100 leones,' the taxi driver told us on the way to the hospital. 'He then sends me to the pharmacy, which charges me 250 leones for four tablets. How can I pay that? Then four tablets will make no difference. I'll need another four. That means another 250 leones. Where can I find that money?' And 250 leones is only the price of a packet of cigarettes.

His brother's wife, he told me, was in labour for nearly two days before he found a retired midwife in the next village, but she was so old she couldn't come to them. He had to help his wife walk ten miles through the bush to the main road. Then they waited over four hours before a truck gave them a lift to the midwife. They lost the baby. It was lying sideways instead of head down. But the old midwife saved his wife.

At the Princess Christian Maternity Hospital along Fourah Bay Road patients even have to pay to go to the toilet. 'Who do they pay?' I asked the lawyer.

'The nurses.'

'And what happens if they can't pay?'

'They go outside. They go in the street. They go down the wharf at night.'

'You mean even if they're pregnant or have just given birth?'

He shrugged.

Sierra Leone, the original white man's grave, should not be the black man's grave it is today, with no social facilities, no infrastructure. One in ten children dies before the age of twelve months. One in ten mothers dies in childbirth. Life expectancy is forty-one years. I find it's not unusual to go back to Africa after a couple of years and find that people I knew, who were in their forties and fifties, have died in the interim. In Freetown, it happens after a couple of months.

I used to know the production director at one of the fish-processing plants in the so-called industrial zone along Waterloo Road. The whole area is largely a shambles, apart from the brewery which is modern, organised and quite hi-tech. But then there is a law somewhere that says that the poorer the country the better the beer.

What fish-processing machinery they had was decidedly spartan. Offices were definitely not offices; facilities were basic or nonexistent. Yet somehow it functioned. Trouble was it couldn't get sufficient fish to operate at anything like near-sensible production levels. One hour, maybe two hours every morning, and they were finished. Because they couldn't produce, they couldn't sell. Because they couldn't sell, they didn't make any money. The workers couldn't be paid. The production director wasn't paid. He was forced to give up living in one of the few wooden homes in the city and he and his family moved in with his brother's family in a lean-to shack they built themselves with sandy, home-made bricks.

When I returned to see him, some months later, the production director was dead. He was only forty-one. He had had a leg infection, and couldn't afford to have it treated. Gangrene set in. Within a month he was gone.

Then there are the power cuts. Most countries in Africa have power cuts. Sierra Leone has made them an art form. The last time I was in Freetown the temporary power cut had already lasted ten months. 'But that's not a power cut,' I was told by one minister. 'We still have electricity. It's just that we are not supplying it.'

On one occasion even Lungi International Airport had a power cut. We took off in the middle of the night with the help of headlights provided by a motley collection of cars, vans and trucks lining the runway.

If the offices or shops or banks or government buildings have stand-by generators they look as though they run on coal. Wood and charcoal fires are everywhere.

The whole economy, the whole country, is just falling apart. Prices are soaring, inflation is booming, the currency is falling faster than gravity. On my last visit, within just three days it had crashed from 120 leones to 175 leones to the dollar.

Freetown was supposed to be a home for free slaves. Today

it is dirt, poverty, destitution. It is everything you can imagine wrong with a city. There is in fact practically no city. It is a sprawl. There are almost no decent houses, no services, no drinking water. There are practically no real roads. There are trucks and what pass for trucks. If you ask the way in Freetown, the directions are related to tin drums, palm trees and car wrecks.

'For us, happiness is cooking rats in the sunshine,' my driver told me once as we drove along Pademba Road towards Government House.

Everybody is trying to help them – the IMF, the World Bank, a dozen different aid organisations – but in vain. I've seen hard-nosed World Bank officials, who've solved the most impossible situations in the four corners of the world, sitting in their candlelit office practically weeping into their last dirty glass of warm duty-free whisky because they can't even make the government see the problems let alone begin to solve them.

Sierra Leone is supposed to be the land of lions. They are more like lambs waiting to be slaughtered. They don't seem to have the energy to complain, to fight back, to try and solve their problems. And the crazy thing is, Sierra Leone could be one of the richest countries in Africa. It is virtually built on gold and diamonds.

Land at JFK and the best way into New York is by helicopter. Land at Don Muang and the best way into Bangkok is by ferry. Land at Lungi International Airport and the best way into Freetown is to cross the Atlantic on a very, very old ferry. Nothing like the *Ayatthaya Princess*, the luxury catamaran lavishly decorated Thai classical style, which shuttles guests between Don Muang Airport and the Shangri-La. It is packed with passengers, overflowing with luggage and overloaded with cars and trucks. Temperatures are in the 100s.

There is a helicopter link between the airport and the big

French hotel on the beach, but it only seems to work when the airport is closed. For whenever I arrive at Lungi I have to take the fifty-mile absolutely non-scenic Atlantic route and risk my life on that old ferry.

In a break between meetings in the City and drafts of the prospectus I was working on, I landed at the airport early one morning. By then we were up to draft six – or was it seven? I was drenched with condensation which had been pouring out of the overhead panel above my seat.

I try to be last off planes in Africa. In the old days I always tried to be one of the first out: get through the so-called health check first; get through customs before the rush; change my money before the crowds. Not any more. When I was first off I still managed to be delayed by the health check, taken apart by customs, taken to the cleaners by the money men and pushed to the back of the queue. Now I take my time. I saunter through the whole business as if I haven't a care in the world, even if I'm overtaken by three more jumbo loads. It usually also means I get the nice, civilised taxi drivers who are not prepared to wrench your suitcase from your hand or tear the shoes off your feet to get you into their cab.

This time, however, because I was drenched, I was in one of the first groups. I'd cleared the health check, or rather the unhealthy health check had cleared me. It took two days, however, to get the stains off my vaccination book. I'd survived customs. I'd got my money changed. I was now being routinely searched. A routine search in Lagos virtually means losing your wallet as well as your dignity. In Freetown it usually means just losing your dignity.

Way behind me I noticed Irving. He was wearing a ten-gallon hat, a Hawaiian tee-shirt, yellow jeans, what looked like prototype Doc Martens and carrying a fishing rod; no luggage, just a fishing rod. He sailed through. All the customs officers and policemen waved and shook him by the hand. Nobody searched him. No questions. He was out the other side in two minutes. Which must, I thought, be a world record for any African airport.

'An old trick I learnt in the New York police,' he grinned at me, and walked outside to where a car was waiting for him.

I fought for a taxi. I fought to get my luggage back from every other driver who wanted me to use their taxi. I fought to get inside the taxi. Finally we chugged off for the cross-country rally and ferry towards Freetown.

If Freetown is bad, the countryside outside is worse, even the so-called road from the airport. It announces straight away to the visitor that Sierra Leone is probably the poorest country in the world, bottom of the World Bank's table.

Yet everywhere there are diamonds – diamonds which even de Beers say are among the finest in the world. And just about everybody is selling diamonds. In other parts of Africa you have to travel days across the desert, smuggle across frontiers, make friends with the local tribesmen to get a sniff of gold or diamonds. In Freetown people sidle up to you in the street, waiters come up to you in restaurants and offer you diamonds. Bank managers, even policemen all carry tiny felt bags in their jacket pockets full of diamonds. Even government officials and ministers try to sell you diamonds.

Which, of course, is why Sierra Leone is in such a mess. Instead of having a well-organised, properly controlled diamond market, the whole country is one vast, grossly inefficient, disorganised smuggling operation. The controls on the Komo and Tongo Field mines are minimal. Gold panning is as popular as fishing in this country. Kenema, Koho and Bo, the diamond triangle, illegally export, it is estimated, over US$100 million of diamonds a year into Liberia, Burkina Faso and Côte d'Ivoire.

If ordinary Lebanese traders can routinely smuggle around US$500,000 a month of gold and diamonds out of the country, just think how much the multinational diamond companies, run by former Israeli army officers who were thrown out of

Zaire for guess what, are taking out.

After struggling for survival, diamond smuggling is Sierra Leone's biggest business. The government claims only – only – US$200 million worth of diamonds are smuggled out of the country every year. If the government says US$200 million, it must be US$400, or US$800, or maybe US$16 billion.

You've only got to go into any government office to see why. In fact, judging by the government offices I've been in and the government equipment and machinery I've seen, I'm amazed they can even begin to estimate their losses. They hardly have two drawing pins to hold the office together, let alone the back of an envelope and a chewed pencil to calculate their losses. Instead they blame everybody.

They blame the World Bank. 'They can't even monitor gold mining let alone gold smuggling,' one World Bank official told me. 'There are supposed to be any number of gold mines in the northern province but they can't afford even to go up there and look at them.'

They blame the Lebanese, who are supposed to have ministers, officials and even security and customs officers in their pockets. They blame the Israelis. They blame Indian and Pakistani businessmen. They blame middlemen and agents and dealers and anything that moves in the night. But even though one government minister after another is accused of smuggling and wanting commissions of US$12 million for negotiating government loans of US$500 million, they never seem to blame themselves.

After my cross-country rally and my heartstopping trip on the ferry, I got to the hotel. The bed linen looked, as Trollope's mother was told in the United States, as if it had only been used a couple of nights. I took the only two light bulbs left in the room, put them in my briefcase – lesson number two in poor countries: hang on to your light bulbs – and went down to order a taxi.

In Freetown hotels don't have televisions; not just not in the rooms, not anywhere. Freetown hardly has a television service. If they have radios, they rarely work. If they have telephones, they most certainly never work. If you want to arrange a meeting with anyone, you have to order a taxi, wait for it, crawl for hours through the traffic to the office of the person you want to meet; wait to see him; arrange a time for the meeting; crawl back through the traffic; pay off the taxi plus a big thank-you for the driver then order another taxi to take you back to see the person you've just arranged to meet.

At reception, a German businessman was desperately trying to check out. His lap-top computer, his worldwide portable satellite telephone, his go-anywhere fax, even his Braun travel alarm clock, couldn't take the non-German electricity supply. He wanted out. 'At office urgently to myself send a fax I must,' he said.

Irving, I noticed, was already sitting by himself at a table by the edge of the pool, still clasping his fishing rod. The hotel was practically empty. With the German headed out, it looked as though we were the only ones left. I strolled across to him.

'Never carry a briefcase. Africans always search briefcases. They never search fishing rods.' He stroked the top of his head. 'An old trick I learnt in the CIA.'

I wondered what an ex-New York cop and ex-CIA man was doing in Sierra Leone. He said he wanted to rent the sports stadium in the middle of Freetown from the government, in order to turn it into a giant open-air cinema. 'But nobody's got any money to buy a slice of bread let alone go to the cinema,' I said.

'It will be free,' he grinned, 'completely free. I want to do something for the people of Sierra Leone.'

I spent the day visiting people and arranging to go and see them the following day; in their offices, at various banks, in their homes. I saw one minister who was sitting in ministerial splendour in a room lined with cheap, warped plywood panels which were peeling off the walls. The air-conditioning unit coughed and spluttered so much that for years water had been pouring out of it on to the carpet. As I walked across the office I could feel the damp, gooey, sodden carpet sticking to the soles of my shoes. It was like walking through a giant pizza.

I met another minister at Goodrich, a fishing village along the coast. Apart from gold, Sierra Leone is teeming with fish; not only expensive shrimp and lobster but also grouper, snapper, sole, tuna, squid, octopus and herring. But because they have neither the money nor the equipment to harvest them, their whole coastline is a free-for-all for unlicensed fishermen from all over the world. Greek, Italian, Korean, Chinese and Russian vessels regularly fish there for expensive demersals, snappers and bream. Sierra Leone Fisheries Department estimates that at any one time there can be 350 vessels at work.

They've tried fighting back, but with little success. Their greatest coup to date was arresting a 600-tonne French trawler, the *Marsonin*, ninety miles south west of Freetown which had over US$350,000 worth of prime tuna on board. Which shows the scale of the problem.

Back at the hotel, Irving was still by the pool, deep in conversation with three Sierra Leoneans, who were lined up waiting to talk to him. Still he was holding his fishing rod.

Later, over a single candle – there was a power cut – he told me about his plans to refurbish the huge outdoor stadium, at his own expense, as an open-air cinema. There would be no charge for entry, partly because nobody had any money and partly because he was convinced he could get his money back by selling soft drinks and beer before, during and after the events. Everybody was prepared to give it a try – the general manager of the stadium, the local brewery and the local soft drinks company.

Could he get the minister to say yes? No way. Again and again he had explained everything to him: how it would create desperately needed income for the stadium; how it would provide desperately needed entertainment – free; how it would help the brewery and soft drinks company; how it would create jobs, how it would – cough, cough – pump money into police pockets – nudge, nudge; how the minister could claim all the credit for the idea by hiring him to do the work. And so on. But no way. The minister, he said, would only smile and wipe his hands across his face, say what a good idea it was, and tell him how much his constituents would enjoy the opportunity of going to the pictures for free. But sign? No way. It was as if he was frightened of even considering the possibility of taking a decision.

Irving said, 'Just give us permission for one concert. See how it goes. Then decide.' Another smile. But still no signature. 'Okay. One concert as an experiment. We'll donate all the money to charity.' Still no signature. Did his wife want to chair the organising committee? Again a smile.

I was out for dinner, but when I got back he was still sitting by the pool, still holding his fishing rod. He told me he had made a lot of money in Guinea Bissau. His local business partner had married the local telephone operator. Whenever anyone wanted an overseas number she had to get it for them, so they knew everybody and everything. 'An old trick I learned when I was working with the FBI,' he said, stroking the back of his head.

'So what made you leave?'

'They're modernising the exchange,' he replied. 'They've fired the operator.'

For the rest of the week we had the hotel almost to ourselves. We'd meet for breakfast. 'Hear the shooting during the night?' he would ask, propping his fishing rod against the table. 'They're taking the Lebanese out.'

A Swiss engineer working for the Food and Agriculture Organisation arrived one morning. He said he had been sent to study timber resources. But I never saw him again.

One afternoon I was coming down Wellington Street in the centre of town. Across the road I could see lawyers in their traditional English lawyers' white cravats and black gowns, strolling up to the Chamber of the Chief Justice. One was carrying a huge plastic bag. 'He's just been paid,' the taxi driver said. The currency is so worthless that good lawyers get paid at the rate of two plastic bags a day. The poor ones don't get anything. Not even the plastic bag.

Usually Lebanese Clubs wherever you go in the world have everything, even in the middle of nowhere. The other beauty of Lebanese Clubs is that everybody is bribing everyone else, so that even if you're not a member or not even Lebanese, they are the easiest clubs in the world to get into. If you see what I mean. The Lebanese Club in the hills overlooking Freetown, however, was nothing like any other I've ever bribed my way into. It was dull, drab and empty. No government ministers, no Japanese salesmen, and no Lebanese.

'I told you. They've been taking them out. You heard the shooting,' Irving said, smoothing the back of his head.

The only person there apart from us was the barman, a broken-down old man with thick, rubbery skin falling in great folds around his face. When he wasn't serving us, he sat on a crate behind the bar slowly winding and unwinding his dirty bandages. Over two warm beers – the electricity wasn't working and the generators had broken down – I discovered that Irving had been and done practically everything. He'd worked for the New York police, the CIA, the FBI, Mossad and probably the KGB as well. He was a judo black belt, a musician. He'd operated on people. He'd lived in the desert as well as in the jungle.

'So what's with the fishing rod?' I asked.

He said he was worried. He thought he had cancer.

Back at the hotel, things were swinging. While we'd been out the number of guests had jumped a staggering 50%.

Another guest had checked in, from the World Bank. Over a couple of shared bottles of fruit juice – don't forget it's Freetown – we discussed Sierra Leone.

'How do you think we feel?' the World Bank man, a Kenyan, said. 'We want to help them. We know we can help them. They won't let us.'

'But why? Don't they trust you?'

He shrugged.

'They don't want the responsibility?'

Another shrug. 'They want to keep their heads down, avoid problems, keep taking their so-called salaries.'

'So how on earth do you get on?'

He raised his eyes to the heavens. 'We don't.'

'You mean nobody says you can do anything or not? You just do it?'

'We have to. Otherwise nothing would get done.'

For years, it seemed, the World Bank and others were desperate to move in, but the official invitation never came. In the end, they decided to ignore the politicians and work with the few civil servants that were left. 'But we can only go so far – minor adjustments, that kind of thing. We daren't even begin to tackle the big problems.'

The following morning when I came down for breakfast, Irving was leaving the hotel. He said he was going into town for important meetings. I walked with him to his car. The hotel manager came up and shook hands with him. The two young men on the reception desk waved at him. One of the porters rushed across to open the door for him. Outside, two policemen sprang to attention. We walked across the car park. The driver held the door open for him. The car shot off towards Freetown with Irving sitting in the front. Clutching his fishing rod.

That afternoon I also decided to check out. I had done as much as I could hope to do on that visit. In any case, I guessed proof number seven (or was it eight?) would be ready when

I got back. I asked the manager to book me a cab to the airport that evening. I asked all the usual questions. Was the airport open? Did they have electricity? Was the ferry running? Were the roads okay?

'Why don't you take the helicopter?' he said.

'But I didn't think there were any flights,' I replied. 'It's not on the timetable.'

'It's not a regular flight. It's a special.'

'So why have they got a special flight this evening?' I wondered. 'Is there something special going on?'

'Oh no,' he smiled. 'It's just that they haven't any money to service the helicopter for regular flights so they run special flights instead.'

Back in London, as proof number 12 progressed agonisingly towards proof number 12a – superstitious lot, these merchant bankers – I kept in touch with what was happening in Freetown. I even re-installed my old telex machine. Fax machines were almost unheard of in Freetown – or if people had heard of them, they certainly couldn't afford them. Things were so bad there I didn't think they could get worse. But they did.

The civil war in Liberia spilled over into Sierra Leone. The Liberian rebels, backed by our good friend Colonel Gaddaffi the Great Jamahiriya, claimed Sierra Leone was supporting their enemies. So they seized Bo, Kenema and other gold and diamond regions in the south and east of the country.

In a nation of nearly 4 million people, around 250,000 must have been displaced, another 250,000 fled to next-door Guinea, and another 500,000 were trapped behind rebel lines living on God only knows what. Bodies were left to rot where they fell. Many were sucked dry of their blood – by Liberian soldiers eager to increase their strength. Sierra Leonean boys and young men who refused to be conscripted into the rebel forces were hacked to death.

If people in Freetown have nothing, people in the rebel

areas have less than nothing. Villages have been destroyed. What few crops there were have been burnt. Those who couldn't run away have been shot. Bread cost 5 leones in 1989; a year later it cost 20 leones even though those salaries that were being paid had crashed from 1,000 to 800 leones and were still falling. The police were being given rice and left to steal what they could from the people they were supposed to be protecting from people who went around stealing whatever they wanted.

One of my contacts suddenly arrived in London. It was the first time he had been out of Sierra Leone. He checked into the Hilton in Park Lane. I called in on my way to the City with proof number 14. All the Hilton trappings he seemed to take without batting an eyelid, but he was clearly very annoyed by the telephone. He kept picking it up and saying, 'It still works. There's still a dialling tone.'

We agreed to meet later, and I headed for my meeting in the City. Everyone had insisted the previous weekend on having copies sent by special messengers to their homes all over the country. It cost a fortune, but I was sure it meant they would have studied it and made up their minds once and for all. Not on your life. Most had never opened the envelope.

'Just too damned busy, you know.'

'Pony Club meeting in the next village. More than my life's worth to miss it.'

'Sorry, old boy. Wife put her foot down.'

Once again we started ploughing through it, line by agonising line, comma by comma, full stop by—

The 'phone rang. It was for me. 'Meant to tell you.' It was my friend at the Hilton, checking the 'phone was working. 'The helicopter crashed last week.'

We were on the last few pages. This looked like it. No more changes. No more proofs. No more—

The 'phone rang again. It was Irving.

'But I thought you committed suicide . . .'

'I escaped.'

'An old trick you learnt . . .'

'But I had to have my leg amputated.'

'So what happened?'

'You're the last person I'm going to talk to.'

'Look, I'm in a meeting,' I stuttered. 'Give me your number and I'll—'

The line went dead.

Kumasi

Bordeaux is the world capital of wine; New Orleans of jazz; Ayorou of camels. And for me, Kumasi is the world capital of funerals. For if anyone has turned funerals into an art form it is the old Ashanti capital in the bottom left-hand corner of Ghana, off towards the border with Côte d'Ivoire.

Every time I go to Kumasi I get trapped by funerals. Either the people I've travelled almost 200 miles to see from the capital, Accra, in battered taxis along some of the worst roads in the world, are not there because they are attending funerals, or I've just managed to see them between funerals and I am held up getting back because all the taxis in town are out on funeral duty. Or I've got a taxi and we can't get across town because the streets are packed with one long funeral procession after another.

All over Africa, probably thanks to the Egyptians, funerals are big news. They are treated seriously. In this country nowadays they tend to be seen as a minor interruption to everyday existence, but years ago even ordinary funerals were grand occasions. As a lad I can remember living with death. I made all my pocket money writing out invitations and memorial cards in my copperplate handwriting. Irish half uncials were extra.

I used to serve solemn High Mass for the dead, walk mile after mile behind coffins to the cemetery, then help the priest at the final farewell at the graveside. The first dull thud of turf on top of the coffin meant extra money for me whatever it meant to anybody else present.

My first ever hangover was acquired at the wake after the funeral of our old parish priest when we all walked five miles behind his coffin to the cemetery and five miles back. I was only ten or eleven at the time, but I was hooked – on funerals. And on drink.

Since then I've drunk my way through funerals all over Africa. In various parts of Kenya they brew special beers for funerals such as *kwete, keka, maemba* and *kebuulo*, as well as for smearing on graves to appease the spirits.

In Freetown you get a good old-fashioned New Orleans-style funeral complete with black suits, bowler hats and a jazz procession. It's the only town I know where people don't complain about their taxis being held up by funeral processions.

Once I went to a funeral in Lomé, Togo where, on the basis that life is too short to drink coffee, we drowned our sorrows in a deadly mixture of *da-ha*, the local palm wine, and Dom Perignon. Cyril Connolly maintained funerals were cocktail parties for the over-sixties. This was a black orgy for the dead.

Kumasi, therefore, is my kind of ghost town.

Ghana, the home of the famous handwoven *kente* cloth, is in a class of its own when it comes to funerals. For ever since that hot sweaty night in 1951 when, wearing his *kente* cloth like a Roman wearing his toga, Dr Kwame Nkrumah, proclaimed, 'Seek ye first the political kingdom', they have been burying their hopes.

Ghanaians, most of whom now wear *kente* cloth as ordinary shirts, were the first black Africans to run their own country, after 150 years of colonial rule. And – I shall probably be buried for saying this – they blew it. Before, they were poor; they lacked schools, hospitals, decent homes. Today, after nearly thirty years of independence they are still poor.

They still lack schools, hospitals and decent homes.

Yet on paper they have everything – gold, diamonds, enormous natural resources (not for nothing was it known as the Gold Coast), oil, bauxite, manganese, the largest man-made lake in the world and more than enough hydro-electricity for everyone. Not to mention coffee, cocoa, sugar and a million *kente* shirts, dresses, hats, skirts, stoles and handbags.

And yet. 'Attention to detail. Never paid attention to detail. Always dreaming. Never interested in what was happening on the ground,' is what an elderly colonel figure from Tunbridge Wells, who was in Ghana at independence time, told me over tea and muffins at the Naval and Military in Piccadilly.

'Give you an example. In Accra we collected the rubbish every day. After the Brits were thrown out they started missing one day. What's a day? What? Can always collect it tomorrow.' He leant forward and nudged me with his stick. 'That's all right for us. But the mosquitoes, those little beggars, they soon caught on. Within no time at all we were overrun with mosquitoes, malaria, everything.' The country, he decided, was going to the mosquitoes, so he hung up his *kente* shirt and headed back to Blighty.

By 1962, only six years after Nkrumah, first prime minister then president, led the Ghanaians to their independence, the warning lights were flashing. Ghana's external reserves were a third of what they had been when he became prime minister. By 1965 they were down to minus 0.5%. Ghana was bust. Which is more than a shame, because I think Ghana should be one of the showcases of Africa.

Accra, the capital, is a lesson on emptying your dustbins promptly. It is full of once-grand crumbling buildings. Imposing government offices, elegant office blocks, fashionable hotels, they've all gone to seed. Floor coverings and wall decorations have long disappeared. Single light bulbs dangle dangerously from ceilings that used to have plaster. Doors no longer open and close – if the doors are still there. Lifts? I can't remember the last time a lift worked in Ghana.

The street stalls are piled high with bread, vegetables and meat – dog, cat, rat, you name it, they've got it. My favourite? Chicken spare parts. That's what they call unrecognisable bits of chicken which make up the Ghanaian equivalent of Colonel Sander's. The thousand little bars in corrugated tin shacks, instead of promoting a happy hour, try to lure you inside with the promise of a Merciful Hour.

Everyone is entitled to their dreams. What I love about the Ghanaians is the way they manage to live their dreams in a dream. Businessmen in Accra will tell you they can produce in Ghana goods and equipment to match anything you can buy anywhere. And I don't mean street traders, I mean serious businessmen. You go into their factories – there's nothing there. Maybe an old Alfred Herbert rusting away at the back, perhaps two old Czechoslovakian lathes. You don't know what to say. Yet somehow they are convinced they can produce computers as good as IBM's, if not better.

I had a meeting once with the new minister of tourism. He told me Ghana was absolutely safe for tourists. They need have no fear of being attacked, no worries about the black market. Everybody wanted cedis, the local currency. Afterwards he walked down with me outside the ministry, waved over a private car that belonged to a cousin and gave him Togolese CFAs to take me to my next meeting.

The minister for post and telecommunications boasts of their technology even though the 'phones don't work and postmen steal practically all the letters. The minister of health claims that the Orobo Herbal Treatment Centre at Nwoase near Wenchi discovered a cure for AIDS before the rest of the world had started trying.

One evening I was at dinner with a group of ambassadors wasting away their careers in Accra. We were joined by a minister. Conversation drifted on to security, how safe different towns and cities were in Africa. The minister assured us that Accra was the safest of them all.

'Because of the people?' I asked.

'No. Because of the security forces,' he replied. He then insisted on taking us to the central police headquarters, a low narrow building off one of the four-lane highways into Accra. All the way he kept telling us about the efficiency of the security forces, their professionalism, the resources at their disposal, how the government would never compromise the . . . and so on. Immediately we arrived we were surrounded by policemen saluting and barking orders at each other. Before I could go into the control room I was searched about three times. I might have been being ushered in to see the Pope himself. Inside, there was nothing. Bank after bank of radio telephones were empty. Cables were hanging out. Loose wires were everywhere. Everything that could have been stripped out and sold had been taken. Yet to him, I'm convinced, this was state-of-the-art technology. His police were the most professional in Africa, if not the world.

In reality the police spend their time either doing nothing, in size thirteen boots, where they do very well, or rounding up all the tramps and down-and-outs in Accra and sending them twenty-five kilometres away to Pantang Psychiatric Hospital, where they seem to do very badly.

The capital of the Ashantis, however, is hard, solid reality. If Michael Caine had fought against them as he did against the Zulus at Rorke's Drift, Ashanti warriors would be as famous today as the Zulus.

For those who easily tire of balls of *fufu* and *banku*, its more reputable restaurants do a delicious line in grasscutters, a giant rat, the speciality of the region. Less reputable places are still said to practise ritual murder of young virgins who are then cut open, various parts removed and, would you believe, eaten.

Apart from funerals, Kumasi also boasts what I reckon is the best beer in West Africa. I once visited the brewery. The managing director was a fantastic real-life Scottish James Robertson Justice figure. It was said he ruled Kumasi jointly with the present Asantahene, the legendary King of the Ashantis, who had actually qualified as a barrister and practised at the London bar before returning home on the death of his father to claim the throne (which, in the case of the Ashantis is a royal stool). On this occasion, however, the supremacy was being challenged. The beer was so popular in the town that the only way the market mamas, the real tough traders, could sell their own cheap, inferior, imported beers was to collect all the empty bottles throughout the town, stockpile them and slowly resell them at higher and higher prices to whoever would pay; either the brewery or frustrated, thirsty individuals.

'The bottles are more expensive than the beer,' James Robertson Justice bellowed at me across his air-conditioned office which was about as warm as Aberdeen in a force 9 gale. He had already bought back one container-load of his own bottles on the basis that it is always better not to fight anything head-on. Especially the market mamas. But he was determined it would be the last. He was confident that market forces would soon begin to bite and drinkers would put pressure on the women to release their stockpile.

I'd come across a similar example of African free trading in Congo. The aid organisations were supplying fertiliser to farmers, who quickly discovered that the fertiliser definitely produced more crops, but also produced more weeds. The farmers told me they didn't have time to look after the extra crops let alone the extra weeds. So they threw away the fertiliser and sold the sacks to farmers from another village who needed them to deliver to market the extra crop they had grown with their fertiliser.

The brewery director, summoned by his secretary, disappeared, leaving me to continue sampling the products from his bought-back bottles. Ten minutes later he returned with another tiny young secretary who was shuddering and stamping and screaming her heart out.

'She's just received a message saying her mother died three days ago,' he boomed above the screams. 'She's got to get home for the funeral. Just outside Accra. I said you'd take her. You don't mind?'

What could I say? She had a howl that would inspire a requiem. 'And I said you'd take her little cousin as well,' he boomed, opening the door to reveal a massive, wallowing, thirty-stone buddha. 'Family. That kind of thing. Means a lot to them.'

'Not at all,' I mumbled in the cold of the moment through the wailing. 'Not at all. Pleased to help.' Disasters, especially in Africa, usually come in sevens. This was already registering 23 on my Personal Disaster Scale.

Kumasi was 200 miles from Accra. Accra was 150 miles from the border with Togo. Ghana and Togo were at loggerheads again, opening and shutting the frontier whenever they didn't feel like it. The following day I had been invited to the Chamber of Commerce in Lomé for the inaugural meeting of the new Togolese Federation of Barbers and Hairdressers. I had to be back across the border before it closed at midnight or I could be trapped on the wrong side for weeks. 'Pleased to help,' I mumbled again, desperately hoping there wouldn't be too many funerals stopping me from getting back. Either mine or other people's.

The drive back was, well, an experience. The car was too small, especially with thirty-stone little cousin in the front seat. We'd tried forcing her into the back but it was impossible. The heat was a million times worse than stifling. The noise was deafening, like sitting next to a loudspeaker at one of those discos. So I am told. The road was even worse. And everywhere there was thick red dust – outside, inside, in my hair, in my eyes. By the time we'd passed our second funeral

I was smelling like an open container of Rommedou, which is the smelliest cheese in the world even when it's chilled and locked inside a Belgian cold store.

The driver was a cross between a New York taxi driver, a long jumper and a kamikaze pilot. The road between Kumasi and Accra is one red dust pothole after another. There was barely 100 yards in the whole 200-mile stretch that was remotely level. A normal taxi driver would have edged gently down the inside of each crater, swerved madly to avoid a gathering swamp in the bottom, clung perilously to the edge then roared up out of the other side. This driver tried to leap over the top of them. By the time we'd passed our fourth funeral I felt like Pearl Harbour.

We'd swing round a dusty corner. Right in front of us, billowing up mountains of more dust, would be three Tojos, the Bedford trucks that act as buses anywhere more than 100 yards from the centre of Accra. In between would be a pothole the size of an Olympic swimming pool. Everything inside me cried, Stop. Not this honourable driver. We did a ski-jump straight into the middle of the pool then reared, revved, skidded our way up the other end and scuttled for the undergrowth before the lorries made their own death leaps. This we did not once, not twice, not . . . Even now I can't bring myself to even think of how many, many times we could have . . . we could have . . .

Inside the car the temperature was climbing, the heat becoming more intense; the wailing of the grief-stricken secretary was becoming louder; the dust thicker. At one time it was like driving through a rain forest in the middle of a massive logging operation. At another, it was desert. Then we'd crawl through tiny villages with tiny babies running, jumping and crawling across the road.

Worst of all were all the official roadblocks. I say official, although in Ghana there is no way of knowing whether a roadblock is official, or just an enterprising group of young men in borrowed Oxfam suits and, would you believe, raincoats eager to relieve you of any surplus cash. Call me a coward. Tell me I'm destroying the work ethic. I don't care. Asking them for their official police identity cards just did not seem the thing to do in the circumstances.

We would hit a clear stretch of road – say 300–400 yards – and the driver would put his foot down. The engine would scream itself up to 35 or maybe 40mph. Suddenly, out of the trees about twenty yards ahead, would shoot about ten young men, rifles over their shoulders, complete with barriers and pole and slap them down in front of us. The driver would slam on what brakes we had. The car, in a cloud of dust, would rock violently, swerve one way then the next. The little secretary would wail still louder. Our fat friend would scream for her Maker. Then we'd shudder to a halt within inches of the barrier.

'Sir,' they would shout as I crawled out of the car and pretended to stand to attention. 'Good day, sir,' one would always step forward. 'Routine, sir, checking for smugglers.'

An officer at the US embassy in Accra had told me they rated Ghana a 'Caution' as far as terrorist attacks and hijacking were concerned. 'Try to avoid using types of cars that might identify you as an American or as someone rich or important,' he told me. I loved the distinction, which, of course, he hotly denied. Was I American? Did I look rich or important?

'But you're not wearing . . .' I would begin, coughing and choking on the dust.

'. . . Because we're under cover . . .' they would grin back.

'Well now,' I would mutter, unfolding yet another dusty bundle of cedis . . .

Corruption is corruption, except in Africa. In Africa, corruption is a way of life. There is only one way to get anything done in Africa – pay for it. In any case my problem was simple. Did I stand in the middle of nowhere, staring at their rifles which might or might not be loaded, asking to inspect their documents which they obviously didn't have, or did I drop them a few million cedis, shake everyone by the hand and get the hell out of there as fast as my broken-down taxi could make it?

In Ghana everybody wants money; police, customs officers, civil servants, everyone. You can't get into the country without paying extra for the privilege. You can't get your passport stamped without a little something. You practically cannot cross the road without being pursued for small change.

Get a taxi and the driver will ask you to guess how much you should pay him. Go into a bar and everybody will expect a drink. Try and cash a cheque at a bank and the clerk will suggest an extra charge for his particular service. Meet a policeman on the street and he will grin and ask to look at your passport. Go into an office building. Sitting in the lift will be an old man. He'll hold his hand out and ask you which floor you want. You grin sheepishly, hand over a couple of thousand cedis. Then he tells you the lift doesn't work.

Ghana must be the only country where the head of state begins his New Year's message by praising the fact that his fellow countrymen have been celebrating Christmas with Christians all over the world and ends by urging them to lay off taking money from people for performing their official duties and holding up vehicles at unofficial checkpoints to steal money from the passengers. 'Let us hope, my country-men and women, that we will all share the responsibility of confronting the re-emergence of some of these negative traits,' he said in his traditional no-nonsense way of laying down the law in terms that would be as easily understood in the dusty sitting rooms of Accra where families are tucking into their balls of *fufu* and *banku* as in the villages of Sefwi Juabeso-Bia where they are tucking into bits of young virgins.

These were the early days of Ghana's structural adjustment programme. There was literally no money in the country. Everything was cancelled. The country had come to a standstill. Practically everybody who had a job was being sacked and taking to living on the streets. At one time there were so many beggars around Kwame Nkrumah Circle in central Accra that what little traffic there was was unable to get through. Others were drifting back to their villages in the bush to survive as best they could on little more than a wish, a prayer and two handfuls of rice a week.

People were stealing light bulbs from shops, offices and hotels. If they worked they sold them for a bowl of rice; if they didn't they still sold them for a bowl of rice. Knives and forks were stolen from restaurants and hotels. People with homes started chaining their own cutlery to the tables.

J.J. Rawlings was president, and the joke going round the bars was to the point. 'What's the latest fashion?' 'A Rawlings' necklace.' 'What's a Rawlings' necklace?' 'Your collar bone sticking out of your neck.' At that time there were lots of fashionable people in Ghana.

Everybody set up unofficial roadblocks. Suddenly a big market started in stolen foreign passports; this being Ghana, the rewards far outweighed the risks. For stealing no fewer than thirty passports, people were being jailed for just two years – less than one month per passport. Bearing in mind that in gaol at least you were guaranteed something to eat, many felt it was worth the risk.

Traditional dowries for new brides, another useful indicator, were officially reduced from four to two cows.

Bodies began piling up in mortuaries, until they were overflowing. Hospitals were refusing to take people in because there was no way, if the worst came to the worst, they could get them out again. Some wrote to the relatives begging them to collect the bodies to bury them themselves. A few went as far as saying that if the bodies were not collected they would all be buried in a heap in one mass grave.

But even in the middle of all this, the Ghana National Commission on Children meeting in Kumasi felt it necessary to pass a resolution calling for a ban on the importation of toys that were harmful to child development, objects of aggression or objects with racial connotations.

Today things are better. Ghana has rejoined the world. It is now a World Bank favourite, a basket case that came back from the brink. Things are still bad, but not as bad as they were. Industry is beginning to move again, gold mines are operating. New official gold mines are opening up all over the country which makes sense. For a time Togo, next door, was exporting more gold than Ghana and they didn't have any mines. And there are hundreds, maybe thousands, of smaller 'galamsey' – small-scale, unofficial miners.

The once all-powerful but grossly inefficient Ghana Cocoa Board is being completely revamped. Over 12,000 people have been made redundant and overheads slashed. The market inside Ghana has been opened up to competition.

With nothing but a blackboard, a piece of chalk and a room the size of a classroom, Ghana has also launched its own stock exchange, designed both to put a realistic price on what assets are left in the industrial sector and to attract more, especially foreign, investment.

Many small and medium-sized companies are back in business; old ones have been rehabilitated, and new ones have started up against all the odds. And not just corner shops. Ghana is now exporting pineapples, wood, rubber, shrimps, prawns and lobsters. Hotels have been built and opened, mainly by the French. Even the mortuaries now have spare room.

The economy has grown 5% a year since 1984. Exports have doubled to nearly US$1 billion, which is unbelievable. Rawlings' necklaces seem to be going out of fashion. When I went to Ghana in the mid-eighties, this would have seemed an impossible dream. But they've done it.

The secret, I believe, lies in the unlikely combination of 'JJ', the President, Flight-Lieutenant J.J. Rawlings, a casual, freewheeling ex-Marxist, son of a Ghanaian mother and a Scottish father and a man of the people; his Finance Secretary, Kwesi Botchway, a technocrat if ever I saw one, who has in a very professional way charmed the World Bank and IMF into supporting Ghana; and Kojo Tsikata, the mysterious Head of Security.

Rawlings seized power on a leftist platform, then secretly negotiated behind the backs of his supporters with the IMF to put the country on a sound financial basis – or as sound a one as possible. Botchway then worked wonders with the World Bank and the IMF. He made them come across when in other countries they would have, oh so politely and diplomatically, packed their bags and gone home.

The interesting gossip among the more up-market stall-holders along High Street, Accra, is how much contact there actually is between JJ and Kwesi. Most say the contact is very much arm's-length. Some even say that JJ never understands what Botchway is saying. He lives in his castle spending the occasional night communing with the spirits. Botchway lives in his country house. Nobody seems to know where Kojo lives. All I know is, it has worked.

Now we are climbing into yet another giant pothole. I reckon Madonna could have held a concert inside it. All the time the sun is roasting the outside of the car; mountains of dust are piling up inside; our passengers are howling and bawling. All the time the driver is telling me about his boss, the size of his house, how many wives he had, why he shouldn't have married the last one. And all the time I'm pulling leeches the size of whelks out of my leech-proof calico socks.

Slowly it began to get dark. Climbing out of the millionth crater I spotted what looked like the start of a candlelight procession.

It was Accra. For Accra, the capital of the country that advocated seeking first the political kingdom, forgot to order light bulbs. There is no street lighting. The whole city seems to be lit by candles. All the tiny rickety wooden stalls are lit by flickering kerosene lamps.

It had taken us nearly ten hours to cover 200 miles. My passport was covered in sticky 'security' thumbprints. All my small change and notes had gone. All I had left was a FF500 note in my shoe which I wouldn't have wished on any security policeman, official or otherwise.

'Okay,' I said to the driver. 'So where's the ...' The little secretary erupted into another fit of tears. 'Well, ask her,' I said. 'It's no good me ...'

There followed ten hysterical minutes of argument and outbursts of pure hatred between the three of them before they finally agreed on the house where you-know-who had just ... erhm.

It was nearly 8 o'clock. I had another 150 miles to go to the border, safety and the inaugural meeting of the Togolese Federation of Barbers and Hairdressers.

I know Accra well, but that evening I saw places I never dreamt existed. We drove round and round the Pink Lady, the Yugoslav-built international conference centre on the site of the old racecourse opposite the Kwame Nkrumah conference complex. Why is it called the Pink Lady? Because it is covered with pale pink ceramic tiles. Or it was. It was here, during the tenth ministerial meeting of the Non-Aligned Movement, that Niger donated seven cows towards the cost of the show.

We drove a thousand times past the Golden Tulip Hotel which was specially built for an international conference and completed four days after it ended. Up and down we went in front of the old Lonrho guesthouse. Once we even managed to come out facing the new luxury Lonrho guesthouse, where on one visit I lived in splendour. We circled round and round Ussher Town which has its own unique collection of colours, smells and street stalls selling goat stew.

To me one open sewer looks very much like another. But

we passed one particular one with a somewhat unique attraction so many times even I knew we were lost. The driver started stopping for long, animated often hysterical conversations with anyone who would talk to him.

'He told you where the house is?' I asked nervously, after one particularly heated exchange.

'He is my brother.'

'We're not lost?' I hesitated.

'I am Ashanti. I know my country.'

It was almost pitch dark, but after we had circled another block another three times I swear I could recognise the same palm tree outside what looked like one of those bush night-clubs. 'We're lost,' I said. Silence. Even the secretary had stopped crying. 'So we're lost, aren't we?'

'No. I am going there now.' He spun the car round and shot back in the direction we had just come from. 'I just want to be certain of the area.'

The house was already thronged with people wailing their hearts out. I say, house; it was two small rooms built of rough home-made bricks in the corner of a yard. Other similar shacks were dotted around it. I tried to say goodbye and disappear. No way. I was ushered into the crowd and shoved into the house. 'Don't go away,' I shouted back at the driver. 'Stay by the car.'

I was introduced all round by the little secretary, who was now the only person not crying. She was suddenly remarkably composed, brisk and efficient. I was offered a bowl of goat stew and a cigarette. A television in the corner was garlanded like a household god. I didn't like to ask if it worked.

'So sorry . . . terrible news . . . awful shock,' I muttered as I bowed and shook hands with everybody. I was pushed towards the inner room where the wailing was at its loudest. 'Now she is at rest,' the secretary said. I nodded.

An elderly lady collapsed on her shoulder; she disappeared from view. My chance, I thought, and fell back into the crowd.

Within seconds I was outside in the street, by the car. And of course the driver had disappeared. Frantically I ran up and down the dusty track. It was nearly 10 o'clock. The border was still 150 miles away. I had to get there by midnight or I was in trouble. At best, no inaugural meeting. At worst, another three months in Ghana.

An old man with a threadbare *kente* over his threadbare shoulders waved from the broken gate of another yard. Inside the driver was eating goat soup.

'Must eat,' he said. 'I'm sick. Need food.'

'But the frontier—' I gasped.

'Very sick,' he grunted.

I put my hand inside my jacket pocket.

'But not too sick,' he grinned.

To the croaking of a million bullfrogs we spun down the lane, shot past the bush nightclub, leapt six open sewers, skidded through Ussher Town, rocketed through the middle of an empty Accra and headed for the border.

Just over the bridge past the Volta River, suddenly out of the trees about 20 yards ahead of us shot ten young men with rifles over their shoulders complete with barriers and pole and slapped them down right— The driver slammed his foot hard on the accelerator. We headed straight for the— 'Hey, watch,' I screamed. We were through the barrier and zooming down the road, careering wildly between lumps of wooden barrier, potholes, ditches.

'But . . . but . . .' I gasped.

'You want to reach border. We have to go fast,' the driver grimaced. His knuckles, I swear, were white on the steering wheel.

'Yes, but . . . that could have been . . .'

'Pirates,' he snarled. 'Not real police. Pirates, I tell you.'

It was now almost midnight. It was another fifty miles to the border. Should I tell him to take it easy? Maybe we should stop at the next . . .? On the other hand, you never know what's

safest bet. If it was still open, I was okay. If not, I had problems, but they would be the least of my problems.

They all looked at each other, shrugged their shoulders. 'Okay,' the driver said. 'If that's what you want.'

The smallest of the three grinned. 'But we will show you the way in case …'

'In case,' I grinned back.

We all climbed into the car and for what seemed the next three days slid, skidded and swerved in pitch darkness until we climbed out of a ditch in to what I recognised as the outskirts of Aflao, the border town with Togo. The three climbed out. We exchanged greetings and gifts. Actually they exchanged the greetings and I exchanged the gifts. We then drove gently along the main street. Everything was quiet. The occasional street light was on. There were a few dogs rummaging around. People were slumped on tables, along benches, huddled by the side of walls, all fast asleep.

The frontier was bathed in floodlights. Soldiers were asleep outside the customs hut. A policeman had his head across the barrier. A dozen fat old ladies were asleep on top of each other by the side of the road.

I grabbed my briefcase and made the traditional farewells you make to any African taxi driver. The car purred gently into the good night. Shall I wait, I thought, like a good boy, until the frontier opens in the morning? Then probably another three hours to get across? If it opens. Or maybe three weeks if it doesn't open. Or shall I . . .?

I began walking. I bent down under the frontier post with its sleeping policeman. Not a murmur. I was in no-man's-land. I walked slowly the 100-odd metres to the Togo frontier. Deliberately I kept in the middle of the track. If I walked along the edge, in the shadows, I thought, anything could happen. I could fall over somebody on the ground. A guard could suddenly wake up and fire into the shadows. In the middle of the track, in the light, it was still risky. But it was less risky.

I reached the Togo frontier. Nobody was around, not even a sleeping policeman. I stopped and turned round, trying to look the innocent traveller who didn't know he was breaking every rule in the book. Pretend you're looking for a policeman, I thought, just in case.

I ducked under the barriers. I was now in Togo. Again down the middle of the track, I ambled as casually as I could in case the Togolese police spotted me. This side also everyone was asleep. I walked along the side of the customs office. Policemen were asleep on tables, customs officers were curled up on chairs. Dozens of old men, fat old ladies, dishevelled travellers were stretched out on benches, on the ground, huddled under trees. Nobody stirred. My casual, absentminded stroll became a brisk walk. I turned the corner. I was on the road into the centre of Lomé.

I was safe. At least I wouldn't be going to my own funeral. Yet.

Lagos

'I want to launch the Nigerian version of *Time* magazine,' said the voice on the 'phone. 'But better.'

Nigerian businessmen are always so modest and unambitious.

Who but a Nigerian minister of finance, in his capacity as chairman of a private company, could build a £270-million aluminium smelter in the middle of nowhere, against World Bank advice, at practically double the price anybody else would anywhere else, and get away with it?

'And I want to start in three months, my friend. Is it possible?'

'Well,' I began nervously.

'Come to my home, I'm in Onslow Square. We'll discuss it.'

Well, if Alhadji has a home in Onslow Square he must be worth something, I thought. Might as well go and talk. Nothing's ever lost by talking.

There was a house in Onslow Square, that much was definite. Whether it was his home or not I never found out. I did find out that the curtains were always drawn, the heating always on full blast and it was continually full of people: Africans, Europeans, rich men, poor men. One man who looked like a finance director turned out to be Alhadji's live-in mini-cab driver who came one day to take him to Harrods and just stayed on. Oh, I nearly forgot – and thousands of babies and children.

Finding an opportunity to talk business was a problem. 'But Alhadji,' I kept saying, 'if you want to launch a magazine in three months . . .'

'Later,' he would say, pointing to the mini-cab driver. 'Talk to my business partner. He has some good ideas.' And we'd be shuffled off into the kitchen to join 500 babies for their afternoon chocolate drink.

Eventually I nailed him. I turned up at 8 o'clock one morning. Everybody was asleep, even Alhadji. A girl let me in. I waited in the stuffy lounge with its drawn curtains. About an hour later Alhadji arrived, in what I think is known as a traditional dressing gown.

'Look, Alhadji,' I started. 'If you're serious, I'm serious. If not . . .'

'You don't believe?' He looked so shocked I almost felt guilty. 'My brother,' he came towards me and we shook hands. Beware, I thought, of brothers who call you brother. 'I am so serious.'

Then he told me his plans. He had been an assistant in the Ministry of Information in one of Nigeria's state governments. One of his cousins was in the Ministry of Defence in Lagos. The minister wanted to buy some military cranes. The cousin had deliberately delayed ordering the cranes.

'But why would he do that?' I asked.

'So that when the minister realises, he will have to buy them from whoever can supply them straightaway.' I looked blank. 'My cousin and I have bought them,' he explained with laughter. 'When the minister wants them he will have to buy them from us, and we will sell him them at a big, big price and with the money start the magazine.'

'But launching a magazine is expensive.'

He waved his hands in the air. 'When we sell the cranes we will have no problems.'

'How much are these cranes worth?'

'Millions and millions,' he shrieked. 'We can launch ten *Time* magazines.'

'But if they are worth millions, how were you, an assistant in the—'

'No problem,' he howled. 'I borrowed the money. I have another cousin in a bank in Lagos.'

'But if you can't sell the cranes?'

'Can't sell!' He leapt to his feet. 'You saying my cousin is wrong?'

'No, no,' I protested. 'I'm just . . .'

'Look,' he jumped up and down on the spot. 'You saying I'm not a rich man, I cannot launch this—' he threw a booklet towards me. 'Look. Ring my bank manager. Ask him how much money I have.'

'Oh no, I'm sure that's not . . .'

'Yes. Yes. You call. You say . . .'

I turned the booklet over. It was a deposit book for the Bristol and West Building Society in Fleet Street. 'Well, if you insist,' I said quickly. 'Perhaps I will.'

'Actually, the account today is £3,702 overdrawn,' the manager's assistant drawled down the 'phone.

'There you are,' shrieked Alhadji. 'I must be a rich man, otherwise they would not allow me to borrow so much money. You agree?'

I agreed. How can you argue with such Nigerian logic? We agreed to meet in two weeks in Lagos.

Known affectionately as 'the armpit of Africa' – at least in polite society – Lagos is perhaps the least loved, most despised hellhole – sorry, city – in the world. It's filthy, overcrowded and violent. It makes Calcutta look like Cheltenham. And it's still a million times worse than you think. It's the largest, ugliest, most dangerous city in West Africa. It has the fastest growing population, the highest crime rate, and is probably the most corrupt place on earth. Everybody is looking for tips, inside information, back-handers, fake university degrees or just good old-fashioned commissions. Everybody wants to introduce you to everybody else. And everybody is related to a state Governor or cabinet minister who is just dying to place a multi-million-pound contract with the next good guy who comes along. Which is probably why the country has run out of petrol even though it's Africa's largest petrol producer.

When Nigerians talk about the country needing a dash for growth, they definitely don't mean what we mean by dash, and they are not interested in our kind of growth either.

Groups of up to 150 businessmen get together to organise illegal loan syndicates. Vital import documents with millions of dollars regularly dash through the doors of the Central Bank of Nigeria itself. Cash dashes out of envelopes in the post. Practically every businessman in the country is busy dashing off all over the world to unsuspecting companies trying to persuade them to put up seed money for bogus business deals and Mickey Mouse currency transactions.

Legislators in state assemblies refuse to approve government appointments unless they are bribed beforehand. Faked bank drafts and cheques are as common as, well, faked loans and transfers.

Even the man in the street will dig up the very street for the telephone cables underneath and ship them off to Belgium. And in broad daylight as well. Things are so bad that thieves are now desperate to return stolen money for fear of being beaten severely by the police to reveal where they have hidden it.

One French expat in Lagos told me that when he went to report the loss of his wallet, the thief, who had already been caught, pleaded with him to tell the police that it only contained 10,000 naira and not 100,000 so that they would stop beating him until he produced the remaining 90,000.

I've known experienced travellers walk out of well-paid, well-cosseted jobs rather than face another trip to Lagos. 'I've been to hell and back,' a World Bank agricultural adviser told me after his first, and last, visit.

I know a man who used to bathe non-stop for a week after coming back from a visit there, which I thought excessive until in 1991 Glaxo Nigeria actually produced a report claiming that 'legions of bacteria', which would cause anything from boils to conjunctivitis, were living happily on Nigerian bank notes. The Department of Microbiology at the University of Lagos followed this up in a report which claimed that 'any organism found in faeces can be found on Nigerian currency notes.'

A friend was asked to open an office there for his company. He quit. He now spends his time serving drinks in a country pub, painting pictures of World War II fighter planes, and telling anybody who will listen that his enthusiasm for Lagos is infectious.

Me, I think Lagos is fantastic – as long as I keep coming back alive. I've been there in the heat and unbearable humidity when it's been up to 45° centigrade. I've been there when the heavens have opened in the rainy season, and thought seriously of building an ark. I've seen garbage piled so high it has practically obstructed the Kingsbury Rendez-vous restaurant next to the old First Baptist church. I've seen starving women and children huddled under the motorways too weak even to lift a bowl of rice. I've seen the end of a necklace job.

'What's a necklace job?' I asked a young policeman leaning against a lamp post in Broad Street, picking his nose.

'Fellow snatched a necklace from a lady, but the crowd caught him.'

'So why do you call it a necklace job?'

'They throw a rubber tyre over him, then set light to it.'

'You mean . . .'

'Don't worry, old chap,' he tapped my shoulder, with that

finger. 'Everything's all right. They got the necklace back.' He smiled. 'Out of the ashes.'

I've been there when you've had to fight gangs of screaming youths, not to mention the occasional policeman, the moment you step outside the airport, just to hold on to your briefcase. I once had to fight dozens of tiny kids who were trying to take my shoes off. And I've been there, amazingly, in the last few years when, maybe thanks to President Babangida and his military rulers, it's been a most pleasant, relaxed and courteous place; still filthy, and much too hot and humid, but at least nobody tried to steal the shoes off my feet.

'No wonder we've got problems in Africa. Look at all the Nigerians we have on our side,' an African diplomat once told me confidentially. But not in Lagos.

Some British businessmen I know prefer to fly into Karno, over 1,000 miles to the north, then drive into Lagos. French businessmen are more logical. They usually fly into next-door Lomé, Togo, or Cotonou, Benin, and cross the border by car. They all want to avoid Lagos Airport, which must be the worst airport in the world. It is the only one where planes are held up by armed robbers on the runway as they are taxi-ing to take off, and all the passengers robbed of their valuables.

That's not all. With nine seaports, five international airports and twenty-four land borders, Nigeria is a 'major drug transit country', according to the US Drug Enforcement Agency. Any day of the year, according to government statements, 5lb of heroin are seized being smuggled out of Nigeria, either hidden in clothing or swallowed in balloons or condoms. If that's what the government figures say you can guess what the real figures are.

Lagos Airport couldn't be worse. You always arrive at the same time as three other jumbos. Three thousand people descend on three tiny desks, two of which are closed. You wave your health card at a grubby man in a dirty white coat, and are carried by the mass of heaving, frustrated, sweating humanity towards passport control. A thousand hands are waving two thousand passports – if you have two passports, you wave two, to increase your chances of having one examined by the laid-back police officers. Once and once only I was lucky enough to have my passport grabbed by a policeman after only forty-five minutes of heaving and shoving.

'It's not valid,' he said, throwing it back into the crowd.

'What do you mean not valid?' I tried to shout politely, scrambling for it over three huge market women and fifty-three children.

'It's in pencil,' he smirked.

'Pencil!' I shouted, a little less politely, snatching it from a polite Lebanese trader who looked as though he had already re-sold it three times. 'It's in pen.'

'Next,' he smirked.

Two hours and you're through passport control. You're exhausted. And if you're lucky all you've lost is half a kilo. Now, however, the real excitement begins. You've got to change at least £50 into naira before they let you in.

The throbbing, heaving, sweating mass of humanity now turns like the tribes of Israel in the desert towards passport control because – who says the Nigerians haven't got a sense of humour? – the passport officials always keep only two or three finance forms on their desk for the thousands who tramp through Lagos every day.

'Why haven't you got any more forms?' we all mumble under our breath, hoping that to the police we all look the same and they won't make us unpack our baggage and repack it six times before letting us through. 'This is nonsense,' I remember an irate British military type bellowing at a poor slim girl of a customs official. 'Absolute nonsense. Just needs a bit of planning, that's all.'

Eventually more forms appeared – and disappeared into six thousand grabbing hands. The first-timers, poor, innocent things, settle down to fill them in. We professionals leap and hurdle our way ten times faster than Daley Thompson to the tiny, grubby exchange window hidden behind piles of abandoned luggage on the right of the immigration hall, because – oh this glorious Nigerian sense of humour – you must have at least £50 in naira, and the Nigerians only have 5-naira notes. You end up with bundles of notes stuffed into your pockets and bursting out of your briefcase, easy prey for any pickpocket south of Watford let alone in Lagos. And each note has to be counted out at least twice. Work it out for yourself: three jumbos – 2,500-odd passengers; 50 naira per passenger; that's 125,000 notes. How long does it take to count 125,000 notes? Twice? At the end of one busy day in Lagos I met some people arriving at the hotel from the plane I had arrived on that morning. They had just collected their naira.

Naira bulging out of every crevice, you rush back, hopefully the same day, to customs. Then with a prayer to Mohammed and an accidental stumble which just happens to shower every customs man in naira, you're finally through the formalities and into Nigeria proper.

In the old days I used to stay at the old Eko Holiday Inn on Victoria Island. I arrived there late one evening after landing at the airport around mid-morning. 'Good evening, sir,' said the smart young man at reception. 'Welcome to the Eko Holiday Inn. We've given you the best room in the hotel.'

It was the best room, I soon discovered, because it had just been painted. Painted an awful, thick, dull ministry of works green. Everything: the woodwork, the walls, the toilet walls – apart from the patch behind the lid of the toilet which had not been closed. The toilet seat and bowl had even been painted. The room was still thick with fumes. When I opened the door it hit me like mustard gas. I didn't complain; in Lagos you quickly learn there is no point in complaining. But for the next three days, I can tell you, I was first in for breakfast and last out of the bar at night.

Now I stay at the Sheraton at the airport, and after everything I've said you're not going to believe this, but it is honestly one of the best hotels I have ever been in. It's beautifully clean and sparkling. The service is fabulous. The staff are friendly and helpful and courteous. The food is fantastic. And it is so cheap. Because of the exchange rate, it costs me around £30 a night. It's wonderful.

The first evening of one visit, I'd just finished a fabulous meal: *foie gras*, a whole chateaubriant to myself, a fabulous bottle of claret, all for about £17.25. As I was walking through reception, in staggered the now very unmilitary-looking major I'd seen at the airport. Now he looked like a survivor of the Charge of the Light Brigade.

'Problems at the airport?' I enquired.

'Problems!' he exploded. 'I'm writing to my MP soon as I get back. Damn girl at customs ran off with over £10,000.'

'Ten thou—' I began.

'Showed her all this damn Mickey Mouse money. Asked me if I had any other money on me. Told her I had £10,000 in case of emergencies. What. Made me fill in another damn form. Then said she'd have to take it to her superiors to see if I could bring it in.'

'And – you – gave —'

'Thought, why not? She's a customs officer after all. Might be a damn girl, but . . .'

'You – gave —'

'Now the damn hussy's gone and disappeared with all my money. You wait till my MP hears about this!'

It was another of those Lagos days.

You think the traffic is bad in London. Compared to Lagos, London doesn't have a traffic problem. If you want to run a meeting your way, and don't want anybody disagreeing with you, organise it in Lagos. Book everybody who might disagree with you into the Sheraton. It's a long flight. Fabulous hotel.

Give them a chance to have a good night's rest. You know all the excuses. Then arrange for the meeting to be held in town – at the Eko Holiday Inn, if you have to. Then tell everyone it's not fair that the people at the Sheraton should do all the travelling, so to share the burden you've organised special lunches with government ministers back at the Sheraton. Which is after all less than six miles away and, you've been told, about twenty minutes by cab. This, I can assure you from bitter experience, guarantees chaos.

Before they started building the expressway into Lagos traffic used to start building up around 6 am. Today it starts building up about 5 am. By around 7 o'clock, when everybody is leaving the Sheraton early to avoid the rush hour, it is one six-mile-long mass of rotting, rusty, burnt-out container lorries, vans and cars with a sprinkling of highly polished Mercedes hastening oh-so-slowly to meetings that will have been long abandoned by the time they arrive.

To try and solve the problem, the city authorities decided on the simplest of bureaucratic solutions. One day, only cars with odd-number registration plates can come into the city; the next day, only cars with even numbers. Most people rushed out and bought another car. The really smart operators rushed out and bought another registration plate.

The problem isn't so much the volume of traffic, which is horrendous, but the state of the traffic. I don't think, apart from those few brand-new shining Mercedes, I've ever seen an ordinary car without a bump, scrape or jagged dent in all the years I've been going there. The Knight, Frank & Rutley man in Lagos drives around in a battered old Land Rover which he claims is the best possible protection. It has spikes on the bumper.

'Why the spikes?' I remember asking him innocently, before I began to know and love Lagos.

'To stop them jumping on and getting a free lift,' he grunted.

Even so it's been bumped and crunched and dented more times than you've read estate agents' enthusiastic brochures.

Take it from me, old cars never die. They go to Lagos. In Tokyo you never see a dirty car, let alone an old one. In Lagos you never see a clean car, and you rarely see a new car. Stop ten cars crawling along Eko Bridge to Victoria Island any day, ship them back to Britain and you could open up in competition with Lord Montagu. In fact, if you're in Lagos longer than forty minutes and your car is not bumped or scratched you get nervous. More nervous than if it is.

'What's going to happen? What have they got in store for me? What are they planning?' You start going crazy. Luckily the condition only lasts a very short while because you just can't avoid being bumped.

All of which means, of course, breakdowns. I've never tried to get into Lagos without seeing five or six breakdowns. Trouble is, in Lagos if a car is hit by another car or just collapses from old age, the owner – or rather the person driving it at the time – just jumps out, leaves it where it is – in the middle of the road, skewered across a roundabout or parked perilously at the edge of a flyover – and hops into another equally old, dilapidated banger and never gives it another thought. The result: more jams, more delays.

In 1991 the Nigerians finally decided enough was enough. They had to bring in a tough professional to sort everything out. What did they do? They appointed the Nigerian poet, Wole Soyinka, winner of the Nobel Prize for Literature in 1986, as the traffic supremo. His first tough, no-nonsense executive decision was to rewrite the text for the driving licence. His second? To waive compulsory eye tests for motorists.

So what happened when I had my first meeting with Alhadji in Lagos? I can't find a cab. When I do we don't move for forty minutes because of the traffic. I finally arrive stained with sweat at the address Alhadji has given me. Whatever I was expecting this isn't it.

'Are you sure?' I ask the cab driver, suspecting one of those neat little Nigerian tricks where you are taken to the middle of nowhere and don't come back alive.

'You said Ashabi Adedire Street,' he said. 'This is Ashabi Adedire Street.'

'Off Creek Road? Near the Apapa Boat Club?'

'Off Creek Road, near the Apapa Boat Club.'

I was standing in front of a broken-down, ramshackle, one-storey wooden home. If Hitchcock had filmed *Psycho* in Nigeria it's the kind of place he would have used.

I looked back at the driver. 'You'd better wait,' I said.

'No thanks.' He grinned and drove off.

I walked across the scrub to the front door, which was open. Inside the house looked derelict. There were holes in the ceiling, paper was falling off the walls, there were yawning gaps in the floorboards. Well, I thought, maybe this is the Onslow Square of Lagos. I picked my way gingerly across the hallway. There must be easier ways of making a living, I thought – and certainly safer ways. At the end of the hallway was another door. It was splintered and dusty. I pulled it open. Inside was an elegant brass-studded leather door, green and clean and shining. I went to open it when suddenly it swung back, revealing the most elegant of living rooms – deep plush carpet, leather sofas, dimmed lighting, pastel walls. Waiting to shake hands was Alhadji.

'Welcome,' he smiled. 'Welcome to my home. It is so nice to see you.'

'But. But . . .' I stammered.

'Precautions,' he said. 'You are now in Lagos.'

Inside the derelict shell was a luxury home and office that would put the Paris Crillon to shame. There were reception rooms and dining rooms, a library, a suite of offices crammed full of computers, word processors, Reuter terminals. Want to know the price of pork belly futures in Chicago? They could tell you the price of pork belly futures, German aluminium alloys or vanadium, whatever that is, anywhere in the world.

Alhadji had his own independent telecommunications network. He could direct deals anywhere in the world, from a country where you could hardly telephone reception from your hotel room.

'But how . . .?'

'You are in Nigeria,' he smiled. 'Not London. In Nigeria everything is possible.'

He led me into his office, which was dominated by a large mahogany table around which sat his senior executives who, he said, ran his coffee plantations, his sugar mills, his fishing fleet, his trading company. All he did was supply the money. They were all Indians.

'Ranjit,' he said to one, 'tell us how you run the coffee plantations.'

'Simple,' said Ranjit, 'all the workers we divide into teams. Each team has a part of the plantation to look after. We pay them according to how much they produce. The more they produce the more money they make.'

'Doubled production in a year,' grinned Alhadji.

'I'm surprised,' I said. 'I didn't think the Nigerians worked hard. Especially for money.'

Alhadji grinned and wiped his forehead with a large white handkerchief. 'They're not Nigerians, they're all Asians. They work much harder and they're cheaper.'

The same thing was happening with the sugar mills, the fishing fleet, the trading company.

'But won't the government find out?'

Alhadji laughed. 'The government – who's worried about the government?'

'In any case', a senior-looking Indian said, 'we're out in the bush. Nobody has heard of us. Nobody knows we're there. We're all right.'

Secretaries, also Indian, rushed in with piles of telexes and faxes. Alhadji looked at them briefly then quickly dealt them to the players around the table. 'Now,' he said, 'we talk about my *Time* magazine.'

Business plans, projections, piles of paper, whole armfuls of documents suddenly appeared. Everybody had their say. I had mine. But Alhadji was determined to go ahead. He made one concession, however: launch day would be four months away instead of three.

I spent the next ten days trying to put the package together. Trying to put together a financial package in London is a nightmare. Trying to do it in Lagos is a million times worse.

'Go and talk to Chief Bwala, my accountant,' Alhadji told me. 'He knows everything.'

Old Broad Street was packed. The sun was burning down. People jammed the pavements and swarmed all over the road making the slow-moving traffic even slower. Tall, elegant Ibos jostled alongside beggars with hardly two rags to their name let alone two naira. I was looking for the Chief's office. I couldn't see it anywhere. There were no numbers on the buildings, which proves that the Nigerians did learn something from the British. What names there were on buildings had either fallen down altogether or the letters that were left were unreadable. I started asking. Nobody knew what I was talking about.

Then suddenly from the middle of the jostling, stifling crowd appeared what would politely be called a troupe of traditional musicians. For a split second, they looked less like traditional musicians than one of Lagos's highly efficient snatch-and-grab gangs.

'Good morning, sir,' I shouted at the leader of the band as he whisked round and round me, each time pushing his masked face – zap – closer to mine – zap. 'Looking for Chief Bwala. Wonder if you could help?' Zap.

By now – zap – I was the centre of a whirling circle of gaily coloured masks – zap – 100-year-old tee-shirts and grubby jeans whose interest in notes – zap – I was beginning to pray was purely of the musical variety. The leader's mask – zap – which seemed to have been made out of the bottom of a shopping basket was now – zap – practically touching my nose each time it whizzed past my face. The traditional instruments – zap – they carried also contained, I noticed, a brand-new Swiss Army knife and three very rusty sheath knives. Zap. 'Sure man,' he said. 'We go.'

He knew the area inside out. He took me straight to the Chief's offices, where I eventually discovered Chief Bwala in a tiny cramped room overflowing with mountains of dusty paper, three floors up a ramshackle building at the wrong end of Broad Street. He was a giant of a man, of about 20 stones. He sat behind a tiny desk in his long flowing robes.

'I really need the latest set of accounts for all Alhadji's companies,' I began.

'Are you British?' he said.

I didn't know whether to be insulted or flattered. 'I am,' I said. 'Or maybe he has a master company . . .'

'Why did the British stop giving awards and knighthoods to us?' He leant across the table at me. 'We're members of the same Commonwealth aren't we?'

'Of course,' I nodded furiously.

'It was a big mistake.' He leant back, smoothing the papers in front of him.

I nodded again. 'Have any reports been published do you—'

'The French give us medals you know. Made one of our writers a *Chevalier des Arts et des Lettres*.'

'Perhaps I could . . .'

'Invited me to Paris as well.'

'. . . have a look at his file?'

'Prefer an English medal though.'

Alhadji's lawyer I finally tracked down to an upstairs room in the big Lebanese casino on Ikoyi Island. Outside, it looked like a large temporary classroom; inside it was deep plush red carpet, deep plush red wallpaper and lots of deep plush well-oiled Nigerians.

'Dom Perignon?' he asked me as we sat down to eat.

'Dom Perignon?' I started. 'I thought all imported wines and spirits, and especially champagne, were barred by the government?'

'So they are,' he roared. 'I just happen to have some left over from my daughter's wedding.'

'You mean it's been in the cellar for years?'

'Since last weekend,' he exploded again, slapping the table.

'A big wedding was it?' I murmured.

'Only about a thousand people,' he said. 'Lasted three days. A traditional Nigerian wedding. And we drank Dom Perignon for three days.'

Undaunted, I next tracked down one of Alhadji's bankers in Union Bank on Marina. 'Can't stop, old chap,' he said as soon as I explained what I was doing. 'Got to go to the polo club. Give me a tinkle some time.' Fortunately, the Lagos stock exchange was less evasive.

Research completed, I settled down to prepare my report. I wrote for two days non-stop. I drew up a strategy document, wrote the business plan, proposed a sales campaign, outlined the approach to advertisers, sketched out the editorial plan. I even drafted a prospectus. Alhadji had said he wanted a comprehensive package.

I proposed a Nigerian company as the master company, as this would enable us to tap local investors, raise funds from international institutions and ultimately float on the Lagos stock exchange. The operating company would be based in the UK, together with the editorial, sales and advertising departments. A Dutch company would raise further international funding. The Business Centre at the Sheraton had it all typed and photocopied and beautifully bound. It was a work of art.

I booked a car for the following morning, and it turned up on time. Amazingly the traffic was light. It took us only one hour and twenty-three minutes to travel four miles across Lagos to Alhadji's ramshackle luxury headquarters. I was ushered straight into his presence.

'My friend,' he said. 'I've had a better idea. Forget *Time* magazine. I'm going into films. I have lots of sugar here I can't sell. You take the sugar, for free. You sell it in England. You keep the money in England. We then invest the money in films. Good idea? Yes?'

Nairobi

We were lucky. It was only 93° Fahrenheit and there was a gentle breeze. We'd driven miles over rough terrain, and had had a couple of near misses, but we were safe. We parked the Land Rover under a tree. In the distance I could see a huddle of zebra-striped Volkswagen buses. It was getting hotter by the minute. The mosquitoes were beginning to gather.

'Let's go,' I said to the driver, a tall, thin Kikuyu.

Outside it was hotter still. The heat was already coming up from the ground. We tried to keep to the shade. Suddenly the driver nudged me. '*Bwana*. Over there, can you see? There's one of the old bulls. They say he's trampled many to death.'

Four hundred miles away to the south east, in Mombasa on the Indian Ocean, and along the coast on some of the world's best beaches, the tourists who had come to Kenya to see the real Africa were dragging themselves out of their air-conditioned rooms and downstairs for orange juice, dried figs and Weetabix, flown in specially from Europe to make them feel at home.

We were in the real Africa, the Africa of blood and gore, life-and-death struggles, the quick kill. The old bull ambled along, stopped, looked left and right. He raised his head and sniffed, then continued his constitutional. He knew where he was going. 'Some say he can be very dangerous. You have to watch out,' the driver continued. By now we were standing behind a tiny cluster of trees. I pushed the branches apart; I'd definitely not seen many like him in Africa.

In the safari lodges in Tsavo National Park, the largest game reserve in East Africa, all the modern Hemingways on their rough, tough safaris, having spent the night huddled under the bedclothes for fear of lizards are pushing back their delicately laundered mosquito nets and flip-flopping in their slippers to their balconies to catch a glimpse of the backside of another waterbuck disappearing into the bush.

'Quick,' gasped my driver. 'Here come the stags. Look.'

They all looked young, well-groomed, fleet of foot. The slightest hint of danger and they would be off.

The sun was climbing rapidly. It was getting hotter by the second. Suddenly another bull arrived. Through the branches I could see them eyeing each other warily. The stags were in a group on one side, watching, and keeping their wits about them. Suddenly the bulls began to follow them. '*Bwana*, we can't stay here. We must move.'

The Nairobi stock exchange was open for business. Two mornings a week in the centre of the city, in the New Stanley Hotel, in the reception area surrounded by mutinous indoor plants and trees, at a corner table, the bulls and stags of Nairobi – they don't have bears – make up one of Africa's tiny struggling stock exchanges.

Although African stock exchanges list more than 1,000 companies employing nearly a million people and with an annual turnover of more than US$40 billion, they are largely ignored by foreign investors – and most also have a tough time winning the trust of investors at home. Only two exchanges – those in Lagos, Nigeria, and Harare, Zimbabwe – are included in the International Finance Corporation's survey of the world's emerging stock exchanges. Nigeria is in fourteenth place, Zimbabwe in sixteenth. In terms of market capitalisation, Nigeria's US$1.1 billion puts it in the fifteenth place while Zimbabwe rates twenty-eighth with capitalisation of US$410 million.

India, the leading emerging market, has 5,460 listed companies (compared, for example, with 8,403 in the United States). Brazil is the number one new market in terms of capitalisation, worth around US$42 billion (compared with US$2,636 billion in the States).

Either way, African stock exchanges are out-gunned and out-classed. Five – those in Casablanca, Tunis, Abidjan, Cairo and Nairobi – are not even included in the ratings. The remaining two, in Mauritius and Botswana, have only recently opened.

An elderly man, another old bull, now settled down in another chair in the corner. Three others had been watching. Slowly they ambled across, settled alongside him and began looking at their watches. Briefcases are opened, papers appear on the table in front of them. One man takes out a pocket calculator. Other businessmen join them.

The director of one of the big Swiss consultancy firms with offices in Nairobi saunters in, shakes hands with a stag. Both saunter out and collapse in a gleaming white Mercedes waiting outside.

A group of Asians bustles in, looking as turbane as they do anywhere. One is accompanied by his wife. You can tell it's his wife; she walks five paces behind him. The door suddenly opens and a smart Asian accountant-type shoots through, darts across reception and drops into a chair alongside the waiting group.

The lobby is now filling up with tourists heading out for what they think is the real jungle.

Dealing is under way. This is the real jungle. One false step or too hasty reaction and you're trampled underfoot. I've seen more killers, red, raw, naked greed, life-and-death struggles and spilt blood in the boardrooms and ministers' offices of Africa than playing Hemingway trampling round after elephants and buffalo and elusive white rhinos.

* * *

Nairobi is by far the biggest, most developed, most successful and most unashamedly capitalist city in East Africa. It doesn't just believe in free enterprise; it believes in a rampant, no-holds-barred free enterprise. It is Thatcherism at 90° Fahrenheit. It is also Britain's favourite colony, the West's staunchest ally, the jewel in the crown of independent Africa. Or was until recently when things began to go wrong and innocent people started killing themselves in car crashes, money started appearing of its own accord in people's bank accounts and the *wananchi*, ordinary people, started demanding something called democracy.

But more important, especially to anyone married to a vegetarian with an excess of tofu baloney sandwiches in their bloodstream, in Nairobi National Park, just ten minutes from the city centre, is the Tamarind restaurant which serves every kind of meat you can imagine – and some you would never want to imagine, let alone eat.

Nairobi's rival, Harare, the capital of Zimbabwe, on the other hand, is small and pleasant and still terribly, terribly English. If Nairobi is like Liverpool or Southampton Harare is like Gloucester and Cheltenham. The high street running through Harare actually boasts, in a terribly refined sort of way of course, a Woolworth's, a Norwich Union, a Freeman Hardy and Willis and even, would you believe, a Toc H. The frightfully swish upper-class suburbs of Highlands and Mount Pleasant with their villas, bougainvillaeas and snarling dogs, look like a cross between Wimbledon and Virginia Water. There are still portraits of the Queen all over the parliament buildings; probably more than in Cheltenham town hall. The hills of Maronders still echo to the accents of Jesus College, Oxford rather than to the purr of jaguars.

Which is surprising because the president, the Hon. Robert Mugabe, the St Paul of African politics, began by preaching Marxist-Leninism and prophesying a 'socialist transformation', and ended up turning capitalist and embracing a donor-funded five-year structural adjustment programme with the World Bank designed to turn the country into a market-driven economy.

Expats over G and Ts in Meikles Hotel will tell you Harare has more class because Nairobi was built by officers while Harare was built by the ranks. If that's true I can see why I was never invited to become an officer.

In between the two come Tanzania and Uganda. Dar es Salaam, the capital of Tanzania, is a Methodist, well-meaning socialist that got itself completely chewed up and spat out. The old President, Julius (the Teacher) Nyrere, was an honest, innocent man who virtually destroyed his country with silly, impractical ideas before he finally quit in a blaze of failure. In twenty years, he turned a country rich in land and mineral resources into a poor miserable patch of dust. He believed all men were brothers. He created collective farms so that everybody could work together as brothers, live together as brothers and share the fruits of their labours as brothers. It didn't work. They produced fewer crops than the peasants had produced before. He stopped shopkeepers making profits. Everybody had to share. The shops went bust, the shopkeepers fled. The customers were forced to pay higher black-market prices to survive. Factories were not allowed to ... well, not allowed. Unemployment soared. So what did Brother Nyrere do? He insisted the employed shared their work with the unemployed. Under the benign, faltering direction of a man who genuinely had the interests of his people at heart, the whole country took a step backwards to virtually nothing.

Kampala, the capital of desolate, beautiful Uganda, once hailed by Churchill as the 'pearl of Africa', is lined with trees and sits precariously on seven hills. The nearest I've been to it is, like the Israelis, Entebbe Airport.

Today after fifteen years of horrifying dictatorships – fancy being rescued from the clutches of Obote by Idi Amin – and desperate economic chaos, Uganda is full of ghosts. The Nile Hotel, next to the conference centre, is empty. People are frightened to stay there any more. After a hard day at the office, Obote used to turn up there to see his enemies thrown off the roof one by one. Now everybody heads for the Sheraton, a twelve-storey white block on the top of one of the seven hills.

On paper Kenya, Zimbabwe, Uganda and Tanzania have all been star pupils of the IMF, notching up average annual growth rates of 4.2%. Admittedly Uganda and Tanzania started from practically zero, but don't knock them. They tried, and got there. Not even Kenya, however, one of the few African countries where per capita income has risen during the eighties, is a patch on Hong Kong, Taiwan, South Korea, Singapore or even Malaysia.

Forget the Flame Trees. The great thing about Thika, thirty miles from Nairobi is its leather industry. With backing from the Aga Khan, this is one of the most modern, hi-tech tanneries in the world producing nearly 500,000 cow hides a year. But it is not another Hyundai. Neither is any of Kenya's food, tobacco, glass, beer, textile, engineering or chemical companies.

After independence in 1963 the economy boomed under Kenyatta and foreign investment poured in. It has huge tea, coffee and sugar plantations. The fruit, flower and vegetable industries account for 11% of GDP and employ nearly 10% of the population.

Tourism, providing you can forget that Lake Victoria, the second largest freshwater lake in the world, is slowly dying from a lack of oxygen, is organised, civilised and very well developed – for wimps, not machos. In the old days people went to Kenya to hunt, kill and glory in the wild life. Now they go to criticise.

Once between meetings I was on safari in Tsavo, 8,000 square miles of killing fields – as big as Wales. On a clear day you can see Kilimanjaro, Africa's highest mountain. Suddenly out of the grass burst a cheetah. With the speed of light he bore down on a gazelle.

'Quick! Do something,' two elderly American matrons screamed at me.

'Wha ...' I stammered, as the cheetah brought the gazelle crashing to the dust.

'Men,' they hollered. 'Typical. Not interested in animals.'

In the old days the wild life used to stop, sniff and nervously approach the mini-buses like they would a suspicious interloper in the herd. Now we're as common to them as bankruptcies in the steel industry. If you want to see black rhino, lion, cheetah, you no longer stalk them for days, hoping you might spot one disappearing into the bush. You tell the receptionist when you check into your safari lodge: 'I'll have a *Financial Times*, *Guardian*, an early morning call at 5.30 and a black rhino, a giraffe and an elephant, please.'

Room service will then call you as soon as one ambles up to the watering hole in front of the lodge. If, however, they deliberately refuse to put in an appearance then no problem, sir, we'll arrange to take you to the black rhino instead. There are now more zebra-striped mini-buses bursting with tourists criss-crossing the fragile plains than there are zebras or black rhinos. In fact many of the great wimp white hunters you see dragging themselves on safari deserve conservation orders more than the animals.

One great white hope of the dark continent, who I swear spent the war teaching elocution, spent the whole of my safari playing regimental sergeant major. As we were about to slump into the van he would walk up and down barking out his comments. 'Tie's at half mast.'

'Sir,' we'd bark back in an attempt to humour him.

'Shoes need cleaning. Call them clean? What?'

'Sir.'

'Same shirt as yesterday, Biddlecombe.'

Whenever we stopped, he would march up and down in the boiling heat inspecting us all again.

'What day is it today, Biddlecombe?'

Whatever the day, he only wanted to hear one thing. 'A new year's day, sir.'

'Very good. Very good. Carry on.' And we carried on until the next time.

The hotels and safari lodges are all first class, especially the big Swiss-managed ones in Mombasa which in spite of everything still seems to be the ivory capital of the world. Unfortunately they are full of Hemingway types wearing cowboy shirts, kepis and shoes that look like duck-billed platypus, who invariably turn out to be non-executive directors of captive insurance companies in the Isle of Man.

One I came across drank all his duty-free between the airport and the safari lodge. Then lunch after lunch, night after night, we had the same ritual with the barman.

'Did you put the water in first or the whisky?'

'The whisky.'

'I thought I'd come to it sooner or later.'

His wife stood by just looking at him.

He liked to regale us all with his wit and wisdom. 'Of course the Queen is going to have to abdicate. Why else would the Mall be built wide enough to take a plane?'

Or: 'Of course, you know Neil Kinnock is worth a fortune?'

'Never.'

'Got eight bank accounts, all in different family names. In the Abbey National, Fulham. Wife works there. Told me all about them.'

She smiled at him. Slowly.

'So where did he get the money from? He's only had his MP's money and his salary as Leader of the—'

'The trade unions all pay him retainers. Probably only lives off £10,000 a year. Rest is paid for. House is in Glenys's name.' His wife nodded but didn't say a word.

In the mornings the talk was always about animals, but they were discussed in stock exchange terms. 'I have black rhinos. Now I'm looking for cheetahs.'

'All I want to see now are lions.'

'Have you got hyenas? Not many people get hyenas.'

'Sure, I've got hyenas. Everybody gets hyenas.'

One morning as we were heading for the safari bus he broke the routine. 'Worried about the wife,' he grunted. 'I think it's *après* children.'

But in spite of its tourism potential, Kenya has nothing like Sir Y.K. Pao's Hong Kong-based empire.

As recently as 1983 South Korea, Taiwan and Singapore were merely primary producers at the mercy of commodity traders and markets worldwide. They had hardly any factories, and those they had produced out-of-date and wildly uncompetitive goods. Exports were practically zero. Their economies were disaster zones. Now look at them. They have been so successful they are very quickly dragging the rest of the region, especially Thailand, Malaysia and Indonesia, up into the first division with them.

As I watch the Nairobi stock exchange in action, I can't help wondering why Kenya couldn't do the same. Friends of Africa say it is a question of culture. Others, who are not friends of Africa, point out that human life began in the Rift Valley four million years ago and has not made any progress there since.

The legacy of colonialism? Arbitrary and plain bad government? The collapse of law and order? Corruption? A spectacular decline in living standards? Lack of the protestant work ethic? Then comes the even bigger question: what's going to happen to Kenya, *après* President Moi?

The Nairobi stock market, like the rest of Africa's stock exchanges, has very little stock and hardly any market. Companies that have any cash, and there are some very rich companies in Africa, prefer to keep it on deposit and finance their development from their own funds. Pension funds, and there are some very rich African pension funds, prefer either to keep it under the bed or to hand it over to foreign banks to invest in Wall Street. The result is that the stock markets in no way reflect the industrial activity of the country.

Some say they are more like casinos than markets; the much respected Zimbabwean Minister of Finance, Bernard Chidzero, who was once in the running to be Secretary General of the United Nations, refers to them as 'the whore of Babylon'. It's true that people only play them to win, and handsomely. Nobody is interested in markets settling down or adjusting to the right level, let alone putting a realistic value on a realistic industrial activity. They want to make money, nothing else.

I've seen socialist Chinese and North Korean diplomats and advisers playing the markets with the same abandon as they bet on whether one fly climbs to the top of the wall faster than another. 'That wouldn't happen in London,' I told a Chinese diplomat in Lagos. 'We have Chinese walls.'

'Where there are Chinese walls there are chinks,' he said.

Most African stock exchanges are controlled by a Capital Markets Authority, but these Authorities are controlled by people who would never take a decision unless they agreed it with you-know-who-runs-the-country first. So, if you're in the know, you're in the know; if you're not, you don't even think of playing the game. Except that with stock markets anywhere it is still a case of trying to guess whether the man who says he is in the know is really in the know or just kidding.

'What shall we do about Kenya Commercial Bank?' asks one of the old bulls. The bank had just issued 7.5 million shares to the public, the biggest share issue in Kenya's history.

'The Zimbabwe exchange has now jumped over 600% since '86,' butts in one of the stags.

'Power and money, money and power. It's all in the Shona North,' somebody whispers.

Not for Harare a table in the corner of a hotel lobby. The

Zimbabwean whore of Babylon occupies two floors of nondescript modern office block.

'But it's all South African money. They're trying to get as much out as they can.'

'They'll buy anything.'

'They won't buy my holdings.'

'Look at the price you paid. I don't blame them.'

'Thought any more about the Seychelles? René can't last much longer. Mancham is on his way back. Maybe now is the time to start offering to help.'

'Could buy a couple of hotels. Ideal for development.'

The Nairobi stock exchange is finished for the day. Everybody scatters; the bulls to their exclusive clubs for lunch, the wazungu stags in search of another Lady Isadina and her Happy Valley set.

In the east, the tourists are still complaining about the tea and threatening to write to their MPs about the lack of marmalade. In the safari lodges, the Hemingways have missed seeing a herd of charging buffalo, three pink flamingoes, two giraffes and a bush buck, although they did catch sight of three zebra-striped coaches, three giraffe-print buses and a luxury personnel carrier containing fifty-two towel-bearing German sun seekers.

The Asian businessman and his wife, I notice, leave the hotel, climb into separate cars and drive away – with the wife's car five lengths behind. We wander back to our Land Rover parked under the trees in Kenyatta Avenue. My financial safari is over.

'She is from Texas. But I tell her straight. She must look after the children of my first marriage. She must have lots more. And she must look after my mother.'

'What does she say?'

'She says nothing yet. I have given her deadline. She must decide by next Friday.'

'And if she says no?'

'She cannot say no. If she does, I must marry a Muslim girl. My mother has arranged it. She works for Salomon Brothers in New York. She is stockbroker. Her dowry is three office blocks in Kuala Lumpur.'

Sunday afternoon, and I was on an industrial safari around Nairobi with the eldest son of one of Kenya's secretive Asian families – 'We don't believe in chauffeurs' – who are the driving force in the economy. In a Land Rover, mark you, not a Ford. It is dangerous to drive a Ford in Kenya nowadays. Ford stands for Forum for the Restoration of Democracy, one of the groups opposed to the president. A FORD rally, which attracted 250,000 stomping, rejoicing supporters in Nairobi's famous Kamukungi grounds, compared to a mere 5,000 for the president's official ruling KANU (Kenya African National Union) celebration, was described by a local journalist as like Macbeth's 'Birnam Wood coming to high Dunsinane hill'. Ministers call upon their supporters to tour the beer halls crushing FORD supporters. Opponents, according to the vice-president, are traitors. Everything to do with FORD, therefore, is dangerous.

'That's mine.' We drove past an office block on City Square, 'I've got 80% of that.' Now we were on Moi Avenue. 'We're negotiating to buy that. I was in London last week to sort out the finance.' We turned into Kenyatta Avenue. 'My uncle has that.' We shot along Parliament Road. 'I have a cousin. I think she owns part of that . . .'

While he was busy reviewing his investment portfolio, as we all do on Sunday afternoons, my multi-millionaire driver, who looked like any Asian running a chemist's shop in Wimbledon, kept complaining that his family wouldn't let him marry whomever he wanted. We stopped in front of a field near the airport. 'Here I'm building offices and warehouses. I have some big companies interested, international companies. They're talking about making this their headquarters for India, East Africa and the Middle East. It's the ideal location. And we're much cheaper than the Arabs.'

We swung back towards the centre of Nairobi, past a field full of soldiers who were clearing the ground. Two or three were struggling with a tractor, others were watching. A few were smoking, most were lying on the grass fast asleep. 'See. We haven't forgotten the lessons of our colonial masters,' he laughed.

'What are they doing here?' I wondered.

'Clearing the ground for roses,' he said. 'It's a good business. Export around the world, plenty of hard currency.'

'So who's behind that?'

'Must be getting back,' he said.

One of the reasons Africa is behind, according to some experts, is not because there is a shortage of money, but because there is too much money looking for a home. The problem is finding the best home for it.

International Finance Corporation, the World Bank operation for investing in the private sector, has only been able to invest US$750 million in business in Africa in twenty years. By comparison the World Bank and others have poured in over $12 billion in aid over the same period.

Africa is full of traders. Dhows have been ploughing up and down the East African coast for centuries. Africans know how to trade; it is in their blood. I remember once in Mombasa, the ancient, steaming, sweaty port from where the single-sailed dhows shipped frankincense, ivory, slaves and coffee all over the Indian ocean before Somerset Maugham was invented. Some of the old hotels, retreats for the old white settlers, still keep fish in the lavatory cistern to eat the mosquito larvae. In the old Ivory Room, off Treasury Square, I asked the tall, slender, impressive Masai waiter how he decided what to charge. 'I look at the people. I guess their weight. Then I charge them for every pound,' he said.

But they don't know how to set up the boring, run-of-the-mill industrial companies every country needs to survive and prosper in this day and age.

'So if you can fund projects to invest in, why can't everybody else?' I asked the multi-millionaire – who was still under his mother's thumb – as we swung back to the Intercontinental.

'First, because we're here. We know the system. We know how to make it work. Second, we know how to look after our money. And third,' he grinned, 'we know how to insure our investments.'

'So if you can't insure your investments, you won't make them?'

'What do you think?'

There's corruption and corruption. In many African countries, ministers – and practically everybody else down the line – take the money and get it out of the country as quickly as possible. In Kenya, they tend to keep it there and invest it in office blocks, hotels, farms, enormous ranches.

One evening I was at the Tamarind putting away more reserves for the day I returned home to mung-bean pizza. I had already bombarded my white corpuscles with lamb, pork and goat. Now I was trying to decide between Thompson's gazelle, raccoon, buffalo's tongue and monkey's glands. At the bar I had a beef encounter with an old Dutch banker. 'If it don't bleed, it is not dinner,' he said.

When he had first decided to move into East Africa, he told me, Kenya was in a class of its own. Kenya and Zimbabwe had a well-established and fairly well-regulated infrastructure; Kenya more than Zimbabwe. Controls were minimal. You could get things done. Tanzania and Uganda had nothing at all. You were lucky if two people could agree which day of the week it was. Now things had changed. Bureaucracy was deadening. A pound here, US$10,000 there. It was the only way to get anything done. 'I bribe everybody to begin with,' he told me. 'If they deliver, I go on paying. If they don't, I find somebody else.'

By now we had demolished the buffalo's tongue and were heading for the raccoon. My white corpuscles were turning a gentle shade of pink. He told me about army life in Zimbabwe. 'Psst. Want to pass your staff college exams and pass out as a fully-fledged army officer? No problem. Z$1,000 cash and it's yours, Captain.' Which apparently is the examiners' approach to exams. 'Everybody's doing it, everybody knows about it, and everybody benefits,' he said.

A businessman had told him his son was worried he wouldn't pass his examinations. In desperation, he handed over the Z$1,000. Afterwards the son found out and was so ashamed he tried to shoot himself. He survived, but was badly injured.

'So what happened?'

'He got promoted. They didn't want anyone to know what had happened.'

Army tractors and trucks are said to be more common on farms in the Sudan than in military barracks in Zimbabwe.

I once met an Italian from Danieli, the big steel company, who was working in Uganda. He had actually supplied and been paid for nearly US$20 million of equipment for a steel mill in Jinja which was still in its packing cases. But that's kids' play. Kenya is for grown-ups. Everybody was now trying to start their own bank. The trick then was to get one of the big state-owned companies to deposit part or all of their funds with you. You then lent most of the funds back to the politicians, government officials, your wife's brother-in-law, or whoever.

As a result, he said, some banks had not been charging interest on their loans. Most loans were not being repaid, many probably never would be. Most loans were unsecured, others were secured against questionable office blocks or shopping centres. Most were way over normal, or even generous, banking limits.

During one visit to Nairobi all the talk in the Intercontinental bar was about a consultancy contract landed by a British company with Kenya Power and Lighting Corporation, which the World Bank claimed was 'five times what such services should normally cost'.

On another occasion I was in Nairobi with a big African delegation, most of whom couldn't believe they were still in Africa. One Nigerian, as soon as he arrived, rushed up to reception. 'Quick,' he screamed. 'What time do the lights go out? I've got a speech to write.' The rest just behaved as they do at home – and started lifting all the ashtrays, unscrewing the light bulbs and telephoning their friends and extended families all over the world.

When the conference was over and delegates had begun drifting away, heading home, making for Mombasa and a few lazy days in the sun, or preparing for the next international jamboree, a Kenyan minister invited a group of us to lunch. On the way from the hotel, he showed us the companies he owned outright, the office blocks he had a share in and the land he had just bought in his wife's name. We arrived at his house which was, well, terribly Kenyan. As we sank slowly into the ankle-deep carpets a Nigerian minister who obviously knew about these things stopped and gasped. 'My God. These Kenyans are giving corruption a bad name,' he said.

Now, of course, the party is over and Kenya is suffering one hell of a hangover. Everything is going wrong – or right, depending on your point of view. The economy is faltering, inflation is soaring. Former vice-presidents are arrested for spreading rumours. Foreign ministers are murdered. Everybody is nervous. Tribalism seems to be bubbling up to the surface again. In central Nairobi a Kalenjih can be hauled off a bus and hacked to death by a bunch of Kikuyus. Under President Moi, a Kalenjih, they have changed from being a small disadvantaged tribe into a tight-knit dominating elite, controlling most of the government and most of the big jobs. Which, of course, the Kikuyus do not like. The Luo, another big tribe, are flexing their muscles. The Luhaya, a minority tribe, are looking edgy.

Many local Kenyan and Asian businessmen are taking over Kenyan companies. They say they are doing it in their own right. Others say they have had a mysteriously sudden influx of money and are busy finding profitable homes for it. They've also been looking after themselves in the process.

'For instance?' I asked the Dutch banker.

'Sure,' he said. 'We've had cases where people have taken £1.7 million on contracts of £380 million.'

By now floods of red corpuscles were surging through my veins and I was beginning to feel like a Würtemburg foot soldier in the Napoleonic Wars who 'as soon as a horse plunged, fell upon it in heaps and often cut at it alive from all sides'. It was certainly an improvement on the red shiu sensei ginseng, gotu kola, dong quai and ginger that would greet me when I got home. As I dragged myself back to the car, I met the eldest son with the marriage problem.

'Did she call you?'

He shrugged. 'If you're ever in Kuala Lumpur give me a call,' he said.

Bangkok

No I didn't. But I know a man who did. Another who said he was going to. And one poor guy who now wishes the hell he hadn't.

A business trip to Bangkok, which unbelievably means City of Angels, is unlike any other business trip, because nobody believes you are going there on business.

That applies to everyone: your colleagues, your secretary, the travel agent and your wife. Especially your wife.

Worse still nobody believes you, whatever you say, when you get back. 'There's no point talking to him, he's got his mind on other things.'

'No honestly, my idea of happiness is . . .'

'Never seen him smile like that before.'

'. . . driving through the rain . . .'

'He's still out of breath.'

'. . . listening to Steve Race on "My Music".'

I know you're not going to believe a word I say, but I went to Bangkok with a senior Dutch civil servant and his Thai wife. It was during the Gulf War which, in spite of all the security warnings, was the time to fly. Planes were empty. There was all the space in the world to move around, drink champagne and fall asleep. Airports were relaxed. There were none of the usual tensions. Security, in fact, was tighter and more thorough than ever because there were fewer passengers.

'You know the best way to ensure there's no bomb on the plane?' a New Yorker in front of me told the security guard as we checked in at Heathrow. 'Take your own bomb. The chances of there being two bombs on the same plane are just impossible.' Everybody fell about laughing. Just mention 'bomb' to a security guard when there is no emergency and you'll get arrested.

The Dutch civil servant and his wife had met on Thai Airlines. She had been born in the Golden Triangle up in the north where the River Ruak flows into the Mekong to form the borders of Burma, Laos and Thailand. In other words, opium country. She was working as an air hostess. Now they were living in The Hague.

He'd been asked by his political masters whether the Dutch should run a big extravaganza in Bangkok. He was against it but, bureaucracy being bureaucracy even in money-conscious Holland, he knew that they wouldn't believe him if he said so. If an independent consultant said so they would agree. Knowing my opinion of giant international extravaganzas and my more than reasonable charges as a poor English zentrepreneur, he asked me to write the report he wanted for his masters. Long may senior Dutch civil servants distrust the views of their juniors. 'Your report will contain your estimates, which I actually gave to the ministry last week,' he kept saying.

In between redrafting my independent estimates, which he had already given to the ministry, I agreed to accept their services as my personal tour guides. As a result I saw all the things *farangs* or foreigners do not usually see when they visit Bangkok. Yes, I did see practically all 300 temples and buy mushrooms grown on buffalo dung in the floating market on the Chao Phraya river. Kop koon kha – thank you very much.

Yes, I did see the temple of the Emerald Buddha and the Royal Chapel and all the gentle Buddhist monks in their saffron robes in Wat Po nearby, Bangkok's oldest monastery.

Kop koon kha. And yes, I did see policemen holding hands with some pretty unsavoury-looking characters. Kop koon kha.

But I didn't go anywhere near Ping-Pam-Pong what's-it-street with its wall-to-wall you-know-whats and never-ending supply of gifts that go on giving, as they say.

Take one step outside Bangkok's Don Muang Airport, one of the most modern and efficient airports in Asia, and you're gasping for breath. Not because of the view, but because of the pollution. The air is so polluted you can slice it with a rusty knife; diesel fumes, petrol, burning engine oil from a million two-stroke motorcycle engines that power the little three-wheel tak-taks.

They might call it the City of Angels, but in many ways it's hell on earth. Take two steps and you don't have to be told that only 2% of Bangkok's 9 million inhabitants are on proper sewage facilities. Take three steps, if you are able, and you will see why it is practically choking on its dramatic economic success.

Refineries; chemical plants; smelters; electronics factories; electroplating works; textile mills; industry is everywhere. With a sparkling, barely regulated economy, fabulous double-figure growth for three years, per capita income which has doubled in five years to US$1,620 and is scheduled to double again over the next five years, precious few planning regulations, military governments more interested in cleaning up in Switzerland than in Thailand and unparalleled industrial expansion, it is no wonder Bangkok's mushrooming industrial suburbs seem every year to be oozing further and further like some glutinous, toxic sludge over a wider and wider area. Bangkok's angels today account for 70% of the urban population of Thailand, 70% of the bond deposits, more than one-third of GDP, over 90% of Thai trade, and Buddha knows what percentage of you-know-what.

Take four-steps, if you dare, and you could end up a

registered drug addict. Bangkok is supposed to be the jumping-off point for one of the biggest drug operations in south-east Asia. Drug production began years ago high in Doi Mai Salong, where cherries blossom and roses bloom all year round, when a handful of veterans from the Kuomintang's ninety-third Division, which had fled Communist China in 1969, started shipping opium across the border from Burma to make ends meet. Today, however, Thailand has virtually eliminated opium production, having successfully persuaded its farmers, with the aid of grants and incentives, free education and medical care, to switch to other cash crops.

Burma, however, under the legendary Khun Sa and his Shan army, produces around 2,500 tonnes a year; Laos 300 tonnes. Most ends up in Bangkok – in the bottom of suitcases, in the soles of shoes, poured into condoms, swallowed and carried through customs packed into the stomach. The world record for smuggling drugs out of Bangkok internally must go to a Nigerian, Ohuoho Uguta, who somehow managed to smuggle seventy condoms full of heroin past New York customs. He collapsed and died shortly afterwards, but that's no reason for denying him his fifteen minutes' fame.

I had no wish to spend up to four hours in a taxi inching along Vibhavadi Rangsit Highway for 24 kilometres to the city – rush-hour speed is now 4.5 kph compared to 15.3 kph ten years ago. It was Saturday afternoon so I didn't fancy paying US$100 for the ten-minute helicopter flight to the roof of the Shangri-la either. I decided to let the train take the strain.

Take the strain! Bangkok is the only city I know where people are so desperate for space they build their shacks between the railway line and the fence that is supposed to keep them off the track. Every second of the journey I thought the train was either going to slice some stray kid in two or bring every shaky shanty crashing to the ground in its wake. By the time we pulled into Hua Lampong terminus I was streaming with tears. From the pollution, not from what I had seen.

A French professor in the same carriage said it might be the opium in the atmosphere. The day before, the police had burnt nearly £500 million of it, seized from local and foreign traffickers over the previous three years. I knew then I was going to be addicted to it. And I was. To Bangkok, I mean, not opium. Even in the railway station I was stunned by the extravagant traditional costume – smog masks. Everyone was wearing one: pedestrians rushing between the stationary traffic, drivers sitting hoping that one day they would move again, even the traffic policemen, who had practically nothing to do.

'Bangkok is pumping out over a million tonnes of waste every year. By 2001 it will be over 6 million,' the French professor told me as we fought for breath on the way to our taxis. 'On every possible calculation, Bangkok is short of at least four sewage works.'

Surveys show that blood/lead levels among people in Bangkok are up to three times higher than anywhere else in the world. And it is the same story throughout the country. Around the coast coral reefs, even the mango swamps are being choked to death. In Thailand, the four S's of tourism (sand, sun, sex and syphilis) have become five; the additional S is for sewage with the Island of Phuket, once known as the Pearl of the Orient, taking first prize. The gloriously named TAT, Tourism Authority of Thailand, denies it all, of course, though the country's head forester, Seub Nakhasathien, committed suicide as a protest against what the pollution was doing to his beloved forests.

'So why haven't they built the sewage works?' I asked the professor. Our taxis were still alongside each other ten minutes after we had clambered into them. He gave me that reassuring, inscrutable smile of the French. 'Politics,' he said.

My taxi lurched forward two metres. I was on my way.

Before my first trip to the City of Angels I was told again and again by old British south-east Asia hands, 'Remember their damn silly rules, old boy. No shaking hands. Little blighters don't like you touching them. No chat about the Royal family. Royalty to them are gods. Must always squat in their presence. Their heads must always be higher than yours. And whatever you do, don't point the soles of your shoes at anyone.'

Thai businessmen, I found, were more than happy to shake hands, to chat, rather than gossip, about the Royal family – theirs as well as ours – and however much I tried, I found it impossible to point the soles of my feet at anyone, unless I sat at a 90° angle to them and chatted to the wall.

In Thailand, the only 100% Buddhist country in the world, everybody is charming, everyone smiles. Not the have-a-nice-day mechanical smile which is *de rigueur* from Providence, Rhode Island to Pier 39, San Francisco, but a really genuine, benign smile. They seem to have a unique serenity and tolerance and contentment.

In the old days if the King of Siam didn't like you, he gave you a present; a white elephant. Which you must admit is better than a poke in the eye or half of everything you own or may possibly own for the rest of your life. Today they still seem genuinely to follow Buddha's Golden Rule, or Dhamma-pada: avoid evil; be good; purify the mind. And give pictures of Yul Brynner to people they don't like any more.

'Are they really as nice as they seem?' I asked an ICI manager who had been in Bangkok for over twenty years.

'Of course,' he said. 'The nicest, friendliest, most genuine and honest people in the whole world – unless you cross them.'

'Then what happens?'

'They'll kill you.'

'You're kidding.'

He assured me he wasn't. 'Don't gamble,' he leant across the table towards me. 'I never gamble in Thailand. If you lose and haven't the money to pay up there and then, they'll shoot you.'

A big Thai steel company had recently bought 5,000 tonnes of hot rolled coil from a Hong Kong trading company. When it was delivered, instead of being 2 mm thick it was 2.5 mm thick. The Thais went bananas, refused to pay, insisted the hot coil was rerolled. They were told it was impossible. Then they slapped a US$325,000 claim on the Hong Kong company. When executives arrived from Hong Kong to try to work out a compromise the Thais called in officers from Bangkok's famous Bangponnpang police station and had them thrown into gaol on a charge of personal fraud. After six days, however, they were released, surprise, surprise, because the Hong Kong trading company came up with half the US$325,000. In cash.

'They were lucky,' said the man from ICI. 'Sometimes a turtle cannot talk to a fish. Old Thai saying.'

If during the samara, our cycle of birth, death and rebirth, you happen to pass by Bangkok, the best place to reach nirvana on earth – apart from smoking a Thai stick – is the venerable old colonial Oriental Hotel on the banks of the admittedly heavily polluted Chao Phraya river where it all began 116 years ago. The Author's Lounge, the lobby of the original two-storey wooden hotel which was a kind of east Asian Harry's Bar to Somerset Maugham is a little, you know what I mean. But it's still fun.

Failing that, try the Shangri-la, which must be the most luxurious, opulent and elegant big hotel in the world. It has nearly 900 rooms, the biggest in the city, but you'd never guess it from the standard and speed of service. Trouble is, and you can never have everything in this life, it is often full of incentive travellers because Thailand is the ideal incentive country. It has beaches and skiing and boating. It has jungles and elephant safaris. It has rivers and rafting and plenty of rapids. It has fabulous hotels. Gold is for sale on every street corner, silk on every other.

And, let's be dishonest, Bangkok is the ideal incentive city.

Not, I am afraid, for achieving *amaravati*, the Buddhists' deathless mind, or even *cittavivekka*, the silent mind, but for, as the Thais say, *sanuk*.

My Dutch civil servant and his wife were in the Oriental. They wanted to sit in the Author's Lounge and read books. I went to the Shangri-la to sit in my room and write one – about not holding extravaganzas in Bangkok.

Four English businessmen checked in beside me. Three looked as though they were big in double-glazing. The fourth, who looked as though he had just paid the others to double-glaze his bungalow and wanted his money back, was asking the receptionist to have the mini-bar in his room emptied. 'Can't trust 'em y'know,' he was saying to nobody in particular. 'You never know what they might put into them.' The last thing his three colleagues were thinking about was mini-bars.

As I got to my room, I noticed Mr Mini-bar wandering towards me. 'Never like going direct to my room,' he whispered, 'in case I'm being followed. You never know.' He looked as though he was going to spend the evening curled up in bed with a medical dictionary.

From my window, beneath the pollution I could see old Bangkok giving ground all the time to new Bangkok. Conrad and Maugham got out just in time. The temples and palaces by the river look as if they are being pushed into the water by the marauding skyscrapers, hotels and office blocks encircling them. Downstairs, from the back of a tak-tak, the view is completely different. Bangkok from the back of a tak-tak is nothing but tak-taks.

Old Asia hands sneer but I prefer going everywhere by tak-tak. The driver never understands a word you're saying. You've got no idea where you're going. You know you're going to be charged double, treble or maybe even ten times the going rate, depending on whether you're wearing a tee-shirt or a collar and tie. But I don't care. To me, and anyone else who thinks happiness is listening to Steve Race in the rain, it's great fun. Either the traffic roars past within an inch of your life, or you roar past the traffic, stuck in yet another enormous jam, also within an inch of your life. The noise is unbearable, the fumes are sickening, the heat is stifling.

'You'd never catch me in one of them,' one old Asia hand once told me over mint tea at the Oriental Club in London. 'You never know what you might catch.' He reminded me of a British diplomat I met once in Lagos. During the whole time he was in Nigeria, he boasted, he had managed to avoid shaking hands with anyone. 'Never know what you could catch,' he would shiver. 'They've all got every social disease you can imagine under their fingernails.'

I still think taking a tak-tak is safer than hiring a car. In fact, hiring anything in Bangkok is dangerous. A German I spoke to as our tak-taks pulled up alongside each other outside Wat Mahathat, a Buddhist monastery which has its own market selling everything from antiques to aphrodisiacs, told me that in Bangkok every hired car has a girl in the back who begins by stroking your head and saying, 'You're a nice man.' Except that they're not always girls.

Bangkok is also full of tak-taks pop-popping and pumping out their fumes because there are no 'phones – or none that works. It's impossible to get a connection. There is only one telephone for every fifty people. Getting a new one can take six months if you're prepared to be persuasive and forever if you're not. When you've got one, there's no guarantee it will work. Even the official telephone statistics claim only a 60% first-time success rate so you can guess what the real rate is. 'It's so bad that the first thing you say when anybody answers the 'phone is, "what number is that?"' a Thai businessman complained.

But don't think for a moment the Thai Telephone Company is inefficient. Every two weeks, regular as clockwork, it sends out its invoices for international calls. And every two weeks, regular as clockwork, it will disconnect you if you don't pay up on the dot. If you want to do business you have no option; you have to send your telephone messages across town by tak-tak. Just like France used to be until they modernised their network. At one stage, I remember, it used to be quicker to drive from Paris to Le Mans, than to get through on the 'phone.

'Carrier pigeons?' I suggested.

'We're already looking into it,' I was told.

Just as they are looking into modernising what telephone network they've got in the time-honoured Thai way they have given the US$6 billion contract to an agricultural company. And naturally I cannot believe the rumours of US$300 million kickbacks, although even the old military government did describe the communications minister as a man of 'unusual wealth'.

But if the telephones don't work, the traffic hardly moves and everyone is coughing their guts out with pollution, there is one thing the Thais do better than anybody else, and that is, collect dead bodies.

'Please not to fall asleep after lunch lying on beach,' Mrs Dutch Civil Servant warned me over cocktails one evening at the Oriental. 'If you do you wake up in morgue.' Bangkok has no ambulances, so, like zentrepreneurs anywhere in Asia, private companies have moved in to provide the service. Except they are only interested in dead or near-dead bodies, not live ones. It's the ultimate privatisation nightmare.

'What on earth do they do with all the bodies?' I asked her. 'There must be a limit to the number hospitals can use for teaching.'

She came as close to roaring with laughter as sensitive Thai etiquette would allow. 'No,' she said. 'They are not for hospitals. They collect them to bury them.'

Apparently, Buddha he say, 'Give someone a proper burial and good funeral, you get good place in heaven.' So what's happened is that the peace-loving, ever-smiling Thais have turned the City of Angels into a rip-roaring, freewheeling, moneymaking battlefield of death. Various societies are furiously trying to collect as many dead bodies as they can to sell to Thailand's rip-roaring *sias*, or tycoons, for them to bury with all the ceremonies they can afford so that they will reap even bigger dividends in heaven.

'You mean, they believe they can do whatever they want in this world because they know they will be looked after in the next world?'

'Sure. It's insurance policy.'

The two biggest body snatchers are apparently the Por Tek Tung Foundation, which means Memorial to Virtue, and the Ruamkhatanyu, which means Shared Gratitude. Both are huge organisations with their own so-called ambulances, which race like Dutch tugboats to any accident as soon as they hear of it. Both have thousands of policemen in their pockets to ensure that they are the first to hear of deaths from road accidents, natural disasters, whatever. Unless, of course, the nearest and dearest get there first. But even then there is no guarantee the body snatchers will leave them alone. Many Thais believe in matchmaking for the dead.

'Many Thai people pay foundation to find dead girl's body. It is unlucky for man to die unmarried. If dead girl is buried with him it is lucky. It is what Thai people think.' I now had three reasons for treble-locking my hotel room, two of which were not wanting to be snatched and killed, and not wanting to be buried with the dead.

The following morning I was planning to call on Bangkok's big new convention centre, my tak-tak driver permitting. I didn't fancy the idea of being scraped off a Bangkok pavement – actually I didn't even fancy the idea of being in contact with a Bangkok pavement – fought over by charitable organisations, and thrown into a pit alongside some forty-stone harridan to ensure that some *sia* goes to heaven.

'Hey what have you been doing with my wife?' the leader

of the double-glazing delegation, who looked as though he wouldn't take yes for an answer, bawled at me across reception. 'Quick, your flies are undone,' shouted number two. The third made a gesture most unlike a Thai gesture of greeting. I couldn't see number four. He was probably fast asleep after sitting up all night in case the trouser press caught fire.

Drinks appeared from nowhere. I had a drink in my hand. Three paces I had two drinks. Six paces we'd practically taken over the bar. A group of Japanese businessmen in their salarymen suits were already in the corner slugging back non-stop whisky. The double-glazing salesmen turned out to be European service engineers for a big British engineering company. 'Europe?' I said. 'So what are you doing in Asia?' 'Changed the tickets. Supposed to be in Zurich this weekend. Big machine to service. Decided to come here instead.'

'How did you do that?'

They swore me to secrecy. But what they had done was book first-class tickets to Zurich through the company. They then got their local bucket shop to cancel the tickets and rebook them on a cheap three-day special for Bangkok.

'Won't the company know you've been in Bangkok?'

'No way. We hand in the ticket with our expenses.'

'But surely the company you're supposed to be visiting will complain you weren't there?'

'No way,' the three of them grinned. 'Meet the client.'

The fourth man, who had been up all night with his trouser press, suddenly appeared at reception. He was the client.

Given the fact that I've never met anyone who wants to go to the Churchill bar in the British Club which is supposed to serve the best pink gin in south-east Asia, Bangkok is the easiest city in the world in which to plan your evening. Either you're going, or you're not. And I don't mean to the Churchill bar.

Now, if you're quiet at the back, purely – if that's the right word – out of academic interest, I'll explain what it's all about. I think.

There are three Pat Pongs squeezed between the Suriwong and Silom Roads where, incidentally, you can buy the best and cheapest counterfeit Rolex watches, Cartier handbags and Hermès silk scarves in the world. Not, of course, that you are interested. Number one Pat Pong – now pay attention or you'll be getting a white elephant in the post tomorrow – is your conventional Pat Pong. Number two Pat Pong is your queer Pat Pong where, I am told, the Rome Club is home to some of the most breathtakingly beautiful transvestites.

While I was in Bangkok an Italian, Paolo Eduardo Poeris, managed to obtain a divorce from his wife, Riam Khuemchau, who turned out to be a man. He told the tribunal that for three months he had been making love to his wife in the dark. It was only when he turned the light on that he discovered the truth.

Pat Pong number three is the Japanese Pat Pong where one evening of inscrutable pleasure is designed to turn you into an ecstatic, slathering workaholic thrilled with the idea of living in a rabbit hutch for another twelve months. The real enthusiasts told me there was in fact a fourth Pat Pong. She was the legendary Bangkok madam Chintana Bunnag, who half convinced the government to invest in a chain of Feelings Banks until somebody realised she wasn't thinking of the usual deposit-taking institution.

The three salesmen had already decided where they were going. That's why they were in Bangkok. Their client was still drinking his St Clements, probably the most innocent mixture of orange and lemon juice ever served in Bangkok. 'You going as well?' I mumbled to him.

'No, not for me, not this time,' he muttered sheepishly. 'Thought I'd spend the evening checking the fire escape procedures. I also want to check if the stairs are blocked and if the exit is easy to open.' I couldn't think of anything to say. Of all the dangers you could face in Bangkok, a blocked hotel fire escape was the last anyone would think of.

Mr and Mrs Dutch Civil Servant suddenly arrived. I'd been rescued. We were supposed to, you'll never believe this, go to a restaurant called Cabbages and Condoms owned by Mechai Viravaidya, a former director of the Planned Parenthood Association of Thailand, who had switched his energies to turning out the best crab poo, duck pet, goong choop and something called – honest, no kidding – pang turd, in south-east Asia.

Instead we spent the evening in another one of Bangkok's red light districts – the traffic lights at the junction of Sukhumrit Road and Rama IV Road, by the new 65,000-square-metre National Convention Centre which can accommodate over 10,000 delegates. It took hours to reach the traffic lights.

'Normally not like this,' Mrs Dutch Civil Servant gave me a serene Buddhist smile.

'Nonsense,' grinned her husband. 'It is so bad when you go by car in Bangkok the government tells everybody to take emergency supplies of food and water with them. Even toilets.' We edged a few inches forward. 'The other day it was worse than usual. Parents could not get to school to collect their children until 11 o'clock at night. Then it took them another six hours to get home.' Another few inches. 'Planes were late. The pilots couldn't get to the airport.' Another few inches.

'People are turning their cars into offices. They spend more time in them.'

When we actually got to them, the lights stayed red for seventeen and a half minutes. As soon as they changed, we shot across and had barely reached the other side than they were red again. Half the cars behind us were empty, I swear; the drivers had hopped out, grabbed a tak-tak, dashed across to Pat Pong, taken in a couple of clubs and were planning to get back to their cars before the lights changed to green.

Breakfast next morning was deserted. But then Sunday

mornings in any hotel are always fragile. I sat by the riverside soaking up the pollution. There was a heavy blanket of foam over the city. Maybe the police had been burning opium paste again. The Japanese businessmen appeared as I was about to leave, wiping their glasses and staring straight in front of them. They must have been preparing for re-entry into the world of non-stop working and rabbit hutches.

We did a tour of Bangkok's klongs, or canals. Mr Dutch Civil Servant said they were as good as those in Amsterdam; Mrs Dutch Civil Servant said they were better; I kept talking about Venice. We also visited – well, at least 299 of those 300 temples. Some were stunning. The five-and-a-half ton, ten-feet tall, solid gold Buddha at Wat Trimitr near Bangkok's Chinatown is spectacular. For centuries it was covered in bricks, and everyone thought it was just another common old Buddha, until one day a bunch of Thai Murphies were moving it and dropped it. The bricks fell off to reveal the gold. Most of the temples, however, looked like poor relations of Italian churches or rich Mormon temples.

Not neglecting Mammon, I also saw about half a million share shops, which look and feel like betting shops, even down to the middle-aged women running them, where it is as easy to buy and sell shares as it is to back a horse. Which, I suppose, is the way it should be.

The best restaurants in Bangkok, I discovered, were not the award-winning Ma Maison at the Hilton, the Shangri-la, La Tache, the legendary Normandie on top of the Oriental, or any of the more discreet ones favoured by the military where any old Château Petrus costs £1,000 a bottle, but tiny roadside restaurants which look like mini-aircraft hangars. Until you've eaten sky prawns, sublime curries, lemon grass and lime leaves on a tin table decorated with delicate strings of threaded jasmine and pineapples sculptured into exotic flowers, you haven't lived. Except that sky prawns are not prawns, but grasshoppers. Admittedly corn-fed, 100%

genuine Thai, but they are still grasshoppers. And of course much, much cheaper than other prawns.

I also discovered from Mrs Dutch Civil Servant, over another dish of crab poo, that Mr Dutch Civil Servant admired the British so much that he videoed all the British comedy programmes shown on Dutch television in order to play them back slowly and try to find out why we are all laughing. As she was telling me this in her delightful, serene, open, non-violent Buddhist way, she kept receiving non-serene, delightful, closed, violent, non-Buddhist looks from Mr Dutch Civil Servant.

I didn't see the double-glazing delegation again until I was checking in at the airport four days later. Their poor long-suffering potential ex-client, who looked as though he'd been drinking bromide in his tea since he arrived, had already checked in. He got there early, he told me, to check if there was ice on the wings.

'How do you check for ice on the wings?'

'There is supposed to be a piece of yarn fixed to the wing. If there is an icing problem, it becomes rigid and hangs from the wing. If it's okay, it will be blowing in the wind.'

His three very fragile potential ex-service engineers arrived, and slapped their poor client around the terminal. 'Hey, what have you been doing with my wife?' screamed number one, who still had testosterone coming out of his ears. 'Quick, your flies are undone,' shrieked number two, who had obviously lost all hormone control. Number three was wandering all over the departure lounge, endorphins bursting out of his head like dandruff, handing out his potential ex-client's business cards. 'If you're ever in Zurich, look me up,' he was saying. 'No, I insist. You're very welcome.'

I said I thought they only had a weekend ticket.

'New economy measures, old boy,' number one slapped me on the shoulder. 'Told to cut costs.'

'Chairman's banned us from flying business class,' said

number two, 'so we've had to stay here four days until economy tickets were available.'

Their potential ex-client was asking the girl at the check-in desk if he could have his suitcase back. 'Just remembered I hadn't seen the old pink shirt when I was packing. I'm certain the laundry hadn't returned it,' he said turning to me. 'It never does any harm to check.' The three others fell about laughing.

'Do you ever get fed up with them?' I asked as they headed off to the bar.

'I'm not worried,' he said. 'I've already sent faxes to their chairman saying, "Urgent, urgent". She says they should see a doctor immediately.' Suddenly his smile was infectious.

Canton

Marco Polo. Colin Thubron. Hans Dieter Lotz, an export manager for Mercedes Benz. Everybody else travels the legendary Chinese Silk Road. Me? I only get to travel the New Chinese Washing Machine Way.

Not for a me a glimpse of the mysterious Jiayuguan Gate in deepest Xinjiang. All I see is the inside of dusty factories and the outside of a million trucks and lorries. I don't even catch a glimpse of Tashkurgan, the Clapham Junction of the Silk Road that led south into India, west into Afghanistan and the furthest east Ptolemy ever travelled. Although I must admit, it invariably happens during my Buddhist period when I am fairly serene about everything.

The Old Chinese Silk Road starts high up on the edge of the Gobi Desert and runs all the way to the Mediterranean. For centuries it carried what everyone thought was a magic down washed off the leaves of mysterious silk trees and not the guts of a billion worms. Anyone who has ever had a yellow fever injection, or cashed travellers' cheques east of Watford, wants to travel the Old Chinese Silk Road. Worse, they then want to write books and make television films about it.

When I travel, though, I like doing things nobody has done before, visiting places nobody has visited and meeting people who have never appeared on radio or television or been passed over by Alan Whicker. Do you know anybody else who has toured the Electricity Supply Company in Shenzen, or thrilled at the sight of the Lo' Pa La garment factory in Guangzhou? Hence my great expedition along the New Chinese Washing Machine Way.

I was in Shenzen, which is about the nearest you'll get to a Wild West frontier town in China. I was in the Electricity Supply Co at the Ha Fa Enterprises Co Ltd. The offices were dusty, full of rusty bicycles but displaying, would you believe, various bits of compressed-air breathing equipment from Gent, Belgium. The staff were wearing Western suits, the new free-enterprise state uniform, which were all wittily cut two sizes too small.

In spite of all the colour photographs you see in wall newspapers of shiny, sparkling offices and factories, every Chinese work premises I have ever visited looked as though it had come off a production line covered in dust. 'They're so dusty even the rats wear overalls,' an American engineer who was looking for a *guanxi* or agent told me. They are also flat, faceless and empty, like offices in the UK during the early 1990s when the government kept insisting we weren't suffering from a recession.

We swing into the traffic and pass the great marble entrance to Shenzen railway station with its giant red sign actually written by Deng Xiaoping himself during one of his eight-yearly tours of inspection. The Chinese Chinese will tell you he did it to celebrate the enormous changes that had taken place during that time. The Hong Kong Chinese tell you it was because he needed the money, and the pay for even a signwriter in Shenzen is better than for a politician in Beijing.

Chinese trains are not the best in the world. Apart from their old-fashioned net curtains they are very standard, rush-hour British Rail in-the-middle-of-a-snow-storm type trains with not enough seats, too many people and not enough air to breathe. To be fair, though, they are better than African trains, which have as many people outside as inside, hanging on to the railings, the roof, even open windows, with the people inside unpacking their belongings, rolling out prayer mats, spitting on the floor and boiling water on dangerous little stoves.

On Chinese trains, to help you forget the experience, and because there has been an acute shortage of opium since 1839, they serve thick, hot muscly whelks, cardboard boxes of vegetables and mugs of tea, made with hot water poured out of giant bottles, which would make poor old Emperor Shen Nong, the man who invented tea in 3000 BC, turn in his grave.

Legend has it that Shen Nong was a Chinese Isaac Newton. Instead of apples falling to the ground while he snoozed, seated one day in his garden, leaves of the *Ithea sinensis* fluttered lazily into the cup of boiling water he drank daily for health purposes. Before you could say teabags, the first cuppa was born.

Now we pass a Mobil, then an Esso petrol station. So far it could be any run-down hardworking industrial town anywhere in the world. Apart from Britain, of course, where we no longer have hardworking industrial towns. We shoot past factories, more factories, a science park, an enormous curved block of flats and some smart-looking villas tucked away behind marble walls.

Deng Xiaoping says he doesn't believe in socialism or capitalism. He believes in socialist-capitalism. To me this is proof that while he was running his China Beancurd shop in Paris in the 1920s to finance his studies, he picked up the French facility for making words mean just what they want them to mean.

On the other hand, Confucius he say, you must see all the angles. 'There was a peasant who raced his three horses against the king's three horses. Everybody say he must race slowest against the king's slowest, middle one against the middle one and fastest against the fastest. But he say, no. He race his best horse against the king's middle horse, his middle horse against the king's slowest horse and his slowest against king's fastest. That way he won two out of three races.'

So far Shenzen looks more socialist-socialist than socialist-capitalist. Apart from those villas, which look definitely capitalist-capitalist. Now we are passing an open-air street market. A Buddhist nun has obviously decided she's had enough raw monkey brains for the week, not to mention bats or stir-fried bees. She is choosing exactly the right frog for the evening's meal to go with the owl, snake and dog she already has back home.

'Don't ask for a hot dog in Guangzhou,' I was told by a German businessman who had been in Honan Province trying to buy 2,000 tons of barium carbonate, an essential ingredient for stopping white salt from coming out of brick-work and spoiling the colour. 'In Canton they eat everything.'

He wasn't kidding: macaques; pangolins; practically any rare species of bird you can think of (which, of course, is why they are rare); snake they eat raw – even drink the blood; crickets – if the crickets are no good for fighting. I'm not kidding, the Chinese are crazy about cricket fighting – then they're for the pot as well.

Even a French engineer whispered to me once as lunch was served, '*Les excréments des chauve-souris.*' I guessed the meaning of the first word, but was too terrified and embarrassed to ask the meaning of the second.

In Shanghai, apparently it's different. There, instead of buying Porsches, Chinese yuppies will spend up to US$2,000, about double the average annual worker's wages, on pedigree dogs. To make a fuss of, not to eat.

Now we're heading out of town. Suddenly a battered old taxi shoots out ahead of us and disappears in the direction of the Xianhu Botanical Garden. Shenzen taxis look as though their drivers are investing their money on the new local stock exchange rather than in their taxis. I don't think I saw one that didn't look socialist-socialist. An American expat running an electronics joint venture told me never to take a taxi in Shenzen. It was too dangerous.

'So how do I get around?' I asked.

'Take the motorbike taxis, they're much quicker. If there's an accident at least you won't be trapped in the wreckage for hours.' Which made me think. Until his secretary told me he was so nervous of China that whenever he went to the hotel swimming pool he took his own bottle of chlorine with him. After that I went back to the taxis.

I arrived in Shenzen from Hong Kong, which is like turning the clock back, say, ten years. For all their smart green uniforms and little red badges, the customs officers were the same as customs officers along the Old Silk Road.

Will the Chinese merge Guangdong and Hong Kong come 1997? Maybe. It would certainly at a stroke weave Hong Kong into the very fabric of China. The freewheeling Hong Kongers might not like it, but it would be better than more drastic alternatives – such as abolishing it altogether; merging it with another Province; or making it just another Province. And it would deliver to their doorstep an enormous, like-minded market for their products; one which, to a large degree, they already manage and own.

Any businessman in Guangdong Province will give you the facts: over two-thirds of all companies are already privately owned. Over 2 million people are working for companies already owned by the Hong Kong Chinese; another million are in associated activities; nearly 15,000 Hong Kong managers and technicians are already working there; 15,000 vehicles cross the border every day between the two areas and, even more of a clincher, about 20% of Hong Kong's currency is already circulating and accepted as legal tender in Guangdong.

Shenzen is now waiting for 1997. It is already a booming frontier town, almost opposite Hong Kong, with a life of its own. The frontier in this case is between capitalism and socialism of the old Chinese style, Tiananmen Square included. Not only is the whole seething mass of building sites, new roads and, yes, sewage works crammed already to bursting point with people and buses and bicycles, it is also choked with packed restaurants, overflowing nightclubs, and mobile telephones. They are even building twenty new hotels. At the same time. Shenzen is the only place in China which doesn't know the meaning of *bu keneng* – impossible.

As a result, the Province of Guangdong, or Canton as it used to be known, is not really China. It is China/Hong Kong. It is one of China's five special mini-Hong Kong economic zones, licensed by the signwriter to flirt if not actually fall in love with capitalism after years of being restricted by Maoist central planning.

Shenzen has over 2 million inhabitants, tower blocks, a stock exchange, traffic jams, a GDP per person of around US$2,000 a year and a growth rate in trade and foreign investment of a staggering 40% a year.

Guangdong as a whole is the Hong Kong of tomorrow. It is packed with people; over 60 million at the last count, already one of the densest populations in the world. It is working day and night. Factories are churning out shoes, toys, electronic goods of every possible size, shape and chip power. Even groups of doctors are getting together, drawing on China's 2,000-year-old tradition of herbal medicine, and selling their own mix of bark, root and shrivelled fungus for curing everything from backache to the common cold.

'It is very good,' Hans Dieter told me, 'it has to be.'

'Because it is based on herbs?' I said.

'No, because in China people only pay their doctors if they are well.'

Industrial and agricultural production generally is growing at practically 30% a year. It exports US$45 million, a third of the total exports for the whole of China, and that is growing at the rate of 12.5% a year. Thailand, always hailed as the Asian superstar, can only notch up 7.5%. If it continues to grow at the present rate, by the year 2000, together with the next-door Province of Fujian, opposite Taiwan, Guangdong will be as rich as southern Europe.

Yet thirteen years ago, Shenzen had fewer than 100,000 inhabitants, most of them farmers or fishermen. It wasn't even rated important enough to be given any ailing, inefficient, loss-making Chinese state industries. How come they have managed to achieve such staggering success?

Part of the reason, of course, is location. A smart US real estate operator would say there were three reasons: location, location and location. Obviously being opposite Hong Kong, forty-five minutes by train from Hung Hom or fifty minutes by hydrofoil from Kowloon, helps enormously. Part of the reason is the language. Cantonese is the language of Hong Kong and Guangdong. Part is emigration. Chinese from Guangdong and Fujian have traditionally been the traders, willing to go anywhere, suffer any hardship to do the deal and get the business. Part is good old-fashioned pounds, shillings and pence. Guangdong is five to ten times cheaper than Hong Kong for manufacturing. Land costs 2–3% of even the most depressed Hong Kong prices. Wages are one tenth the wages in Taiwan. As a result Hong Kong companies with a handful of staff in head office will often have 20,000 workers in Guangdong. For practically the same price.

Partly because, like everybody, they want to back a winner. Partly because even if the ageing Politician in Peking cannot see it, the man on the shop floor in the restyled Mao Tse-tung suit knows that things must change. Some provinces have closed down the odd collective. Others are allowing one or two state industries to fire people. A few provinces will only undertake to buy half the output of their state-owned enterprises.

Now for the big question. If this is what Guangdong is like

today, what on earth is it going to be like in another ten years? Remember that 1992 was the Year of the Monkey, and everyone born in such a year is guaranteed good luck, lots of money and a long and happy life. Now I know it's all a lot of silly feudal nonsense, as the *Beijing Evening News* said, and that Chinese families are allowed to have only one child, but just imagine how many Guangdongs we will have in 2012 if all the 1992 babies are lucky and end up making a lot of money. It's enough to make you plant a forest of incense sticks for the return of the good old unlucky Year of the Sheep.

And all this, don't forget, is still pre-privatisation. China's state sector, the backbone of socialism according to Prime Minister Li Peng, numbers as far as anybody knows over 10,000 inefficient and massively overstaffed companies which find it easier to generate massive debts than even tiny profits. They range from colossi such as SIMOPEC, China's ICI, which has sixty-eight subsidiaries, nearly 70,000 engineering and technical staff and exports every year 46 million tons of oil and petrochemical products to over 1,000 companies in fifty countries, down to tiny corner shops. They are all trying to sell as much as they can wherever they can. As a result, you find Chinese goods everywhere, always in bulk, always at the lowest possible price. They might not look terribly attractive or be the most consumer-friendly goods in the world but as Henry Ford said, 'What difference does it make if a cat is black or white so long as it catches mice.'

I've been inside one Chinese embassy after another, especially in Africa. Whether it's Washington, Bonn or Ouagadougou, they are all the same; huge, sparsely furnished offices with shelf after overflowing shelf of every cheap fan, saucepan, raffia mat or tin of lychees that China can produce.

It's the same with offices of the New China News Agency. Whether you're in Rome or Lomé they all have the statutory minimum stock of Chinese products plus, in the case of the real journalists, a typewriter. What the journalists did who were not issued with typewriters I never did find out. 'We must sell these,' a West Africa-based Chinese journalist told me one day as I picked my way through a Chinese Wall of cardboard boxes in his office. 'If not we don't eat. You buy a box?'

Not everybody in the public sector in China necessarily wants to be in the public sector. Some are chained to it. Socks, clothes, sportswear, even packaging for expensive bottles of cognac are all being produced in Chinese prisons. It's against every rule and law in the book including the Foreign Prison-Made Goods Act of 1897, but they still do it. China has even turned many of its prisons into factories and pressed thousands of prisoners into earning hard currency from the West. Got a Red Star sweater? Chances are it was made in a Chinese gaol. How about that New Life pair of jeans? They were made in the New Life Cotton Cloth Mill of Nantong County – which is inside the gaol in Jiangsun Province. And what about that glass of white wine produced by Remy Martin's joint venture in China? You're right. The grapes were grown behind bars. Cheers.

Different people, as a result, have different views about privatisation. You've only got to battle your way along Zhongsha Road with its masses of tiny shops to see the beginnings of red raw market capitalism in action. One man buys a big store. He splits it up into twenty, maybe fifty smaller shopping units and resells or re-lets them, then buys another big store and starts again. Everybody who wants to get in on the ground floor can get in.

In spite of the attractions of working for the state sector – lifelong job, subsidised food and free housing, health care, schools and leisure facilities – the new wheeling-dealing private sector which, in 1991, for the first time for forty years, produced more than the state sector, seems to have no problem attracting labour.

'Fir-first everybody w-wants a j-job,' I was told by a German engineer who spoke fluently in German b-but st-stuttered like mad in English. 'Su-second, the Chinese are a nation of g-gamblers. They know a w-winning st-streak when they see one. The p-private sector is now the w-winning st-streak. They are p-prepared to jump.'

Fifteen thousand new businesses, worth US$20 billion, have been started in Guangdong over the last fifteen years. Admittedly over 75% were established by their brothers in Hong Kong. Similarly out of over 4,000 new businesses, worth nearly US$4 billion, in nearby Fujian Province, one third came from Taiwan. But there was still a fair number which were home-grown. Of course there were the inevitable one-man trading companies, but there were plenty of serious players as well. Colgate Palmolive have set up a joint venture with Guangzhou Jie Yim Daily Use Chemicals Factory, Guangdong's leading toothpaste manufacturer, to build a big plant in the south of the province. Honda are going to employ 1,500 people to build motorcycles, also in Guangzhou.

But Shenzen's fortunes were built on washing machines and refrigerators. They even built washing machines and refrigerators when Beijing told them not to. Then when they got permission, Beijing wouldn't let them build as many as they wanted. One factory wanted to increase production from 400,000 to 600,000 units a year. The Central Committee said No. But they went ahead anyway in secret. Two years later, when Deng Xiaoping visited the town, they decided to wash their clean linen in public and admit their errors. He stopped them. They did the right thing, he said. Which was probably also his way of getting a washing machine before the others on the Central Committee.

Today, Shenzen is the supplier of washing machines and refrigerators to practically the whole of China. In 1978 only one in 10,000 Chinese owned a washing machine. Today seven out of every 100 have them. Which with a population of 400 million is an awful lot of washing machines. Or, looking at it the other way, there is still a long way to go.

Most of the washing machines that leave Shenzen head first for Guangzhou, and from there they are distributed throughout China. I was following them on the first leg of their journey as the Old Silk Road hands would say. As we set off along the route of the planned, privatised, six-lane superhighway which will one day link Shenzen and Guangzhon, through the boom towns of the Pearl River delta, I can't help noticing all the Mercedes and luxury Toyotas speeding past. Somebody is making big money.

Then it's like driving in Africa. Patches of scrub, occasional tiny, well-cultivated fields, here and there neat little vegetable plots. Then huge areas of nothing interrupted by building sites; enormous water towers surrounded, or perhaps supported, by bamboo scaffolding. No planning, no organisation, just put there. Sprinkled everywhere are broken-down cars, burnt-out vans and piles and piles of rubbish.

The Chentien Industrial Park in a sea of red dust looks more like an industrial graveyard for lorries. The factories look like a dress rehearsal for a concentration camp. They are all long and low and built of concrete blocks. Inside everybody is working furiously to destroy the factories in the West. Leaning precariously against practically every concrete wall are more, smaller, precarious concrete huts. Presiding over everything is a gaudy sign proclaiming, Sunrich.

Whenever and wherever I come across Chinese, in banks, offices or even take-aways in New York, or deep in the middle of the Sahara, they are always reserved, polite and velly, velly self-contained. It's as if they all know one day they are going to take over the world so they are quite happy for the time being to see how things tick, work out better ways of doing them and stand by ready to assume control. They always seem more than happy to do things your way, sell at the lowest possible prices to get the business and deliver to the most impossible deadlines.

We also say they are inscrutable. The British taught the

Chinese to be inscrutable. When we arrive giving direct answers to direct questions, we say it is good manners. Everyone else thinks it is either 'two-faced, double-dealing, double-crossing, back-stabbing hypocrisy' – or being inscrutable.

More scrub, this time industrial. Outside Evergreen Industries, another industrial concentration camp, a young woman is walking along the edge of the road, a bamboo pole across her shoulders sloshing two enormous plastic buckets of water. Further along is a small nondescript council house with a satellite dish on the roof. Now we are coming to a residential area. Squat concrete factories give way to high-rise blocks of flats. Chinese families are only allowed to have one child, but that still means a lot of concrete flats.

'You mean there's an enormous birth control operation?' I asked the driver. 'For 400 million people?' The mind boggles.

'No. The government only pays you if you have one child. If you have two children you get nothing, not even for the first child. And the government won't get jobs for your children either.'

Which is a pretty effective birth control campaign. Except, of course, nothing is ever straightforward in China.

'What happens is that if people have two children they kill one.'

'The second one?'

'No, the girl.'

'So there are more boys than girls?'

'No. In Guangzhou there are seven girls for every boy. People still have too many girls.'

Straw hats were now bobbing up and down coaxing a buffalo to pull the wooden plough in a straight line. The soil is so rich that they have two harvests a year. Suddenly we hit a stretch of good road. On either side are odd-shaped fields like an erratic patchwork quilt. A water buffalo is being cajoled along the roadside. We swerve to avoid a whole

family: mother, father, grandparents and one child – a boy –
pushing a cart as if they were refugees. The odd-shaped fields
give way to larger, more rectangular ones. Orange trees
suddenly line the route. A man with his coolie hat is leading
a buffalo along the road, for all the world as if he were taking
his dog for a walk.

We swing into Dongguan, one of the new old towns of
Guangzhou. Everything looks old and dusty. All the buildings
look as though they were thrown together by the same man
who threw together the factories and tower blocks we passed
on the way in. This is strictly the no-nonsense, functional, get-
it-up-and-open public works style of architecture.

In Hong Kong I was told that when in Guangzhou I should
go only to *dai pai dong*, street markets, and eat nothing but
dim sum, the fast food snacks of southern China. A single
restaurant could serve up to 2,000 different types ranging from
steamed dumplings with pork to deep fried bean curd filled
with pork and shrimp. Instead I was dragged into the only
so-called decent hotel in town. Instead of being served instant
dim sums, we had to wait patiently for the waiter. I know
Chinese hotels, but the waiter was like a Brahmin with dirty
fingernails. He was fussy about everything. I musn't put my
plate there, it had to go there. I shouldn't play with the
chopsticks, they should be left here. It was a case of from the
sublime to the meticulous.

I looked at the menu. Instead of a thousand *dim sum*, it
offered 'sheep's foot, meet pi or finced umlat wiv brane.' Is
that what I got?

In the time it took for listeria bacilli to spread halfway across
southern China, I was eventually served with what tasted like
slug soup followed by juicy young grubs covered in an
earthworm sauce mixed with chopped caterpillar. 'Have a
good taste,' the waiter bowed towards me as he put it on the
table. I took one look and decided to stick with it to the bitter
start. When he was in China, Marco Polo thought *mao Fai*, rice

wine, was the best wine in the world. When I asked for a bottle I was told they had none left. Which proves either how thirsty he was or how wrong he was. I settled instead for the local beer.

Afterwards I wandered around the centre of town. The streets were teeming with bicycles; they just kept coming, wave after wave, like Rorke's Drift on wheels.

The Shenggi Electronic Co Ltd factory looks as though it was built of mud. Inside they are probably making advanced micro-electronic equipment for IBM. In the back streets I see a pig hobbling along. Chickens are scratching at the rubbish.

I know it's obvious when you think about it, but the first thing that struck me was that the Chinese are not all Chinese. They don't all look alike. They don't all speak Chinese.

'How do you say hullo?' I asked one driver.

'Joe son,' it sounds like.

I start repeating 'Joe son, joe son, joe son'. Instead of being impressed, she starts giggling. Mandarin has four different tones; Cantonese has nine. Every time I repeated joe son she told me it had a different meaning.

The people are also different. The southern Chinese are the businessmen, the wheeler-dealers. Go into a jewellery shop in Hong Kong, chances are the eager, fluent shop assistant who persuades you to part with HK$10,000 for the latest video camera instead of HK$10 for a Rolex, will be from Guangdong, or some part of southern China. In Guangzhou there is even a thriving white, or I suppose yellow, slave trade. According to the *People's Daily* a number of dealers have been sentenced to death for selling women to farmers in Henan Province in the centre of China. Some farmers can't afford a dowry for their daughters, others can't afford to spend the money looking for a wife. It's the south China logic of the market place.

When I got back to the hotel, an old lady so thin she looked like a corpse which had climbed out of its grave was standing on the kerb shouting at a bus. Some things are the same the world over. As we head for Guangzhou I realise I've only seen one traditional Chinese building the whole length of the New Chinese Washing Machine Way. It was a pagoda.

We cross a river, the largest in the province. The traffic is building up. There are more and more factories, houses and people. We are on the outskirts of Guangzhou. We pass the zoo with its rare panda which pads around its lonely pen, making the occasional somersault and nibbling bamboo shoots. Everybody says he looks unhappy. To me, he seems relaxed, at peace with the world; maybe because, after three million years, most pandas seem to have taken to heart Lord Chesterfield's words to his son – 'The position is ridiculous. The pleasure is momentary. And the expense is damnable.' – and decided to give up lady pandas altogether and lead glorious, uncomplicated bachelor existences much as, a million years ago, they gave up eating meat and became vegetarians.

Forget about Guangzhou and the Opium Wars. Forget about Guangzhou being the hotbed of revolution. (It witnessed the first revolutionary steps of not just Chiang Kaishek, Zhou En Lai but the great Mao Tse-tung himself.) Forget about its obsession with food. (In Guangzhou they eat everything, and every bit of everything – dogs, cats, rats, snakes, heads, toes, tails, and all the unmentionables inside.) Guangzhou is people, people and nothing but people. Any time, any day, it is packed, jam-packed, Guangzhou-packed with people. Every street, every corner, every tiny, jam-packed alleyway.

The Nanga 9 Industrial Zone probably has more workers in four acres than Britain has in the whole country. The Li Po La garment factory, housed in what looks like a large garage with half the wall missing, has more machines in it, working more furiously, more closely together than Birmingham had at the height of the Industrial Revolution.

In the shops, it's a non-stop Harrods sale. Perfect for Chinese washing machine manufacturers. The Friendship Stores look as though they could be more than friendly. There are more shoppers squeezed into a square foot of retail space than in an entire Sainsbury's on Christmas Eve when the frozen turkeys arrive. The shelves are piled high with the fruits of the private sector; shoes from Shanghai, children's clothes from Xiamen and everything else that could fall off a lorry between the factory and the port. The street stalls are packed with fresh fruit and vegetables from private farmers and small one/two-man businesses.

Instead of the old blue Chairman Mao suits, people are wearing Western-style clothes. Instead of revolutionary slogans, the loudspeakers are playing the top of the Chinese pops, 'Hits of the Cultural Revolution', a selection of old revolutionary slogans deifying Mao which have been turned into pop songs. In the Mei Mei barber shop I swear there were so many people you could sit in the chair and the barber could cut somebody else's hair without realising what he was doing.

In the street every spare stretch of brick wall has a newspaper pinned to it giving the latest exciting news about the Leteshi Sports Show and the local song and dance shows. And for every one of the 30,000 characters in the Chinese alphabet, there are a million other Chinese characters reading it. *People's Daily* have on one page an article as big as the Great Wall itself, proclaiming the glories of Marxism. Opposite it is a half-page advertisement for a Sony video cassette recorder.

The roads are choked with traffic. Chong Sun Road, the Oxford Street, Boulevard Hausmann and Fifth Avenue of Guangzhou, is so packed you can't imagine how it can possibly chug, spurt and jerk forward another inch. But it does. An enormous truck looks as though it will spend the rest of its life mesmerised outside a restaurant with a wriggling bowl of live water snakes in the window. But it inches slowly forwards – with two trailers behind it. Two cars with oil drums strapped to the roof look as though they are going to collide. But they move half an inch, another half inch, while the snakes curl and twist and writhe over each other in preparation for lunch. A bus containing happy Chinese holidaymakers back from their three-day summer holiday at the Beeiteng Lake Holiday Village for Peasants, pants slowly along, heading straight for another eighteen-hour day at the factory. Amazingly, in and out of this solid capitalist mass a million bicycles and a couple of thousand motorcycles weave their way at the speed of light oblivious to the danger and the chaos they are causing. And it's like this all day and practically all night.

Confucius only knows why Puccini made all that Nessun dorma fuss about everybody staying awake all night. If he had staged the opera in Canton instead of Beijing there would have been no story because nobody gets any sleep in Canton anyway. So the Chinese are now doing what they always do when they hit problems. They are launching a birth control programme: for cars. The city is jammed to kingdom come. One more Robin Reliant and the whole place would seize up, so now, families are not allowed to have even one car. For bicycles, they have partial birth control. People are allowed to have just one bicycle. But they must get permission first otherwise it's a case of, off your bike.

Everything is beyond my Zen. In search of peace and quiet I head for the Six Banyan Pagoda, which from the outside looks as though it has nine floors but inside actually has seventeen. People are everywhere, Chinese as well as tourists. The Chinese struggle to step over the lip at the door of the Grand Hall, put there to stop monsters from getting in. The tourists rush around panic-stricken for key rings to add to their collections, having already bought all the miniature bottles they can pack on to the top of the mantelpiece. A sign outside says 'It is forbidden to enter a lady even foreign if dressed as gentleman.'

Inside gazing inscrutably down on the throng are Sakya-muni in the centre, Amitabba on the left and Maitreya on the right, the three biggest giant wise men in the province. Some say they are washed down with opium and milk. They certainly look in better condition than all the bronze oxen I've ever seen in Mormon temples.

On one side a group of monks are chanting. An elderly American woman asked her husband – it was the type of temple only elderly married couples would visit – what the monks were chanting. 'I had a good woman but she married Lawrence,' he says. She doesn't say a word.

An eager young Chinese student followed me out into the Banyan Gardens. 'You capitalist?' he says. 'Me capitalist. Not socialist.'

'Great,' I nod, trying to study Liuzu, a giant one-ton statue of an old Buddhist teacher.

'Not socialist. Now capitalist. You capitalist?'

'Church of England,' I mutter.

'Not socialist?'

'Free Church.'

'Capitalist?'

'Salvation Army.'

'Yes. Me capitalist also.' We shake hands. He goes off to make another million.

Behind me now are three old English women living up to Biddlecombe's First Law of Travel: 'Where two or three English travellers gather together they talk about the toilets.'

'You should try Singapore. If you don't flush the toilet when they tell you to they fine you £180.'

'Really!'

'What's more all the lifts are fitted with special urine sensors. The slightest whiff and the door locks tight. There's no escape until an attendant lets you out.'

Eat your heart out, Marco Polo. Not even the Old Chinese Silk Road can rival the New Chinese Washing Machine Way.

Hong Kong

'Quick, quick. The Hang Seng is 2.3% up. Everyone's buying Sun Hung Kai and Cheung. What do you want to do?'

Hit Hong Kong and you hit the ground, not running but racing. The real players are out of the plane as it swoops low over the city for the final approach; it swoops in so low, as soon as they can count the noodles in the bowls being eaten by the Chinese in the skyscrapers surrounding the airport, they're out.

The more restrained players, biting their fingernails, simply wait like greyhounds straining at the leash until after it has banked, plunged sharply to the right, thrown its engines into almost immediate reverse thrust and landed. And the adrenalin doesn't stop pumping until you drag yourself back to Kai Tak Airport shattered and exhausted after the twenty-seven years you have spent in Hong Kong over the previous three days.

For Hong Kong is rip-roaring, undiluted, naked, free-for-all capitalism. It eats, lives, sleeps money. It is money. Lots of money. Hong Kong is one of the world's greatest economic success stories. It is the centre of the Asia Pacific region, the fastest growing region in the world. It is where East meets East as well as where East meets West. And it is easily one of the most exciting cities in the world.

With a population of around 6 million tough, hardworking Chinese, interested only in making money, tiny Hong Kong – it measures just 400 square miles – is the world's eleventh largest trading nation. Amazingly, it is virtually run by a handful of Foreign Office graduates who are forever reminiscing about the dear old 'bedders', male and female, who fussed over them when they were at Emanuel, Magdalene or Corpus Christi between the wars.

Growth is around 5% a year. Unemployment is practically zero. Exports are soaring, re-exports are soaring. They have a trade balance of nearly US$2 billion and massive surpluses.

Kwai Chung is the world's largest container port. Kai Tak is the sixth busiest airport in the world in terms of passengers, handling nearly 20 million a year, and the fourth largest in terms of freight, handling nearly a million tonnes a year. Hong Kong's stock market is the fourth largest in Asia in terms of capitalisation. The colony has over 160 banks, more than anywhere else in the region. It has over 80 luxury hotels and more than 6,000 licensed restaurants, not to mention Buddha knows how many unlicensed ones. It has single shopping complexes that comprise over 120 different shops and cover over 200,000 square feet. It has bustling hi-tech factories working around the clock, a million limousines and probably 2 million mobile telephones.

Hong Kong has the glitter, the glamour, the frenetic, non-stop pace of New York. At first I used to think it was like New York, a Big Apple smothered in sweet and sour. No longer. They are both original cities, both fast-moving and dynamic, but there is a crucial difference.

New York pretends it has a soul. Though Wall Street bankers take their lap-tops to the opera, and are often rifling through their papers before Tosca even lifts her veil, it pretends it is interested in culture, makes out it is concerned with the better things of this life. In Hong Kong they don't bother to pretend. They buy newspapers, read the latest share prices and throw them away. It's a city where everybody seems to play chess in their head, do seven jobs instead of three and earn enough money for six people.

Hong Kong is for grown-ups. Blink once and you miss a deal. Blink twice and you're dead. In Hong Kong their culture is money. 'If Adam and Eve had come from Hong Kong,' I was told by one insider, 'they would have sold the apple and eaten the snake.'

'Sun Hung Kai is now HK$33.50, up another HK$1.25. Cheung Kong is up HK$0.60 to HK$21.20. HSBC is also up HK$1.00 to HK$13.40.'

To me the amazing thing about Hong Kong is that it is actually connected with the British! Yes, the British. Those wonderful people who launched upon an unsuspecting world such things as poor design, bad workmanship, late deliveries and service with a snarl. If Hong Kong had been the product of Chinese or Japanese or American or German efficiency, I could believe it. But the British?

Every time I go there I wander around staring at the enormous skyscrapers, pushing my way through the crowds, visiting super-modern factories, marvelling over the economic statistics. How can the British have created something like Hong Kong? Gibraltar, yes; Accra, definitely; Lagos, most certainly; but Hong Kong? If we can make Hong Kong such a success why can't we do the same thing at home? Turn the UK into an enormous Hong Kong off the coast of Europe?

And what will happen when we hand it over to the Chinese in 1997? The 1984 Sino-British agreement guarantees Hong Kong will remain capitalist for fifty years after 1997. Many people see this as a cast-iron guarantee, but to me it has as much validity as a fortune cookie. What will keep Hong Kong capitalist are the Hong Kongers themselves. No way will anyone change them, not even the Chinese.

What will happen, I'm convinced, is that far from making Hong Kong socialist, Hong Kong will make China capitalist. Already the process has started with Guangdong Province, across the water. Hong Kong has poured its capitalist dollars into the region virtually unchecked. Already there are more than 20,000 Hong Kong-owned factories there, employing 3 million people. And that's before they are officially allowed in.

'Now it looks like its heading for a new peak, it's already up 41% on the same period last year. It was up 6.9% last week. Late buying yesterday took it even higher . . .'

In spite of a British-led government and legal system, Marks & Spencers and, naturally old chap, a British Club, Hong Kong – or Honkers as we say in the Club – is still the biggest Chinatown in the world.

Sure, the skyscrapers, the non-stop traffic, the lights, the never-ending din, wall-to-wall people, remind you of Manhattan. But look again. Across Victoria Harbour is the Kowloon Peninsula and Tsim Sha Tsui, the most spectacular and the most honest shopping centre in the world. 'Imitation Rolex, sir?' three over-enthusiastic young Chinese salesmen rushed up to me as soon as I got off the Star Ferry. 'Sure,' I said. 'I'll give you imitation dollars, okay?'

Behind Kowloon is the New Territories. Behind that is China, brooding like a mass of noodles inching itself slowly nearer.

Now look again. China is already in Hong Kong: in the rickshaws, in the joss sticks, in the temples. On the floating sampan restaurants, in the junks in Victoria Harbour, squeezed between towering office blocks are stalls and street markets open till past midnight selling peacock shoes, eelskin wallets and chicken feet ties. Perched perilously on top of flyovers are gnarled, crippled old women who can probably still remember the day Mao Tse-tung first went to school, pushing their *dim sum* trolleys carelessly through the traffic. Underneath the flyover at Canal Road, hunched over a board, Chinese men and women are playing some mysterious game as if their life depended on it. Which it probably does. Between the *dai pai dong* foodstalls in Temple Street market wizened old men are squatting in the gutters sniffing something suspicious. While I was there one evening a boy of two or three crawled between the stalls singing 'Old Macdonald had a Farm' in Chinese, or something remarkably like it.

In Nathan Road on Kowloon outside the Yue Hwa Chinese Emporium which sells practically everything not made in China such as genuine Chanel, Helena Rubinstein, Cartier watches and Ralph Laurens, an old monk is sitting in the street giving advice to a queue of Chinese. In the Can-do restaurant along Hennessey Road, the young man in a brown coat sitting at the next table eating his vegetarian bean curd roll stands up at the end of his meal to reveal a saffron robe. He is a monk.

Wander around Wanchai on Hong Kong Island, Susie Wong's old haunt, and you are as likely to be accosted by an old Chinese beggar with a plastic mug as you are by a young lady who wants to improve her English. Whether it's just after breakfast, before lunch or late at night after a serious business meeting over four bottles of Johnnie Walker.

And talking of taking risks, everybody in Hong Kong is a gambler. You can bet me as much money as you like, everybody gambles on everything, from the stock market to the horses. Hong Kong gambles more money on horses, over £600 a year for every man, woman and child in the country, than any other place in the world. And this is serious Chinese money for winning. There are more than thirty racing newspapers analysing not just the usual form but also the length of time horses are in training. 'For you, it's a gamble,' I was told. 'For us, it's an investment.'

They also gamble for business. One favourite game is *tin sin kuk*, the perfect set up. You find an innocent businessman and persuade him to play *chong yuan tan*, some mysterious Chinese game which, of course, he loses. Then you offer him a chance to get his money back. He says he hasn't any more money. You say, that's okay, borrow the money from your company. He hesitates. You say, tell you what, because of the risk, if you win we'll place a big, big order with your company which will give you your money back and make you a company hero as well. He falls for it, borrows the money and puts the champagne on ice. You take the money and run. What can the businessman do? He is too embarrassed to go to the police. He spends the rest of his life wandering across Wanchai with a plastic mug.

But, cross my palm with silver, nobody ever gambles with their health. Everybody seems to be a health food freak. Hong Kong may be wall-to-wall people but that means it is wall-to-wall doctors, herbalists, acupuncturists and little old men with packets of white powder. You've got a problem? Thousands of people in Hong Kong can solve it for you. Feeling poorly? How about a mixture of snakeskin, dried silk worms and forty other equally appealing ingredients, mixed into a thick paste to be taken morning and evening, six to eight weeks only every year.

'Silk worms give glow to skin, balance yin and yang forces,' an old Chinese doctor sitting by a stall in Nathan Street told me. I would have bought a couple of tons, but he looked like a refined lizard. His head kept jutting backwards and forwards, his skin was dark and wrinkly and he kept jumping quickly from one end of his stall to the other.

Need something a little stronger? An old lady with two boxes outside the Supreme Court is selling gallstones. Gallstones? You'd be amazed what you can do with gallstones, especially in Hong Kong. Providing, of course, they are not dried in sunlight which burns them and destroys any good they can do. They range from the size of pigeons' eggs to chicken's eggs and cost over £6.50 per gram. You buy now. From now on always you feel velly well, Chinese promise.

A herbalist, Mr Poon Ping Kor of the Cheng Wo Medicine Co in Jubilee Street, Central, told me after I'd downed a mountain of fried vermicelli with chillis and minced pork, that I had too much *yitheh*, internal body heat. He suggested a foot massage, which sounded suspect, like suggesting talcum powder as a cure for piles. Instead I went for the mixture of ginseng, roses and camellias.

Off a sidestreet off a sidestreet in Mong Kok, the most densely populated part of Hong Kong and perhaps the world, I was told there was a dentist who, when he was not performing operations in the street, could conduct a symphony with tooth picks inside his mouth. In fact, I was told there is one shop where you can actually buy kidneys taken from prisoners executed in China.

If I was going native I think I'd prefer *t'ai chi ch'uan*, or *t'ai chi* for short, to anything they sell in the White Fungus Health Food Shop. An ancient Chinese tradition, it is slow-motion meditation. Shoes off, jacket off, undo your tie, stand still. Slowly lift your arms in front of you, wrists on top. At shoulder height, stop. Turn your hands around and twiddle your fingers back to your side again. Now do it again, and again. Now pivot your heels, rotate your hips and take one step forward. It's almost like swimming standing up.

Ten minutes a day, I was told, are enough to keep you sane. But you can go for the ultimate and practise such exotic exercises as White Stork Spreads Wings and Strike the Tiger, which take about thirty minutes to complete. Like learning to play golf, I've never had the time to get beyond the basic preliminaries even though every *t'ai chi* enthusiast I've met claimed it would give me the strength of a lumberjack, the flexibility of a child and the wisdom of a philosopher.

You can scoff: I did as well, until the Chinese banker again told me that in China people pay their doctor if they are well, and don't pay if they are sick. 'Why should we? If we are sick, he is not doing his job. He does not deserve to be paid,' he said, gulping down what looked like a handful of gallstones.

'Inflation is falling. Corporate earnings are up and likely to increase further next year. Foreign money is ready to pour in. It must hit 7,500 before long.'

Quick. Make certain your office is facing the right way. If not, you've got big problems. Check the building next door. If the windows are reflecting back on you, hang a small *ba-gua* mirror surrounded by hexagrams on the outside wall. It will ward off bad luck. Still not working? Hang a couple of wind chimes next to the mirror. And for goodness' sake never paint the whole skirting board. Always leave a corner free. Painting the whole board will mean you are striving for perfection and upset the gods.

Hong Kong is ruled by one thing – no, not money, although that is almost as important. It is ruled by *feng shui*, an ancient Chinese mystery which says that everything is governed by the laws of wind and water, the flow of *ch'i*, the life force. Put a clock in the wrong place and you block off the flow of *ch'i*. Put up the wrong building in the wrong place and you risk blocking off a whole flood of *ch'i*. Crazy? Don't you believe it. *Feng shui* is serious stuff. When the Hong Kong and Shanghai Bank were planning their new headquarters in Queens Road, Central, they called in a *feng shui* master as part of the design team. His advice: the front of the building should face south, the rear should look out on the mountains and it should be the tallest building in the area.

They did exactly as he said. Except that while it was being built in the early 1980s the two bronze lions guarding its entrance had to be put in storage. What happened? Hong Kong was hit by one currency crisis after another, banks collapsed, and the UK handed the colony over to the Chinese. Now do you believe me?

When the seventy-storey Bank of China, the most important Chinese financial operation in Hong Kong, which is controlled more or less directly from Beijing, was completed in 1988 everybody believed its mirror walls were reflecting the evil spirits their way. Even the Governor planted a tree in his garden nearby to ward off the spirits.

Going for an interview? Negotiating a deal? Hoping to sign a contract? Consult your local *feng shui* master. Some days are good days, some are bad. If you really need help he will not only tell you the best day, he'll probably also give you a good luck piece of paper which he has psychically charged and scrawled with magic symbols. But if you insist on going on the fourth you're on your own. Four is *sei*, which means death.

Watch a Chinese being allocated a room anywhere in the world on the forty-fourth floor and you'll see the same reaction many people have about being seated in row thirteen on a plane. I know one Chinese businessman who even counts the windows outside the hotel to make certain the number of floors inside corresponds with the number of windows outside. Everybody goes for three, eight and nine, the good luck figures. Three, apparently, sounds like the word for life, eight for wealth, nine for long life.

I was in Hong Kong once with the director of a big French-based international engineering group. We were in the Man Wah restaurant on the top floor of the Mandarin. Don't worry, I checked the windows. We were watching the *tai fei* making their illegal nightly smuggling trips backwards and forwards to the Chinese coast. The giant Pacific prawns were doing a Duke of Clarence in a delicate basin of madeira in the middle of the table. Waiters were gathering for the precise moment to serve them. We had prudently ordered a mixture of *yin*, cool foods and *yang*, hot foods and *yin*, chilled white wine and *yang*, 'hot' cognacs. As the waiters served the director four giant prawns, he leant across the table.

'I've been demoted,' he said. 'They've given my job to Antoine.'

'Wasn't he the one who failed in personnel?' I asked.

He nodded, and swallowed a prawn.

'And was then put in charge of America and failed again?'

He nodded, and stabbed another prawn. 'Now he's got my job.'

'So what are you going to do?' I asked.

'What can I do? It's just crazy. Nobody can believe it. Even the girls in the office keep saying it's not possible. It's a joke. All the managers who used to report to me have been ringing up saying they're not going to take any notice. They're going to continue reporting to me. It's crazy.' I could see the Star Ferry going backwards and forwards between Kowloon and Wanchai. 'What's more he hasn't even got an office. When he came back from the States he sat in the general office with the girls, and he's still there. None of us see why we should give up our offices for him.'

'So what's going to happen?'

He swallowed another prawn.

The following morning, over my first Hong Kong power breakfast at 7am I heard more from one of his colleagues. 'Apparently the chairman told him he was going to tell him something which would be very difficult to accept and he didn't want him going round the office making jokes about it. He said he wouldn't. Then they told him.'

'How did he take it?'

'He couldn't believe it. He still can't. He thinks it's a joke.'

'So why did they do it?'

'*Feng shui.*'

'You're kidding.'

'He's the only one who doesn't believe it. When the Bank

of China building went up we all said it was sending evil spirits in our direction. We put blinds up in the windows, plants, that kind of thing. He didn't, so he was demoted.'

'It's up 386 points in a week. It's unbelievable. You've got to get in now.'

Hong Kong may be Chinese – expats will tell you the Chinese already have a secret army in Hong Kong just waiting for the signal to rise against the *gweilos*, a not unaffectionate name for their white colonial masters – but its way of doing business is, thank God, definitely British. Unlike many parts of the world, Hong Kong even believes in punctuality, down to the minute on your counterfeit Rolex. From the moment you begin counting birds' nests on the roof as well as on people's plates in the surrounding buildings as the plane comes in to land, everything for business is organised and re-organised to the minute, if not the second.

Cars – I mean, limousines – are waiting to whisk you off to your hotel. The Peninsula Hotel, as colonial as a white suit and plumed hat, is a favourite of old-time company chairmen doing their annual tour of inspection of the south-east Asian corner of their empire. Famous for serving tea on the Veranda Lounge, it is terribly Empire, known to old Far East hands as the Pen. The Regent Hotel on Kowloon is a favourite among jogging chief executives who head for the Tsim Sha Tsui waterfront; one of the world's best jogging routes. At least that's what I'm told. The Grand Hyatt on One Harbour Road in Wanchai boasts not only the best Chinese-Italian restaurant in Hong Kong but also JJ's, the best nightclub in Hong Kong. Which, of course, I've never had time to visit.

At the grande deluxe Mandarin, if you're a regular you don't even have to check in. You just drift through reception with your lap-top computer, receive a courtly bow from the manager, enter the lift which is always waiting and ascend gently to your suite where your luggage is unpacked, drinks served and your every whim pandered to. There is even a notepad and pencil by the telephone. In the bathroom. Some suites, it is said, even have monogrammed fax paper. There will also be a table booked for you in the Man Wah restaurant on the top floor, the best expensive Chinese restaurant in Hong Kong. If you drop the slightest hint they will eat that delicate selection of cuttle fish, satay, fish floss, fish stomach and red melon seeds for you as well.

Junior US marketing managers who still feel guilty about leaving the Peace Corps check in to the guesthouse at Po Lin Monastery on Lantau Island. For HK$15 a day you not only get three vegetarian meals a day, cold and not-so-cold running water and communal bathrooms, but the tallest outdoor Buddha in the world. Asia's answer to the Statue of Liberty, it is 26 metres high, 53 metres in diameter, covers an area the equivalent of half a football pitch and incorporates an ancestral hall as well as its own exhibition centre.

But, *pace* the Peace Corps, most business hotels not only boast an average four staff to every guest, they provide twenty-four-hour room service, laser disc players and even a fax machine in your own room. Hong Kong as a result is power breakfasts, power lunches, power dinners and probably power glasses of whisky and hot milk at three in the morning. The emphasis is on business, Carruthers, non-stop business.

Business meetings are just that, whether at breakfast, lunch or dinner. Even a cup of tea on the Veranda Lounge is business. The Chinese are just not interested in golf handicaps, where you're going on holiday or photographs of your daughter on her first pony. They want to do business: during the week, running from one meeting to another; with their mobile 'phones out shopping with the family on Sunday mornings; or wolfing down beggar's chicken, the colony's most famous dish, while waiting for the Star Ferry.

Over dinner in the Man Wah nobody talks about art, literature or, thank God, Princess Di. Everybody is discussing the stock market and the Hang Seng Index, and timing the *tai fei*, the jet-propelled speedboats which, powered by up to six 300hp outboard engines, can go at over 70 mph, and which busily smuggle goods through the South China Sea and into mainland China – televisions, video recorders, air-conditioners. Each boat, which has to outmanoeuvre the Hong Kong police as well as the Chinese, can carry up to £10,000 of goods at a time, which is worth double as soon as it is unloaded. In a night, with good luck and the right friends, each *tai fei* can make the one-hour journey three or four times.

They are so efficient, and so good at making friends, they even smuggle Mercedes cars. What's more, when the super-efficient Hong Kong police trap them, inefficient, badly equipped Chinese police suddenly appear and prevent them from seizing the cars or arresting anybody. The super-efficient, law-abiding Hong Kong police back off. The smugglers escape to smuggle another day. The Chinese police disappear. And some top Chinese official who frowns on the evils of capitalism in Hong Kong gets a Mercedes.

Trouble is nobody believes the Chinese police are Chinese police except the Hong Kong police. The Dragon Heads or Triad Chiefs, Hong Kong's all-powerful mafia gangs who run the smuggling operation, are virtually above the law. At least Hong Kong law. How they fare under their own legal system seems to be their very private affair, apart from the occasional bombing of a restaurant or club which goes wrong and involves innocent by-standers. People say there are fifty different gangs or societies, but nobody really knows.

Thanks to the British, Hong Kong is suit, collar and tie country, especially among the Chinese business community who tend to be more *gweilo* than the *gweilos*. Not for them the backslapping Hi Chuck howayatoday bonhomie of the casual

Americans. Instead it's the formal handshake, a touch of reserve and ever so conservative suits, collar and tie. Preferably black. Be warned, blue suits are for funerals, not for wheeling and dealing.

> 'It's the Chinese New Year next week. There is always a
> bull market at the New Year. You can't lose.'

The middle of Victoria, Hong Kong's capital, on a Sunday morning is just as noisy as on any other day of the week. Except that instead of the constant roar of traffic there is the twittering of millions of tiny Filipino housemaids. From every apartment, bungalow and home they descend like a cloud of locusts on Statue Square, in the gardens around the Legislative Square, along by the Star Ferry, sitting on the pavement, gazing at shop windows, laughing and giggling along the road.

There are so many the streets have to be closed to traffic. So great is their chattering and giggling that early morning even high in the Mandarin behind air-conditioned windows it sounds like an enormous human dawn chorus.

With the maid having her day off, what else is there to do but go shopping? But first of all I decided to go to Mass. I asked the concierge at the Mandarin for the nearest Catholic church. He looked at me as a Catholic would look at a Buddhist asking for the nearest temple. It was the only time I've ever known the Mandarin to be less than Mandarin perfect. I grabbed a *South China Morning Post.* In the Church Notices section I spotted the Catholic Centre Chapel in Connaught Road about three blocks away. It turned out to be a huddle of rooms in an office block sandwiched between Ying Kong Enterprises, Hong Kong Paper Mills and a Vietnamese restaurant.

The entrance on the ground floor was packed with a thousand Filipino maids also doing their duty before enjoying their day off. The lift, which was made for ten people, must have had thirty in it before I squeezed in. When we reached the floor of the chapel, it was so packed that I thought I would hear Mass going up and down in the lift all morning. But somehow I felt myself propelled through the crowd to the centre of the chapel. There was a lot of giggling. But you can't turn round and walk out because you don't like the people you're going to Mass with. In any case the crowd seemed thicker behind me so I probably couldn't have escaped even if I had wanted.

As it happened I was glad I stayed. Mass was said in Fili Fili, the Philippine national language, which has a curious sing-song lilt. The singing was beautiful, almost haunting. At the end of Mass, when everybody sang 'Amazing Grace' in Fili Fili, it seemed to drift across the chapel, genuflect in front of the altar and soar direct to heaven. The trouble was the sermon. The priest was obviously a cynical, twisted Filipino–American with a warped sense of humour.

'Now I want every young lady here today,' he said, staring above the heads of the congregation directly at me, 'to open her handbag, ignore her make-up, take out her purse and ask herself, do I covet my neighbour? Do I covet my neighbour's goods?' I looked at the red hat with the feather on the not-so-young Filipino maid in front of me and decided it was the last thing I would covet. 'Now, my little sisters,' he leered again at me, 'we must ask ourselves, do we serve our masters faithfully and without reservation? It is not a sin to obey. It is often a sin to disobey. Can we do more in the kitchen? Can we help more with the children? Could I volunteer to do the shopping?'

I could hear my Filipino sisters beginning to giggle again. But suddenly another liftful of late comers was disgorged into the room, forcing us to shuffle up another three-quarters of a millimetre to let them all in. By the time we'd stopped shuffling, the sermon was over.

Afterwards I went shopping. Many businessmen, as soon as they hit Hong Kong, make for Stanley on the far southern edge of the island; in the markets there you can pick up all the brand-name clothes at half the price of anywhere else. Practically everybody in town works for the big textile companies; they buy the seconds for next to nothing from their companies then sell them on for cash in the markets at weekends.

Kowloon is nothing but shops, millions of them – at street level, on the first floor, on the second floor, probably on the roof as well. They sell everything, from gold chains thinner than a human hair to great slabs of rolled gold. Suits are made to measure in six hours. One shop on the fourth floor of a crumbling block behind the Tuxe Top Co Ltd was hiring out tuxedos. On the same corridor was what was obviously a Chinese sweat shop, producing in a day probably more than the gross national product of Africa, and an Indian restaurant. Further along were flats and warehouses.

'You want copy Rolex?'

'Already got one.'

How about tortoise deer wine? Or natural birch juice? Or, if you prefer, ginseng wine, or male kinetic energy tonic? No? Then how about steamed pigeon hearts, turtle jelly or swallow nest double boiled with chicken? Maybe some snake soup containing five different types of snake to thicken the blood and heat the body in preparation for winter?

And I've never seen so many gadgets in my life: calculator radio transmitters, two-way fountain pens, telephone sockets that divert calls to wherever you want in the world. Shops in Granville Road on Kowloon seem to have sold out of electronic items and gadgets which haven't even reached the UK yet and probably never will.

Normally, I never go shopping. An ordinary window display in Oxford Street throws me. In Kowloon my head reels, my eyes buzz. I have no idea what's genuine or fake, what's a good price or what isn't, whether genuine jade is green with a purple tinge or purple with a tinge of green. In panic, I flee to Wong Tai Sin, the gamblers' temple.

Dedicated to a famous healer and health freak, it was apparently credited with being able to forecast good luck. The temple and courtyard are always packed with crowds bringing pictures of racehorses, sports cars, even yachts to burn in front of the Buddha. Some create proper models which they then burn obviously to hammer home their point. In spite of all this burning, it's supposed to be a no smoking temple.

I was about to get on the mass transit railway (MTR), when I discovered a two-storey shopping mall alongside the temple, packed with little booths where you have your palm, your face, your feet or even the bumps on your head read by experts just dying to tell you whether you're going to be lucky.

Instead I headed for Repulse Bay. Everybody and their grandmother was there to pay their respects to the gods of wealth and pat the big pink buddha on his black belly for luck. It is black because it has been patted so often. Repulse Bay gets so crowded at weekends that the local Chinese call it Excuse-me Bay. The big attraction is not the splendid beach, but the temples on one corner of it. I've never seen so many temples packed so closely together.

There are temples or shrines to the god of wealth and the god of prosperity. There is the Horse of Longevity presented by Lion Andrew So Chin Yu 'President of the Tai Ping Shan Lion Club 1987–88'. Leading to it is the Bridge of Longevity, which is not so busy. Nearby is the Pavilion of Longevity. All around them are big queues of people waiting to pat the statues on the head or rub whichever part of them takes their fancy.

The enthusiasts go for the eyes. Some Chinese donate eyes to statues – hoping, no doubt, that the spirits will see them all right. Others have it done for them. 'Mr P. Graham and Mrs P.

Graham and Mr and Mrs O.L. Millar of Chartered Bank'
sponsored a marathon lifesaving race back in 1969. For their
labours, they had an Imperial Lion 'instated' for them. It makes
you wonder how the sponsorship manager of the Hong Kong
and Shanghai Bank should be honoured if the same standard
applied today.

'Can't stop. There are rumours that Chinese money from
the mainland is now pouring in.'

Whatever your plans, the last day is always a typical Hong
Kong day. Unless, of course, your yin is out of balance with
your yang. Breakfast at 7 am. Four morning meetings. A quick
traditional four-course Chinese lunch: boiled bamboo pith
with yellow fungus in egg drop shark fin soup; deep-fried
pork spare ribs marinated with Chinese spices wrapped in a
paper bag; double-boiled superior bird's nest with crystal
sugar in coconut juice with bird saliva as an extra and all
washed down with pigeon-smoked camphor wood and tea
leaves. To make certain everything arrived on time in perfect
condition, the waiters had mobile phones to keep in contact
with the kitchens.

Then on the fantastic MTR – underground to you and me –
for another meeting in Tsim Sha Tsui, and back to the
Mandarin for a farewell dinner with Antoine's predecessor.
The prawns had done their final Clarence trick and were being
served.

'I didn't tell you,' he said. 'I've got my old job back.'

'How come? I thought . . .'

'So did I. But the other guy took the blame for us not hitting
our figures. Paris fired him. Shareholders were demanding
action. Somebody had to take the blame. Paris was having a
bad year. Everything was down. They wanted some good
figures.'

'You mean . . .?'

'It happens. They got the chairman here to deliberately inflate his forecasts to get them out of a hole.'

'But I thought that was—'

'Of course it is. But what was he going to do? A few years off retirement, big pension coming up, lots of hidden bonuses, non-executive directorships. Come on.'

'So why all the changes?'

'We're not going to hit the figures. Market's collapsed. Now everyone is saying how can you forecast such big figures and then in a couple of months fail to deliver?'

'So someone had to take the blame.'

He smiled.

'And certainly not the chairman.'

I looked down at his plate; eight prawns were smiling up at him, in perfect formation for fending off bad spirits.

Tokyo

Taxis with automatic doors and televisions inside showing sixteen channels. Trains that not only arrive on time but also stop at exactly the same spot every time so that passengers actually form a queue to get on. Department stores with assistants who not only greet you with a bow but are actually interested in serving you. Hotels where room service rings up to see if there is anything you require; barmen who are polite and friendly; receptionists who know your name and the person you are visiting.

Barbers who offer to clean your ears as well as cut your hair, whose chairs have special arms to ensure that the gown around your shoulders catches the hair and stops it cascading all over the floor. Clothes with their own prepaid dry cleaning credit cards. Take a suit to the dry cleaners (computerised, of course) and punch the garment's number into the terminal. It not only cleans it for you, it works out the cost and automatically deducts it from the clothing manufacturer's account.

Golf tees made by a company called Toss Planning that will self-destruct if left behind or lost on a golf course. And, please don't laugh, toilet bowls that tell you if you're suffering from any embarrassing diseases and, if so, which ones.

The Japanese, you must admit, are amazing. Every time I go to Japan I am staggered by their whole inscrutable concept of service, and the amazing standard and extent of the service everyone seems eager to provide.

I'm convinced it's partly to do with Japanese culture, which is geared wholly to the other person. They are honoured if they can bow lower than, and demonstrate their respect to, somebody else. They feel privileged if they can talk to someone for four days without disagreeing with them. They are flattered to be asked to run up twenty-three flights of stairs with a cup of coffee and an orange for your breakfast. And if they can't guarantee to do that at 3 o'clock in the morning they will put a slot machine outside your door so it's there if you want it. Only in Japan would you find temple paintings that look out of perspective – until you kneel down.

It's partly because of their absolute dedication to detail and their beautiful economy of style. We all know the Japanese sense of style and rhythm in everything from placing a single flower in a slim vase to sumo wrestling. But watch a Toyota engineer on a clapped-out clockwork machine in a modern eighteenth-century Midlands' engineering works demonstrating the Japanese way of making motor components and you see the same concentration, rhythm, economy of movement and gentle organisation, dedicated to cutting down wasted effort and achieving maximum productivity. In twenty-three seconds he gets a much, much better component than the one produced in two minutes thirty-three seconds by the British operator who had been using the machine since Stevenson was a boy.

Partly it's because they are Shinto. The Shinto religion, as practised by the Japanese, is a mixture of superstition, goodwill, courtesy, patience and St Luke's Golden Rule writ backwards. They honestly seem to believe it is better to give than to receive, to honour than be honoured. Or rather to receive than give, to be honoured than to honour. You know what I mean.

Tokyo car-hire companies, for example, ensure that if a

pedestrian suddenly walks in front of one of their cars, the driver reacts correctly. 'When the paddenger of foot leave in sight, tootle the horn,' read a sticker alongside the steering wheel in one car I hired. 'Trumpet him melodiously at first but if he still obstacles your passage then tootle him with vigour.'

I'm also convinced it's partly because of the unique conjunction at the end of the war of a proud nation of largely crow-eating rice growers, peasants and farmers sitting on a pile of rocks and volcanoes, desperate to rebuild itself, and General Douglas MacArthur. Japan, I believe, is the enormous success it is today because of the combination of traditional Japanese culture and American marketing techniques. Traditional culture puts the other person first because the other person must always be put first. American marketing puts the other person first because he is the customer, the man with the money, he is the guy you've got to persuade to come across otherwise you'll go out of business. It's because these two philosophies came together at a crucial time, when Japan was rebuilding the fabric of its society, that the country has been so successful. Do you honestly believe that if MacArthur had been a Belgian, or a New Zealander, Japan would be what it is today? It is this blend of Japanese and American philosophy that has made Japan a unique paradise for quality and service – except for one thing. They don't have any photocopy shops.

One of my first trips to Japan was with a big African Development Bank delegation, trying to persuade the Japanese to increase their investment in Africa. I had prepared all the documentation: investment opportunities in Africa; rules and regulations; an analysis of Japanese investment throughout the world; a comprehensive 250-page briefing on Japan itself, its economy, foreign investment policies and incentives. I was going to prepare everything in London and ship the lot to Tokyo in time for the arrival of the delegation. Then it struck me. Organising a mission to Tokyo is not like organising a mission to Ouagadougou, or even Birmingham. Tokyo is the most organised, the most hi-tech city in the world. I decided to take the top copies with me and photocopy and spiral-bind everything when I arrived. It was more straightforward, and would save a lot of money. Documentation for the twenty members of the delegation, plus twenty hangers-on, as well as for the Japanese, apart from utilising a couple of rain forests, was going to cost a fortune to ship halfway round the world.

So what happened when I arrived? 'Photocopy shop? Sorry, we don't have photocopy shop in Japan,' the receptionist at the Okura Hotel, probably the best if not the most expensive hotel in Tokyo, told me. 'But ask at the Business Centre. They will know.'

'No photocopy shop in Tokyo,' the very smart manager of the Business Centre in his morning coat told me. 'Everybody buy machines direct. You want to buy machine?'

'No I don't want to buy machine. I have lots of documents which I want to photocopy. Do you have shop for photocopying documents?' He stared at me. 'A Fuji Xerox shop. A Xerox Shop. A shop for . . .' He grabbed the Tokyo Yellow Pages and flicked through it like a fundamentalist preacher searching for a quote to damn you to the eternal fires (St Matthew VII, 12). 'No photocopy shop in Tokyo,' he smiled in triumph. The Yellow Pages had proved him right. He had satisfied himself and his ancestors that he was providing the best possible service to his client. But it wasn't helping me.

'Okay,' I said as inscrutably as I could. 'Give me the address of the Tokyo office for Xerox. I'll ask them.' I grabbed the address and ran for a cab. If there were no photocopy shops in Tokyo how was I going to produce copies of the documentation for the mission? Which was arriving the following day. The taxi crept through central Tokyo.

Tokyo is bang up-to-date and, apart from one or two spectacular office blocks, such as Century Tower designed by our very own Norman Foster, almost faceless. It is also very, very expensive. Gone are the days when the young Rudyard Kipling could march into a Japanese bank, slap a cheque down on the counter and walk out with £10 to pay for his honeymoon. The most expensive meal I've ever had was in a traditional Japanese restaurant just down the road from the Okura Hotel. There were four of us. We didn't have anything spectacular. We only drank beer and sake. The bill came to a definitely non-traditional £1,000.

In spite, or maybe because of that, it's really the ultimate in business cities. It's lean, it's functional, it's clean, it's polite. There could be a million people walking down any Tokyo street: nobody pushes, or tries to barge past you. Nobody will even touch you. Except in the subway, which is a different world – rough, tough, elbows to the fore, and to aft and port and starboard. While I was on one trip the Tokyo newspapers were full of stories about a middle-aged man who died of a heart attack in a crowded rush-hour train. And nobody noticed. He did two complete circuits before, five hours later, it was discovered that he was dead.

On the other hand, Tokyo couldn't be safer. It's the ultimate machine for doing business in. And in spite of the unbelievable traffic jams – average traffic speed is just 17 kph – everything works. On time. Efficiently. No hang-ups. No excuses.

Even the slot machines work, and does Tokyo have slot machines. Japan has more slot machines than any other country, with one for every twenty people, compared to one for every 200 people in Europe. I know, I've tried them all. They sell everything from Coke to whisky, from meat pies to watches. At the Kabuki Theatre, for example, you can hardly get into the building for the slot machines in reception, up the stairs, along the balcony. In any street, in between a thousand little shops and stalls selling everything from souvenirs to genuine Kabuki hotdogs, there are millions of machines. I even spotted one selling Unicharm nappies for old people. Which, now I remember, was the one I didn't try.

The other thing that strikes me about Tokyo is that you never ever see an old car. They are all brand shiny new, even the brand-new 1950-style Minis which, for some reason, are very popular with the *nijuu-ritchi*, the Japanese yuppies and young housewives. Partly because the traffic is so bad. There are fewer than 15 metres of road for every car in the country – not enough space. One Japanese institute has worked out that it would take less than 2% of all Japanese cars to fill the country's 5,000 kilometres of motorway – parked nose to tail.

Besides, every three years every car has to undergo a *Shaken*, a Japanese-style MOT test which, in a country which produces probably the most reliable cars in the world, is inevitably far more comprehensive and thorough than anything our Ministry of Transport could dream up. As a result, most cars are sold before they have to face the *Shaken*, when they have on average fewer than 12,500 miles on the clock.

Nevertheless, for all Tokyo's up-to-date, clean – you never see any litter – efficiency, it is not a carbon copy of anything. It is still 100% Japanese.

Of course you see millions of slightly old-fashioned Brookes Brothers suits pouring out of the trains as well as the occasional *shinjinrui* (modern manager) who not only dresses like a *gaijin* (a foreigner) but acts like one too. Sure you see thousands of elegant *sumuaatos* tripping along the Ginza and having coffee or a soft, sweet drink called, would you believe, Pocari Sweat, in Mitsukoshi and other fashionable department stores that make Harrods look like Woolworth's.

But even on scorching August days, with temperatures up to 33°C, you also suddenly see trotting along the pavement the plastered white faces, the piles of jet black shining hair and the kimonos of traditional Japan that look as though they are as thick as two short planks and weigh twice as much. Alongside them are invariably little old men who always look like the old Emperor Hirohito's brother-in-law, wearing morning suits that could have come from an Oxfam shop.

Even the way they count is different. When we count on our fingers we start with the thumb. The Japanese end with the thumb. I'm convinced that behind all the big modern office blocks there is still hidden away the real Tokyo, the world of ancient rituals, elaborate ceremonies, silence, peace, everlasting contentment.

In the US you get the impression that behind every McDonald's is another McDonald's. In Tokyo, I feel that behind every wall is a traditional garden and a contemplative monk deep in prayer.

Forget the tea ceremony; the most elaborate, stylised Japanese ritual of all is the Japanese business meeting ceremony. The inscrutable Japanese have turned the quick chinwag by the photocopier into the commercial equivalent of the *dohyo-iri*, the ring-entering ceremony at the start of a sumo wrestling competition. In Japan a quick chinwag is out. A business meeting is for real. Short of the Lord Buddha himself turning up at the door with his Walkman blaring, nothing could be more important. This is high ceremony.

None of this turning up late, grabbing a chair and sprawling over the table. Every meeting has to be conducted according to an age-old ritual. First, the introduction ceremony. It takes longer to seat everybody at a routine Japanese meeting than it does at a French wedding. Should the *kacho*, or chairman, take precedence or should the chief executive? Should the younger but more senior export manager sit further up the table than the older but non-executive former chairman who has just been appointed chairman of the French subsidiary so that he can take three round-the-world trips a year on expenses as a retirement perk?

The Japanese Minister of Foreign Affairs had a heart attack when the former Dutch prime minister, Mr van Agt, was appointed the EC's ambassador in Tokyo. Should he be given the precedence and honour accorded a prime minister and one, surprisingly to the Japanese, untainted in any way by corruption? Or should he be dumped at the end of the table with the other ambassadors? The solution was typically Japanese. When he attended any meeting or ceremony on his own he was to be treated as a former prime minister. When he appeared with other ambassadors, he was to be treated as an ambassador.

Finally everybody is seated. Now the meeting begins. Not on your life. Next there is the official speech of welcome ceremony. Every name must be mentioned, everybody has to be honoured. You smile. You then all get up and shake hands again with everyone in turn. The Japanese keep nodding and saying, *hai hai*. Do they mean *hai hai*? Or do they mean, hi hi? At last you sit down exhausted. Your hand aches. You're desperately trying to remember who is who; who is the guy you've got to smile at and who is the go-for?

At one meeting I got so confused after all the handshaking that I sat down in the wrong chair. Did the *sushi* hit the fan? The salaryman next to me sat down in the wrong chair, presumably to cover my mistake. So did everybody else in turn, until the only person left standing was the company chairman. Did they move when they saw him helplessly staring at the table wondering why the earth had moved for the wrong reason?

At last everyone is seated. Now the meeting begins – if, by now, you haven't forgotten why you travelled halfway round the world and spent a million pounds on staying at the most expensive hotel in the world and eating quick snacks for what at home would buy three numerical machine tools, Japanese of course. Does it hell. Now comes the *meishi*, Japanese exchange business cards ceremony. The chairman puts his hand in his jacket pocket and takes out an elegant twenty-four-carat gold business card holder from which he neatly extracts a tiny envelope of exquisite tissue with a watermark of the company's logo running through it. He unfolds the envelope, extracts a card, refolds the tissue in exactly the same folds, places it back in the holder and puts the holder back in his pocket. He then leans across the table and presents his card to you.

You fumble in your back trouser pocket, grab your thick, lumpy, greasy wallet and plomp it down on the table. Your bus pass falls out revealing a photograph of an inane lager lout hunched inside a photo booth at East Croydon station. You open it up. Three weeks' parking tickets at Gatwick Airport slip across the table in all directions. You struggle to pull your single business card from between your driving licence and your National Trust annual pass for 1967. The corners are all bent. You suddenly remember it doesn't include your fax number. You grab your leaky biro from your other pocket, scribble on the card and, you think with triumph, lean across and hand it to the chairman.

Okay, so now you begin the ... Not on your ... Everybody else now produces business card holders of different quality and finish. Those wrapped in tissue are unwrapped and the tissue neatly rewrapped. The cards are then handed to you. Those not in tissue are held gently back to be handed over when it is their turn. Not before. By now, of course, you're cursing the print department for not giving you enough cards. You're cursing the finance director for cutting the print department's budget so they couldn't have given you the cards even if they had wanted to. And you're cursing the export director's wife for causing so much fuss about his being away a mere 360 days a year that you were sent instead.

At last all the cards are distributed. You shuffle the pack you've collected, look round the table and desperately write little notes on them in a vain bid to link names and faces, hoping that the Japanese sitting opposite cannot read upside-down in English the rude comments you are scribbling about him and his lifelong friends and colleagues. You're safe, he can't. But everybody is looking at you. Of course, Confucius he say, you must not scribble little notes on business cards when Japanese sitting with you at meeting. Velly bad manners Japanese.

In desperation you finally begin the meeting. 'So, Mr Chairman, you've received our proposals. No doubt you've discussed it with our colleagues. Are there any points you would like us to discuss?' The chairman smooths down his standard Japanese hairstyle. He brushes the creases from his standard Japanese business suit. There is a long, agonising silence. Everybody looks at everybody else. You begin playing with the business cards in front of you. The Japanese look everywhere except at you. The chairman now leans forward in his chair. 'Interesting,' he says. 'Very interesting.'

That's it. End of meeting. Back to reception, which looks like a Japanese flower garden, but isn't. It's all artificial with a computer-controlled processor pumping out all the natural scents. Stick all the business cards in the back of your bulging, sweaty wallet. Time to head home. You think I'm exaggerating? Every formal Japanese meeting I've attended has been just like that. Maybe not as informal.

To the Japanese, of course, it's quite normal. But they always see everything differently from us. On Valentine's Day, a boy doesn't send a card to his girl; the girl sends him – and every other man in her life – chocolates. To ordinary friends, even fellow office workers she sends *giri*, a duty gift. To that extra special friend she sends *honmei*, special chocolates. A groom doesn't just marry the bride of his choice. The two families are joined together.

Mr Fuyuhiko Maki, a senior adviser to Kobe Steel, told me that many Japanese suffer severe shock travelling abroad and experiencing life in other countries. 'In Japan cars slow down at pedestrian crossings. In other countries, they go faster. Why?' he asked, in a baffled tone.

Is it because they have different terms of reference, or do they do it deliberately? Take Japan's enormous and ever-growing trade balance. For years the Americans have been trying to work out a deal with the Japanese to try and reduce their trade deficit with the US, which is around US$40 billion a year and still growing. What do the Japanese do? They wait until the Americans are commemorating the fiftieth anniversary of Pearl Harbor, then release a report on, of all things, Japanese steel exports to the US. As if that was not bad enough, at least to US eyes, instead of tackling head on the still growing trade imbalance in steel between the two countries, the Japanese talk about partnership and mutual co-operation when they really mean Japanese acquisition of US steel companies, and say they are considering a dramatic plan to increase US exports to Japan by extending the time allowed for foreign companies to tender for Japanese steel contracts from forty to fifty days.

One reason for the trade balance is their emphasis on, or rather obsession with, quality. But are they obsessed with quality for quality's sake? Or because they are being pushed? Every year the Japanese expect more and more salary. Any company paying out annual increases of four or five points above inflation is considered less than generous. Employees realise that to get such enormous – in any other country unreasonable – increases, they have to work morning, noon and half the night, and are more than prepared to do so. Employers, on the other hand, realise that to pay the increases it means more computers, more automation, more robots – so what the hell.

At the same time, customers are not only demanding higher standards, better quality and more and more new products, they also expect to receive bigger discounts the longer a product is on the market. Partly because they don't see why they should buy so-called old-fashioned products when they can buy more up-to-date ones, partly because they believe that ever-increased efficiency and longer production runs inevitably result in lower prices. What can the company do but increase quality, lower costs and increase production?

So why do we keep coming back to Japan and banging our heads against an inscrutable wall, trying to break in where no Westerner has broken in before? 'Because maybe one year, maybe two years later, you'll get a call telling you they've finally accepted your proposal. You've got the business and it is invariably big business,' an Italian minerals trader told me.

'So after that, it's plain sailing?' No way. It gets even worse. The Japanese are never satisfied. They then start squeezing you for higher and higher quality, quicker and quicker deliveries and lower and lower prices.

One company I know supplies antimony oxide and flame retardants to all the big Japanese electronic companies. Antimony oxide contains 25% arsenic. A year after they started supplying it, the Japanese told them they wanted to reduce the levels to 24%; the following year, 23%. There was no reason why they should want to reduce it. It didn't affect the safety value or the cost. They just wanted to reduce it. The company did as they were told. Were the Japanese satisfied? The following year they wanted it down to 22%.

On one trip I bumped into this sales manager after he had spent another heavy night karaoke-ing with his opposite Japanese numbers in a desperate effort to establish personal contact and stop them squeezing his company to death. 'Are they happy now?' I asked. 'No way.' He collapsed at the bar. 'Next year they want us to bring it down to 21%.'

On another trip I met a German businessman who had spent five years developing an integrated lighting system for Nissan cars which involved over twenty different sources of light in order to create a pleasant driving environment. Over a year had been spent just working out a lighting system which would enable people to find things that fall on the car floor and roll under the seat. Another company, he told me, was working on an air-conditioning system which would adjust automatically to sunlight. There was even a company working on a car navigation system which didn't just tell you where you were on an electronic map, it pumped out non-stop quizzes, horoscopes and karaoke music as well.

None of them had yet had a decision from the Japanese – a good example of the Japanese belief in *bushido*, the way of the warrior: in sheer persistence, holding on, sticking to it, never, never giving in. In business, Sony, Shiseido, Kubota and a thousand other Japanese companies have again and again stuck with a policy, an idea or a product rather than admit they made a mistake. They stand still, keep quiet, stick with it through thick and thin. Again and again you come across the stoic in the Japanese. I suffer, therefore I am. Finally, there is that good old-fashioned non-British virtue of winning. The Japanese, I am convinced, are more than prepared to suffer, to work long hours, to put up with failure and rejection because they know that in the end they are right. They are going to triumph and to be rewarded. In the Christian West we are happy to receive our reward in the next world whereas the Japanese want, and are ferociously determined, to receive their reward very much in this Walkman world, even if it means a few extra hours' effort.

In the Okura one evening, waiting to meet a Dutchman who runs the Japanese end of a multinational, I asked the barman for something typically Japanese.

'Sake Mozart,' he said. 'Velly good.'

'Why sake Mozart?'

'Because to produce best sake, we play Mozart to vats. It makes it beautiful, smooth, velly good.'

'And musical?'

No response. It obviously didn't strike a chord with him. He gave me my sake Mozart. '*Kan pi*,' I said. 'Cheers.'

About two symphonies and a concerto later the Dutchman

arrived. 'Sorry I'm late,' he said. 'The whole company closes down next week for our summer holidays. It's a busy time of the year for me.'

'What, racing to catch up with orders before you close?'

'No. Persuading the Japanese to go on holiday.'

When he had first come to Tokyo, he told me, the Japanese had refused to take any holidays at all. He called them *shachiku*, company animals. 'They would come into my office and tell me that next week was their summer holiday. I would wish them a happy holiday. Oh no, they would say, we're not going on holiday. We're still coming in. We just wanted you to know that next week was our summer holiday.'

For a few years he put up with it. But it was causing havoc throughout the rest of the group. 'We were trying to standardise everything: pay, holidays, benefits. But the Japanese were ruining it. On top of that our production schedules were going crazy. Everybody else would go on holiday, and come back to find two weeks' production already in the system. It was chaos.'

The solution, they decided, was to close down the entire worldwide operation for a regular two-week summer holiday. Including the Japanese. 'It was impossible the first year. The Japanese turned up just the same. They thought we were kidding; just trying to see who was loyal and who was not. In the end we had to open up because they wanted to work. It was unbelievable.'

'Was it purely and simply because they loved working?'

'Partly,' he said, and partly because they had a warrior mentality dedicated to building a strong company in a strong Japan. Partly also, he guessed, because of fear. 'The Japanese,' he said, 'have a proverb. The nail that sticks out will get hammered.'

Over the last few years, however, things have changed. The Japanese have changed slowly from being *shachiku* to salarymen, they are no longer prepared to risk *karoshi*, death from overwork. 'Now it's more acceptable to take a holiday, but only a short one.' And he still has problems. 'Once everybody comes back, they work like mad to make up for the two weeks' production we lost because we were on holiday.' Which again throws all the worldwide schedules out of sync.

I told him about my traditional business meetings. 'You mustn't forget that the Japanese believe in harmony, unity, trust, considering always the other person's point of view,' he said. 'Nobody is going to say anything at a meeting in case they upset their colleagues by saying something they are going to disagree with, and especially in front of strangers. They are very Victorian.'

'So what are they like in private? Open, frank, brutal, to the point?'

'I doubt it. People like the Japanese cannot switch off in private. It would be impossible.'

'So how do they ever reach a decision?'

'I suspect it's the boozing,' he said as we tackled two more sake Mozarts. 'I've often thought the real reason the Japanese eat and drink so much out of the office is that it gives them a chance to talk freely about ideas they can't discuss in the office. If everybody agrees then they discuss it again the following morning in the office, knowing everybody is going to agree.'

'And if they don't?'

'Then they pretend they had too much to drink and can't remember what they said.'

'And because of the Japanese sense of the other person everybody else also pretends they had too much to drink and can't remember what was said either.'

'Exactly.'

We ordered two more sake Mozarts to celebrate our discovery of the inner workings of Japanese business.

The Japanese might work and drink in packs, but do they

really live in what the diplomats call rabbit hutches? They may not be rabbit hutches, but Japanese houses are pretty tiny and, for a nation that has filled the world to overflowing with consumer gadgets, they are still pretty basic. At least the one Japanese house I visited was.

I was at a meeting in the Ministry of Foreign Affairs, which really is tiny compared to Whitehall and the State Department. It employs around 4,500 people both in Japan and overseas; half the size of Whitehall, one-quarter as big as the State Department. Which is amazing when you think of the interests, or maybe control, Japan has throughout the world. On the other hand it is very modern, very spacious and a touch designer-austere. It completely lacks the clutter and squalour and gentle chaos that you find in government buildings elsewhere.

I was going on to the Keidanren, the enormously prestigious Confederation of Japanese Industry. So was one of the ministry officials, who offered me a lift. The traffic was chaotic. For the first time I noticed that whenever the light at the pedestrian crossings turns to green, they all mysteriously play what sounds remarkably like 'Comin' thro the rye'. I'm convinced the appalling Tokyo traffic has spurred on Japan's enormous economic success. Without traffic jams, there would have been no need to invent the fax, the mobile telephone, the lap-top computer.

The ministry official was a graduate of Todai, Tokyo's university, which is like Eton, Oxford, Harvard, MIT, and the Ecole Nationale d'Administration rolled into one. But better. So many Todai graduates were then in key positions in Japan that the government had actually put a block on recruiting any more.

'Know, how you say, short-cut,' said the official as we swung into a side road. The buildings were still big and impressive. We drove through the trendy Harajuka district, the home of government ministers and *yakuza*, gangsters, with *mai hommu*, detached houses with garages for *mai kaa*, my cars, electronic massage chairs, all bathed in gentle electronic music and overflowing with videos, televisions and CDs. Or maybe satiated, for research shows the Japanese are using their videos for thirty minutes less a week than they did two years ago. It was difficult to believe that at one time they used to chop the heads off live monkeys and eat their brains.

Second right. Another left. We were now driving along a dingy road that looked as though it was leading to a small town American factory estate. The buildings were two and three storeys high. Some were offices. There were showrooms selling printing machines. A few looked like the back doors of restaurants. Another right, left and second right and we were in a single-lane, one-way road. The pavements were about a foot high. I kept thinking they were going to scrape the car. On either side of us were tiny houses no wider than a large single garage. Inside I could see traditional polished wooden floors, traditional Japanese screens.

Most Japanese, the man from the ministry told me, live outside Tokyo. Usually it takes them two or three hours each day to travel in and out. The people living in the houses we were passing were like him; junior government officials, earning an above average salary and with very good prospects. That, he said, was important, because the property was very expensive and most people had borrowed money to buy their house. He wouldn't tell me how expensive, but I gathered later that property prices in Tokyo are among the highest in the world.

A house the size of an average council flat can cost up to £500,000. But on a square-foot basis I reckon they must easily be the most expensive in the universe. The official's own house, which we visited very briefly to meet his wife, who was dressed in traditional Japanese costume, was probably no larger than two large double garages. It had been built by a company owned by Toyota. He said he was working from 8 o'clock in the morning until 9 o'clock at night to pay for it, and had so little time he paid a special substitute family service to visit his mother in Osaka on his behalf. 'She likes it,' he says. His wife just smiled.

I wanted to stay and perform the famous Japanese tea ceremony, but I had another Japanese business meeting ceremony to attend. I arrive at the Keidanren the statutory five minutes beforehand to be ushered into a swish, modern office where they are already waiting for me. 'Good afternoon,' I say to Mr Mastaka Nishi, the vice-president of Hitachi, who looks as though he is chairing the meeting.

'Good morning,' he replies. That's all. Then he just sits there smiling at me. And smiling. And smiling. But does he mean it? Is he saying it because I said it? Does he mean the morning is going to be good but the afternoon isn't? So who told him about the afternoon? Isn't he telling me about it? And why does he keep smiling at me?

'You got my report?' I say eventually, turning to Mr Soichi Kobayashi, general manager of Mitsubishi Heavy Industries.

'Yes,' he says, raising his eyes, presumably not in disgust but in perpetual gratitude to his Shinto heaven for having delivered me out of the clouds to solve all their problems.

'Everything okay?'

'Yes,' he says, this time lowering his eyes, no doubt dazzled by my brilliance. Does he mean yes, yes? Or does he mean yes, I understand? Perhaps he just means yes, I got the report, but I haven't read it. Should I have asked him if he has read it? But if I do and he hasn't will he tell me he hasn't? And, if not, why not? Doesn't he want to read it?

'I can let you have the additional figures and samples by the end of the month,' I tell Mr Tsugib Tsukaamoto, senior managing director of the Nishimatsu Construction Company. 'Is that all right?' He's just looking at me. No reply. Didn't he hear what I said? Shall I repeat it? But if I repeat it will he think I think he wasn't paying attention and be upset? Or maybe he can't remember the Japanese word for additional? Or perhaps he's not interested in the whole damn business and is sick to death of all these meetings? If he is, why the hell doesn't he tell me, so I can get the hell out of here and stop wasting my time and money? Wait a minute. He's now closed his eyes and is nodding his head backwards and forwards.

The problem with Japanese meetings is that they are all give and take. You give, the Japanese take. There is no interaction, no feedback, no way of actually knowing what the guy thinks. You spend all your time interpreting and re-interpreting everything they say – or don't say.

In Britain meetings tend to be crisp and to the point unless the office troublemaker is present. The yes men say yes. The maybe men say yes because they don't want to rock the boat. The rest go along with the majority because they're having lunch at the club and don't want to be late. In Germany it's much the same, but for other reasons. Everybody has already agreed the overall objectives. Does the proposal fit the overall objective or does it not? If it does, they say yes. If it doesn't, they say no. They can then get back to work.

Holland and France are different again. The Dutch will discuss everything; analyse implications, assess alternatives. They will debate whether there is a better way. Once they have decided there isn't – and there usually isn't – they will say yes. The French will go round and round in circles for the pleasure of hearing themselves speak. Until, of course, it is time for lunch.

Only in Japan do you encounter such deliberate ceremonial formality, whatever and wherever the meeting, whatever the subject. No one's *tatemae*, self-respect, must be insulted – again that concern for the other person.

At the end of one visit I was vainly trying to understand what makes them tick. Were they really inscrutable? I've known plenty of pretty inscrutable British companies. You can talk to them for twenty years and you still don't know whether you're going to get the business or not. Were they really ruthlessly efficient or just organised? Could you trust them? Did they really mean what they said? Did they really say what they meant?

The 'phone rang in my hotel room. It is Mr Eiji Fukunaga at the Bank of Tokyo. Suddenly I find myself standing to attention on the fourteenth floor of Frank Lloyd Wright's famous Imperial Hotel midway between the Ginza and the Imperial Palace, bowing up and down to him on the other end of the line.

Almost one hour and £35 later, I was in the Xerox head office.

'No problem,' the *nijuu ritchi* young manager told me. 'I can photocopy document for you now.' But I didn't just want one document, I explained. I wanted sixty copies. 'Very sorry. One document, yes. But not so many. Not possible,' he smiled. So where was the nearest photocopy shop? 'We have not photocopy shop in Tokyo. Everybody has own machine. Very sorry.'

I got the Xerox receptionist to give me the address of Gestetner. They might not be in the photocopy business but they would be bound to know a man who was. Two minutes later I was in another taxi inching my way towards another balance of payment crisis. The Gestetner showroom turned out to be in a back street surrounded by showrooms and workshops and warehouses.

'Not know photocopy shopping,' said another very helpful manager who looked more a salaryman than a *nijuu ritchi.*

For the rest of the day I visited parts of Tokyo I never knew existed. I drove up and down Marunouchi, the business area. I drove all through Nihonbashi, the banking area. I toured the back streets of Shinjuku and off towards the vast industrial estates. I saw the inside of small, traditional Japanese printers. In one company everybody was wearing white surgeons' masks because they didn't want other people to catch their colds. I queued in department stores. I waited in the backrooms of what looked like Chinese laundries. At one stage we drove under a big red arch near Shinjuku station which judging by the electronic slot machines – again – looked like Tokyo's red light district. I could only assume that my interest in finding machinery for reproduction had gained something in translation between the *nijuu ritchi* at Xerox, the salaryman at Gestetner and the taxi driver. All I know is that when he passed one office – well it looked like an office to me – he suddenly took his gloves off and started miming like Marcel Marceau and muttering *soapo-soapo etchi etchi* which might or might not have been good clean fun if I hadn't been so desperate to find the reproduction machine of my choice.

In the process I'm also convinced I bought the equivalent of three and a half taxis (US$40,000 each including tax and a year's fully comprehensive insurance); and I saw how quickly the drivers' white gloves can turn black with perspiration. But in the end I got everything photocopied. By getting the manager of the photocopy department of a big insurance company to do the insides for me. By getting a small printer to do the covers. And by getting a tiny gift shop to spiral-bind everything together. The spiral-binding machine I discovered not because the shop was offering the service but because the taxi driver couldn't find the insurance company and I went in to ask directions. He was too proud to do so – loss of face and all that – which was just as well. I spotted the machine under a pile of Western hats and coats. It took a while to explain what I wanted. You try miming, I want to spiral-bind five copies of sixty books. Can I bring three tons of paper here and do it by four o'clock? But in the end, I did it.

The following morning I staggered under mountains of photocopying into the conference room in the Okura so that it would all be laid out neatly for the delegates when they arrived.

'Any problems?' said the manager of the Business Centre, holding the door open for me. 'We are here to help.'

Like the Japanese, and in spite of the Japanese, I'd delivered everything on time. I didn't have to commit hara-kiri and rip my stomach open with a Samurai sword before being beheaded.

Auckland

Excuse me, I didn't mean to yawn. It's just that somehow whenever I think of Auckland I start ... I start ... nodding off. It's not that the people are not nice and friendly. They are. It's not that the country is not pleasant. It is. It's not that the climate is not nice. It is very nice. It's just that somehow ... somehow ...

They say first impressions count. For my first visit to New Zealand I flew out of Honolulu on an eight-hour flight to Auckland. When I landed the airport was deserted. Well, maybe two or three people were wandering aimlessly around. We went straight through customs and passport control – no queues, no problems. Outside the terminal there were a few people standing by the car hire desk; a couple looking at the departures board; a Japanese businessman counting his small change.

I checked my ticket. It said Auckland. Could I be sure I hadn't landed on some remote South Pacific atoll by mistake? The signs all said Auckland. But it certainly didn't feel like the fourth largest city in the world, even though it is calculated in terms of area.

I strolled outside. It was not the kind of airport that makes you rush around like JFK, Narita or even Hull, where they have only about two planes an hour. In the rush hour. There were a few taxis in the distance. A couple of small coaches were tucked around the corner of the terminal. One or two cars were parked over yonder. I stood there and took in the early morning sunshine. Nobody rushed up, as they do in airports, offering a shoe shine, a better exchange rate, dollars, a two-day in-depth tour of the country, their sister, or even a taxi into town (which invariably costs more than the others put together and certainly takes longer). I wandered across to what looked like one of those weekend camping vans with a rickety trailer on the back for the tents. It was a genuine New Zealand taxi.

'Going into town?' I asked nervously.

'Sure thing,' replied a middle-aged weekend camper in a coloured shirt. I piled everything in the trailer and climbed into the van. Then I waited. And waited. And waited.

'Just a few minutes more,' the driver kept saying as one plane after another landed, discharging a maximum of two or three people into the empty terminal, who obviously then found alternative means of transport. I was beginning to nod off. Suddenly I came to with a start. There were three of us in the bus; me, an American student who looked like a Mormon on holiday, and a retired English bank manager who'd come to New Zealand to visit his retired sister. I nodded off again.

Again I came to with a start. The bus was moving. We were heading to Auckland, away from the airport which had really begun to buzz – two taxis were now waiting for passengers. Off we went towards the big city. Except it didn't look like a big city. It was small and neat and very tidy. It looked more like an English country town than one of the major business centres of the southern hemisphere. And it looked deserted.

We turned into Great South Road. Did the curtains flutter in the window above the supermarket, or was it my imagination? Down a sidestreet I glimpsed a cyclist, but ours seemed to be the only car in Auckland.

Just eight hours before I had been in Honolulu. It was Friday night. The streets were packed, the shops and restaurants full to overflowing. As I rushed back to the hotel to pack, the pavements were jammed with people laughing, talking, eating Big Macs and french fries and aloha-ing anything that moved. It was hot. But now! It was like touring the Deserted Village in the *Marie Celeste.*

'Is it always like this?' I nervously asked the driver.

'Always,' he said solemnly.

'You mean no traffic?'

'No traffic.'

'No people?'

'No people.'

The Mormon continued studying his Bible. The bank manager continued staring out of the window. But then the English always do if anybody talks to anybody in a bus or taxi wherever they are.

We now drove along what looked like a high street. I spotted a poster. It said 'Reliability. Onwa sell over 18.8 million TV sets per year to 1.8 million satisfied customers.'

'So is this the centre of town?' I asked the driver as the Mormon ploughed through his Bible and the bank manager swivelled round to look out of the window again.

'Yes.'

'You mean even the centre of town is empty?'

'Yes.'

New Zealand was only discovered about a thousand years ago. If the rest of the country was like this I didn't have to guess why the Polynesians, usually such enthusiastic travellers, avoided it for so long. And it has really only been in the real world for the last twenty years, since the UK joined the EC and forced them to stand on their own feet. Before that they were really one vast off-shore farm for the British housewife.

Now we drove along a long wide avenue. Trees on both sides, Victorian-like mansions hidden behind them. But still no people. I began to wonder whether Auckland was expecting more French visitors interested in inspecting fishing boats in the harbour. Or whether they'd been and were just leaving.

'Much happen here?' I thought I'd try the indirect approach.

'Big match,' he grunted. Ah, I thought. That's why the place is empty. Everybody's gone to the match. But would *everybody* go?

'Just started, has it?'

'Was yesterday.'

The taxi swung in front of the hotel. At last, I thought, the real Auckland. But there were no porters, no staff. I unloaded my bags myself, paid off the taxi-and-trailer, and stumbled inside. There was a girl at reception. I'd been in the country over three hours. I'd driven through Auckland which according to the guidebooks is 'the commercial centre of an open and internationally competitive economy offering not gimmicks or incentives but an investment-friendly environment, characterised by consistency, stability, low costs and low inflation.' She was only the second New Zealander I'd seen.

'Exciting place you've got here.'

'We think so,' she grinned sleepily.

One of the most boring books I've ever read was *Station Life in New Zealand* written by Lady Barker in 1865. It was all about the thrills she experienced burning the countryside and turning the land into 'perfectly black and barren country, looking desolate and hideous to a degree hardly to be imagined'. I began to feel I might have misunderstood her.

I signed everything the girl wanted me to sign, carried my bags up to the room and switched on the television. This was obviously going to be the kind of town where for excitement one stays in one's hotel room and watches the Epilogue on television. But what was this? Not rugby. Not cricket. Not football. A church service. Of course, the time difference. I'd crossed the date line. I'd lost a day. My eight-hour flight had, in fact, taken thirty-two hours. This was not Saturday morning after all, but Sunday morning. No wonder Auckland was dead.

* * *

'I've been to the Aquarium three times already,' I said. 'So what else is there to do?' In Auckland everyone insists you go to the Aquarium. They tell you it is one of the wonders of New Zealand and certainly one of the most famous and spectacular in the world. Don't you believe it. An aquarium is an aquarium. But just for the sake of peace, I went to the Aquarium. In fact, Auckland is the only place in the world where I have visited the local aquarium three times in a week. Which tells you more about Auckland than my interest in fish.

The lady at the hotel information desk looked puzzled. 'Well, you can wander along Queen Street and look at the drug addicts,' she said. 'Some of the bars along there also serve cold tinned spaghetti sandwiches.'

I was trying to put together a hotel deal, which was taking longer than it should have done. I was going to endless meetings: meetings to discuss proposals; meetings to discuss strategy; meetings to discuss meetings. Obviously something about the Maori *marae* – open-air debate – had got into their bloodstream and they were constitutionally incapable of doing anything without having a dozen preliminary meetings. And it wasn't as if the meetings were organised.

I turned up for one, and the chairman of the hotel group wasn't there. 'He could have gone out for his morning tea,' his secretary told me. Oh shades of 1920s' Cheltenham, I thought.

When we did get everybody together, the discussion went round and round in Maori circles. At the time I thought I was just unlucky, but since then I've attended conferences all over Africa chaired by Robert Muldoon, an ex-New Zealand prime minister, and exactly the same thing happened. Speaker after speaker droned on and on and whole rows of delegates fell asleep. But each speaker was praised by Muldoon, after they finally slithered to a halt, for their perception and incisive analysis. At least that's what the official reports of the conferences always said. I was never awake long enough to hear what he had to say. Once I even bumped into David Lange, another ex-New Zealand prime minister, drinking coffee at an all-night coffee stand in Covent Garden. He wasn't exactly a bundle of laughs either.

Thanks to all the meetings I had to stay much longer than I had planned. In one way it was good for me. It meant I was able to catch up on my sleep. In fact, I seemed to do nothing but sleep. Also, I thought, it would give me a chance to explore another part of the world. Trouble was, I found nothing worth exploring.

Normally when I visit foreign countries, I find they are foreign. New Zealand, however, is just like home. There is nothing foreign about it at all. If I had been paying my own way I would have demanded my money back. Even worse, I found everything was about ten years behind the UK. It was like visiting a time warp.

The centre of Auckland could be the nondescript centre of any nondescript English country town. Practically every evening I wandered along the infamous Queen Street. There's more danger in a crowd of old age pensioners leaving church on a Sunday morning. In one shop I actually saw a copy of the *Daily Telegraph* with the headline, 'Heseltine makes bid for Tory leadership'. Gee whiz, I thought, he's taking on Major already! No way. It was a paper left over from when he made his bid against Mrs Thatcher. Over six months later, not only had they not sold the newspaper, they had not even thought of removing it from the rack.

The only excitement was getting a cab back to the hotel in the evening. Whichever route we took it was always the same routine. Whenever we passed a grocery shop, the driver would slow up. 'Asians,' he would whisper. 'They stay open all day and night y'know.'

All the New Zealanders I met seemed to be afflicted by a kind of upside-down mentality. Instead of ignoring the fact that they were dull they seemed to want to glory in it. I am boring, therefore I am. I've only ever come across one New Zealander who wasn't boring. That was Des Wilson. I worked for the Great New Zealand Campaigner for just forty-seven days shortly after he arrived in London. We were both at R.F. White, an old-established family-owned financial advertising agency in Fleet Street. Des was responsible for PR. As soon as I arrived he turned us into a Division. In spite of all the nasty, unfair remarks people make about Des, I must say I thoroughly enjoyed working for him – for the first two and a half days. Somehow I didn't feel secure with someone whose management philosophy was based on, not even the book, but the musical, *How to Succeed in Business without Really Trying.*

Not only did he go to the musical, which was on in London at the time, he took a notebook as well. The following morning he regaled me with the notes he'd taken, especially one about getting your name tannoyed throughout the agency. 'That way everybody thinks you're busy,' he giggled.

'So how do you get your name tannoyed?' I asked in all innocence.

'You go outside and keep telephoning yourself. You're not in the office so the girl on the switchboard puts out a call for you.'

'But she'll recognise your voice.'

'Not according to the musical,' he squealed.

Within two days, you couldn't go anywhere in the agency without Des Wilson being tannoyed all over the place. I decided to look for another job. Des went on to succeed.

Auckland offices were nothing like that. In one, I met a group of New Zealand businessmen who were definitely not being tannoyed all the time. Which is probably why they were still in Auckland. I wanted to ask about the economy.

As a result of a tough, some people have said savage, monetarist policy – Rotorua give people a discount if they dig their own or their relatives' graves – the national government has slashed the rate of inflation to its lowest level for twenty-five years. Within a year they brought it down from 7.6% to just 2.8%. From having the nearest thing to a planned, regulated, protected and distorted economy outside the old Eastern Europe, they had undertaken the most radical free-market reforms of any country anywhere. Prices, wages, interest rates, the exchange rate had all been set free. Tax rates had been slashed. Subsidies had been abolished. One state enterprise after another had been privatised. New Zealand was the first country actually to publish annual accounts just as if it was a public company. Admittedly they were now deep in a recession; unemployment was high and businesses were failing all over the country. But how had they achieved all this? Was it worth the agony?

All they wanted to talk about, however, was the environment. Farmers shouldn't do this, they should do that. Land shouldn't be used, it should be retired and rested. Sheep should be banned; they caused landslides and damaged the land. Pesticides should be banned. All artificial products should be abolished. Animals should no longer be bred for commercial purposes. They should be kept in animal petting farms. Trees shouldn't be chopped down. Anyone who touched a tree was a 'wood butcher'. Grass shouldn't be cut. Mining should be banned. Strip mining should be liable for capital punishment. Pumping carbon dioxide into the atmosphere was dangerous. We should all stop breathing.

Years ago I had a secretary from the middle of New Zealand's South Island. I was organising a big conference and we needed plants to decorate the hall. I asked her to ring up and get some for the day. Three hours later I found her halfway through the Yellow Pages ringing up plant hire companies. Somehow I kept thinking of her while everyone rambled on about the environment.

One day I was lunching with a banking consultant and his

Swiss wife. I wanted to ask about New Zealand's stock market. It had risen by a third in six months. Short-term interest rates had fallen from 14.5% to 9.5% during the same period. Did this mean the economy was finally on the mend?

All they wanted to talk about was the threat to the possum. Not the ordinary American opossum, the wife kept reminding me, but the genuine New Zealand possum which had already destroyed most of the country's forests and was now busily spreading tuberculosis to cattle the length and breadth of both North and South Island.

'Well, surely you trap, shoot or poison the things,' I said.

They recoiled in horror. 'Barbaric,' they cried.

They honestly wanted to burn millions of possums' testicles and fur, mix the ash with some kind of special spray, then spread the lot on the grass when the moon was in the right quarter. This, they felt, was a serious, practical, cheap, effective and environmentally safe solution to the problem.

'But how many possums are there?' I asked.

'Anything between 50 and 150 million,' they said. 'Possums, not opossums. They're American,' the Swiss wife repeated with the regularity of a cuckoo clock.

'And how quickly do they breed?'

'Every twenty-five to thirty days,' they said.

'And you think you will be able to collect enough possums' testicles . . .'

'Not opossums. Possums.'

'That's what I said . . .'

One afternoon between meetings I wanted to take a look at some of the vineyards around Auckland, which boasts it has the largest collection of wineries in the country. New Zealand has some fabulous wines. In all the New World, I think New Zealand is the one country that can concentrate on quality wine production virtually to the exclusion of everything else.

My wine guide told me he was an expert on New Zealand wines. He'd visited every vineyard, knew every wine. 'Fantastic,' I said. 'Let's go to Matua Valley.' He'd never heard of it. 'So how about Villa Maria?' Another blank stare. 'Babich? Collards? Coopers Creek?' He began rummaging in the glove compartment. 'Okay,' I said, 'take me to the ones you know.'

The first vineyard he knew turned out to be a wine shop almost directly under the flight path to the airport. The next was on a motorway about twenty miles away. It had one of the most miserable, unhelpful vineyard owners I've ever met anywhere. Outside looking after the vines was an expat from Windsor.

'So what's it like growing wines in New Zealand?' I asked the Windsor expat.

'All right,' he grunted.

'And the weather?'

'All right.'

'Problems with disease?'

He shook his head. Even growing wines in New Zealand was boring.

The wine expert might not have known any vineyards but he knew every grocery shop. As we passed each one, he would slow up. 'And they stay open late every day,' he whispered each time.

One evening I just couldn't face another visit to the Aquarium. I asked the unsmiling girl at reception, 'So where are the best bars? Which are the fashionable restaurants?'

'There aren't any,' she said.

Which is probably not surprising when you realise that restaurants in New Zealand were not allowed to serve wine until after 1960, and it was another nineteen years before the first wine bar was opened. Auckland is the place to send a salesman if you don't want him to spend all his expenses.

'You could try the Golden Mile,' she said.

'What's the Golden Mile?'

'It's a street with seven hotels in it.'

I decided to go back to the Aquarium. I picked up a taxi at

the bottom of Queen Street by the harbour. The driver was a Maori. At last, I thought, I can find out something of Maori culture from a Maori. I was interested in the *marae*, the formal meeting place, in every village. In Africa they always meet, debate, organise their own legal proceedings under a particular tree in the centre of the village. The *marae* seemed more formal and ritualised. On top of that, I couldn't help being curious about a people that had thirty-five different words for 'dung'. He wanted to talk about rugby.

Did I know that more people had accidents playing rugby than driving on the road? To him this meant that New Zealand was one of the greatest countries in the world at rugby. To me it meant they were one of the worst. If they had that many accidents they couldn't be very good at it, could they? Although the Maoris are supposed to hold with discussion and debate, hence the *marae*, he didn't seem to accept my logic so we drove to the Aquarium in silence.

When I got back to the hotel I spent the rest of the evening watching the water go down the plughole the wrong way round.

The following day while everyone was trying to agree a time for yet another meeting, I took a harbour tour in desperation. Maybe Auckland will look better from the water, I thought. Most cities look more interesting, sometimes spectacular, from the water; in New York you get a clear view of Brooklyn Bridge, the Statue of Liberty, all those skyscrapers squeezed on to such a tiny stretch of land; in Sydney there's the Opera House; Hong Kong's peaks and islets come into focus. Even Marseille looks stunning, especially early in the morning as the boat swings across the Mediterranean towards Tunisia. But Auckland looked the same as it did on land, except it was from a different angle. There was no excitement, no hustle-bustle. There were few boats. The scenery was drab. I stopped feeling sorry for the fish in the Aquarium. They might be condemned to spend their lives in Auckland but at least they didn't have to look at it.

A newspaper was lying on the bench in front of me. Splashed across the front page was a story about an equal rights sex battle in Warkworth, a little village about 70 kilometres north of Auckland. 'Loo tax flushes out a poser,' whispered the headline. For three years the town had been wrestling with 'one of the most complicated conundrums of the equal rights battle'. In despair they were turning to parliament for help.

'The insoluble riddle is this,' said the article. 'When a woman spends the euphemistic penny in the local restaurant's toilet, does she get more for her money in the way of services from the local council than does a male diner visiting the gents? Furthermore, if there is a difference, should this be reflected in the taxes levied by the council?'

There and then I decided: Auckland was too much for me. I couldn't take any more excitement. I had to get out. Especially as the newspaper also said that parliament, under the cover of the Kumeu District Agricultural and Horticultural Society Bill, had recently debated whether biscuits should be served at select committee meetings or not. As soon as I got off the ferry I rushed back to the hotel, booked myself on the next flight out, ordered a taxi and checked out. The taxi was late. Inevitably I sat in a chair and fell asleep.

Suddenly I came to. Three businessmen had rushed into the lobby shouting and waving bits of paper. In came three more – more shouting, more bits of paper. Within three minutes the lobby had more people in it than I had seen all week.

'Foreigners,' I heard the girl whisper loudly across reception.

'Foreigners,' I repeated between yawns.

'From Hong Kong,' she said. 'They're all moving in. Frightened of the Chinese.'

The Hong Kongers turned out to be Taiwanese who were being shown around town by a local management consultant.

He had hit on the idea to tide him over a difficult patch in the economy. He would collect them at the airport, bundle them into mini-buses – Japanese, of course – and show them New Zealand: where to live, where to set up business, where to send the children to school. He would then introduce them to all the important people in town: Taiwanese lawyers, Taiwanese accountants, Taiwanese estate agents, Taiwanese shopkeepers and, of course, other Taiwanese businessmen.

'All like it here velly much,' he told me as I gathered my bags. 'Velly safe. Velly quiet. No problems.'

'And good for business?' I asked.

'Velly good,' he grinned. 'All people I like making happy.'

In the previous year, he told me, he had brought in on average three Taiwanese or Hong Kong families a week, given each the grand tour and introduced them to the right people.

'You must be very happy as well,' I said. He grinned. 'Soon all this will be second Taiwan,' I continued.

'Velly safe. People like it here. We call it Velly New China.'

'But isn't it a bit . . . quiet?' I wondered.

'Everybody like it quiet. Not like Hong Kong.'

Must go to Hong Kong again, I though … thou … th …

Zzzzzz.

Sydney

'Saw some woman, Lady Edna or something, on the box the other night. Thought it would be a good idea to have next year's sales conference in Sydney. What d'yah think?'

'Interesting idea, sir,' I began nervously.

'Wife says bloody marvellous idea. Chance to get some culture.'

'And so it is, sir. So it is,' I quickly recovered. 'Wonderful. Your wife certainly knows how ... I mean, has wonderful ideas, sir.'

This was at a very dull heating and ventilating company in the Midlands that twelve months previously, when the chairman – a Sydney Bracegirdle type of chairman – was being run by an earlier wife, had cancelled a one-day sales conference in Scarborough because they thought it would be too exciting for the sales force.

Don't let anyone tell you any different; Sydney Harbour, the bridge and, of course, the Opera House are spectacular. Three days later as I flew in after a non-stop twenty-two-hour flight, everything was bathed in brilliant sunshine. The harbour was much brighter than I had imagined – more like an enormous puddle of Fosters, with its thousand inlets and coves and creeks, than a conventionally shaped harbour.

Many Australians boast about having a flat overlooking Sydney Harbour. Don't be impressed. Half of Australia could have a flat overlooking Sydney Harbour. It's one of the biggest in the world, stretching from the bridge and Opera House twenty miles west as far as Parramatta, the country's second oldest settlement, and twenty miles east as far as Lady Jane Bay where apparently no lady would dare set foot any more. In fact, it looks more like an inland sea than a harbour.

It was packed with ships and boats of every description – ferries, hydrofoils, passenger ships, giant tankers, tiny little yachts and rowing boats. Some Aussie once said a thousand ships could hide in Sydney Harbour. That, I reckon, was a goodexample of Oz understatement.

The bridge linking the rocks where the British first landed on January 26th, 1788 looks like a giant out-of-date imperial coat hanger. It was designed, would you believe, by a world-beating British engineering and construction company, Dorman and Long, which long ago ceased to exist.

The Opera House, set at the top of Bennelong Point, is undoubtedly one of the modern wonders of the world. Is it a fantastic building, or is it a sham? I don't know. To me it's what happens when a bunch of Ockers get together and hire a Dane to give them something cultural. Apparently when the architect produced his designs it was impossible to build the building. The materials didn't exist to construct that kind of roof in the dimensions he wanted. To me, and probably to the rest of the world, this would be pretty convincing proof that he was 'two sandwiches short of a picnic', as they say down-under. Not to the Ockers. They decided to crack open a tinnie and design the materials to do the job. Which is proof positive, I suppose, that they are more than yobs with cans in their hands. Or at least some of them are. Alongside the Opera House is Circular Quay which is the ferry terminal, bus depot, coach station and general crossroads for everything that goes on in town.

Virtually all around the harbour is Sydney with its 120 golf courses and ninety McDonald's. It's enormous. In fact, it's a

Clive James city. It kind of sprawls everywhere like a technicolour yawn in that floppy, languid kind of way that 17 million Ockers have developed to try and fill out a country the size of the United States.

In spite of 3.7 million Sydneysiders, it's the nicest city in the country in terms of quality of life. The Australian Economic Planning Advisory Council puts it third after Melbourne and Perth; all I can say is, if Australian economists are like economists everywhere else, they don't know one end of a didgerydoo from another.

'Culture?' said Kev, at the Sydney Convention Centre. 'Here in Sydney we've got it all.'

I nodded quietly. Barry Humphries, I remembered, made his name by putting custard in a pair of Wellington boots for a sketch he called Pus in Boots. 'You wanna see some dykes?' Kev asked.

'I've seen enough dykes in Holland,' I said.

'Jeez. They over there as well?'

'Everywhere,' I said.

'The Sydney Tattoo Show?'

'A tattoo? You mean boring army displays?'

'No. I mean tattoos. Tattoos.' I shook my head. 'How about Seven Little Australians? It's on at the Sun Corp Theatre.' I shook my head again. 'The Gay and Lesbian Mardi Gras?' I shook my head again and again.

Kev was not exactly a Crocodile Dundee – more a Reptile Dundee with a couple of sheep short in the top paddock. Finally, eager to please, desperate to show off the city he just knew was the best place in the world to play tennis, surf, sail and between full-on rages to fill in time dropping into the office to catch up on what was happening in the world of sport, he ran into the street and hailed – a bus. Smart operators these Australians, I thought. I went to get on.

'Jeez, hang on, mate,' he grabbed me. 'It's got to kneel first.'
Kneel? Australians expect even the buses to kneel before

them? 'Sure enough, mate,' grunted Kev. 'We're cultured down here y'know. Not like you Poms.' The bus whirred and coughed. It didn't exactly kneel, probably because I was a Pom, but the whole thing tilted over until the platform was the same level as the kerb. 'Great innit?' said Kev. 'Bet you've never seen that before. That's real culture.'

Sydney was bathed in sunshine. Again. Everybody looked as though they were going to the beach to show off their bods, or on their way back from it. There was hardly a business suit in town. There probably wasn't one in the country. People ambling in and out of offices could have been anything from golf professionals to company chairmen – or probably both.

Kev's cultural high spot turned out not to be the Opera House but Writers' Wall on the quayside, on the way to the Opera House. It was a series of copper plates inset in the pavement celebrating Australia's most famous writers.

'So who are your famous writers?' I asked. Kev pointed to a plaque. I couldn't begin to recognise the name. 'Dodgeroo Noonuccal,' he said.

'Who's that? What did he write?' I asked. Kev pointed to another plaque. 'Banjo Patterson,' I read.

'Here's another,' he said. This was C.J. Dennis who, according to the plaque, was famous for such lyrics as:

It 'appened this way; I 'ad just come down after long years, to look at Sydney town. An' struth was I knocked end ways? Fair su'prised? I never dreamed! That arch that cut the skies.
The Bridge!

I moved along the line of plaques. There was one for D.H. Lawrence! D.H. Lawrence, an Australian? Of course, he spent six months in Australia, writing *Kangaroo* in 1922. Of course he's an Australian writer. 'What did he write?' I asked Kev.

'Everybody knows what he wrote,' he told me. 'It's famous all over Australia:

'It's great to be unemployed,
And lie in Domain.
And wake up every second day
And go to sleep again.'

Had he stayed thirty years would Lawrence be commemorated sixty times? Or is six months of D.H. Lawrence equivalent to a lifetime of Dodgeroo Noonuccal or Banjo Patterson?

'What's more, mate, we've got lots of literary journals,' said Kev, thrusting a copy of the *Weekend Australian* he'd been carrying into my hands. 'Look there.' He jabbed the book page at me. 'A topsy-turvy West London home,' it began, 'on the banks of the cold and sparkling Thames is being advertised at £850,000 ($2.1 million), in part because in 1867 it was occupied by the children's writer, George MacDonald (*The Princess and the Goblin*) and stands next door to Kelmscott House which was made famous by William Morris.'

'There you are. That's literary isn't it?'

I nodded as enthusiastically as I could. 'Impressed?' he said. 'Bet you've got nothing like that in Britain.'

'No, you're right,' I grunted. 'Only in London.'

'You're not impressed. You don't think we're a literary nation. So ask me a literary question.'

'Okay,' I said. 'What's the most popular book in Sydney at the moment?'

He drew himself up to his full height. '*The Book of Sydney Suburbs.*'

What could I say?

The business centre of Sydney is a tiny cluster of skyscrapers – like a teenage Manhattan – huddled behind Circular Quay, slap bang in the centre of town. Admittedly it includes the Sydney Tower, at 304 metres high the fifth highest in the

world after Toronto, Moscow, New York and the Eiffel Tower.
But somehow it didn't have the hustle and bustle of New York
or Tokyo or even London. It seemed too laid back.

'Quick, buy a million Hanson. He's making a bid for IBM.'

'Jeez. Did you see the cricket score?'

'I don't care. Buy.'

'Oh come on, you don't care about cricket? What are you?'

I bought the *Sydney Morning Herald* and sat and watched
the ferry boats at Circular Quay. On the front page was a big
story about Sydney's dykes. Which I discovered are not dykes
at all, but gay women. No wonder Kev was surprised by my
knowledge of and interest in Dutch dykes. Alongside it was
another article about – wait a minute, the ferries are ambidex-
trous. They don't turn round, they operate in both directions
– about pokies. Which gave me a start, until I realised it was
more acceptable Oz slang, this time for slot machines.

I've since discovered I'm not the only one who sometimes
finds it difficult to understand what Australians are on about.
The most embarrassing example I was told involved the
Japanese financial newspaper *Nihon Keizai Shimbun*.

If we English think someone is too big for their boots, we
say they are too big for their boots. Australians call such
people 'tall poppies'. The Japanese apparently completely
misunderstood this and concluded a big survey on Australia
by saying that before it could take its place 'on the world
podium, it must shed the tall puppy syndrome and start
wagging its own tail.'

A boat raced into the quay. 'L.J. Hooker', it said on the bow.
'We do it better', it said on its aft. An enormous dial-a-dump
truck was parked between a notice saying Baby Change and
a Two-Way signpost. I collapsed against a 'Stop. Revive.
Survive' notice with a red light camera looking directly at me.

Sydney's greatest conference organiser turned out the following morning to be living in a wooden house on the edge of the

Royal Botanic Garden, which stretches out behind the Opera House into the middle of the city and is one of the loveliest city parks I've ever been in. The last thing he wanted to talk about was conferences. Cricket? Sailing? Not on your life. 'Bloody possums,' he shrieked. 'They're all over the place. And they won't let you do anything about them.'

Such is the Australian concern for the environment that, since they discovered that their cute, cuddly national emblem, the koala bear, was being gradually wiped out by venereal disease, their other cute, cuddly national emblem, the possum, is being given free rein to destroy whatever it likes.

I tried to discuss conference facilities. Would the Sydney Convention and Exhibition Centre at Darling Harbour be available? Originally a mass of derelict wharves and abandoned warehouses, it had been turned into a massive shopping/sports/recreational/convention facility. It seemed the ideal location.

I wanted to know about catering. I'd heard that many conference venues were serving something called Bush Tucker to delegates – a selection of uniquely Australian delicacies such as lillipillies, tosella parakeets, muntharis and quandongs. Could he tell me what it was like? No way. The possums were not only taking over the house but his life as well.

'I keep catching them and throwing them out. But they keep coming back,' he complained.

'Take them over water,' said Kev. 'They say if you take them over water they'll never return.'

'Jeez,' he cried, 'I've taken them to Manley. But the damn things keep coming back.'

'Look,' I said finally, 'this is crazy. Let's go and look at some venues instead.'

'Great,' Kevin squealed. 'Let's go to the State Theatre. It's Joan Sutherland's favourite theatre. Make a great conference venue.'

'You mean she likes the acoustics?' I ventured.

'No,' Kevin shrieked. 'She likes the men's john. Whenever she's in Sydney she holds court there.'

The great Australian soprano had apparently mistaken the pioneers' room, as Sydneysiders discreetly call the gents, for a lounge and marched in smartly to give an interview to one of Australia's top television personalities. According to Kev the theatre was now famous all over Australia – at least its john was.

Sydney claims to be cosmopolitan, but somehow, even though it boasts practically every colour, creed and race you can think of, they all look and behave and act as Australians. Their diversity is their uniformity.

Pick up a cab along George Street or by Martin Place, the big pedestrian precinct in the middle of the city, and the driver can be Croatian or Romanian. Order a beer in a Chinese restaurant in Paddington, the Soho of Sydney, and the student waitress can as easily be from Taiwan, Vietnam or Cambodia as from Hong Kong. Jump on a bus to Circular Quay – sorry, ask a bus to kneel before you – and the driver could be Irish, German, or even English.

Trouble is, everybody seems to find it easier to tell you where they are from than what they are now. Being Cambodian or Romanian or Irish is somehow more definite than being Australian. All the Australians I met seemed to think they were a cross between Californians and English. If the sun was shining – and the sun shines most of the time in Sydney – everybody seemed to think they were second-class Californians. The weather was fabulous, but not as fabulous as in California; the beaches were great, but not as great as in Malibu. Their life style was great, but San Francisco was better. Darling Harbour with its shops and bars and restaurants was terrific, but somehow Pier 39 was out of this world. It was as if deep down they thought Australia was a California created by Englishmen. In other words, it was pretty good – but nothing like the real thing.

It was much the same with businessmen. Sydney was a major business centre, but for real business you had to go to Tokyo, Hong Kong, even Taiwan. Sydney was a thriving financial centre, but for real deals you had to go to London or Frankfurt or New York.

Yet everybody seemed proud of being Australian, of being laid back, of living the good life in the sunshine. The ultimate proof of their relaxed attitude to life is the story of the stained glass windows in Sydney Cathedral. For they were fitted in the wrong order. As a result the Cardinal receives his red hat for building the cathedral before he has even declared it open. But the church authorities just left them as they were. Relaxed or not, however, I found that Sydneysiders were prouder still if they could tell you they were plugged into other parts of the world as well.

Spurred on by its 150th anniversary in 1992 and its bid for the Olympics in 2000, Sydney has suddenly become a major force in the convention business. Whole areas of derelict land have been turned into super-modern convention centres. Hotels have sprung up on every street corner. The Novotel Hotel looks like a giant pink pyramid, the Hotel Nikko like a giant ocean liner. In the last five years the number of first-class hotel rooms has doubled to over 15,000; within the next five years it is scheduled to double again.

As a result, wherever you go you run into conference delegates – from all over Asia, from the west coast of the States (even from California, which I thought contradicted many Sydneysider attitudes), and from Europe. Not many of the ones I met were there simply because it was Sydney. They were also there because Sydney is a great place to get away from. People kept telling me that as soon as the conference was over they were heading off; to the Great Barrier Reef, to Melbourne, to Adelaide, to the Hobart triangle, to Tobruk sheep station. Anything, it seemed, but spend another day in Sydney.

The conferences ranged from massive 10,000-delegate shows like the World Chemotherapy Congress down to a seminar for the Fellows of the Institute of Short People, which Kev maintained was the smallest event they'd ever put on.

One evening at the Hyatt I met a number of senior managers and directors from some of Australia's gold-mining companies, in town for an international conference. Times, they all complained, were hard. The economy was no longer waltzing. It was crawling around the dance floor on its hands and knees. They were deep in recession. On top of that they were being subject to stricter and stricter financial controls. 'Nobody can afford to travel first class any more or get a box at the races,' they kept saying.

Having been the third largest gold producer in the world, they could see nothing but declining production ahead. From a peak of 220 tonnes, one manager was forecasting future annual production levels as low as 90 tonnes. Many were contemplating mergers and acquisitions. A few were considering going overseas and trying to set up mining operations either on their own or in co-operation with others. Indonesia and Papua New Guinea seemed favourite spots to explore. A few were talking about Africa.

But then as one tinnie of Fosters followed another, the recession was forgotten and everybody went on to the second most popular subject among businessmen the world over; the declining standard of education for their children.

'Absolutely appalling,' one hard-nosed company chairman complained. 'Teacher sent us a note. Said she was taking the children on a picnic and would we make certain they all had their Vegemite sandwiches. But she couldn't spell Vegemite. Now when Australians can't even spell Vegemite . . .'

I wanted to ask them about the outrageous stories I had heard of increasing sex discrimination in Australia. In the fifties trams and trains had separate compartments for men and women. In the sixties hotels had segregated drinking areas. Only men were allowed in public bars; women were confined to ladies' lounges. Then in the seventies and eighties all the old male preserves and clubs caved in and admitted women; even, I was told, the exclusive Melbourne Club.

Now, however, with more women taking a leading role in politics and being elected state premiers, the trend is being thrown sharply into reverse and more and more women are openly discriminating against men. Women-only areas are being established in towns and on public transport. Special 'ladies only' seating is being provided in parks and other public places.

But they didn't want to talk. Like a bunch of sooks, they all disappeared to a belt-tightening male-only recession meal of summer salad with galantine of quail followed by smoke-scented lamb loin with a three-pepper ratatouille washed down by bottle after bottle of Penfolds Grange Hermitage, which must be the best value wine in the world at present.

I escaped to the bar for a XXXX. I pushed my way through a bunch of Ockers talking about something called an MPI. Three policemen had been attacked by Aborigines with frozen kangaroo tails in the remote Northern Territory. After the attack, the Aborigines ate the evidence. It was, they kept shouting at each other, an MPI.

'What's an MPI?' I asked the barman.

'A matter of public importance,' he said.

The next two days I spent visiting hotels, checking out conference facilities, trying to put together a social pro-gramme and, of course, desperately thinking of something for the spouses to do other than go shopping.

The best hotels, I thought, were the Hyatt, Novotel Sydney and the Nikko Darling. The best restaurants, out of more than 2,000 listed on over thirty pages of the local Yellow Pages, I thought, were Doyle's at the Quay, a fabulous fish restaurant, and Imperial Peking Harbourside, both on Circular Quay. Alternatively, any of the other 1,998 which serves swags – sizzling beef sausages – and carpetbag steaks complete with oysters or yabbies – freshwater crayfish. The new Sydney Convention and Exhibition Centre was superb; but every hotel could organise a conference. Even the Opera House was for hire at the right price.

Shopping, as I've said, I'm no good at. To me one shop is as boring as the next, and two shops are more boring than one shop. But whatever kind of shop you wanted, Sydney had it. They also had their own special sales approach. One men's wear shop in the Victoria Centre simply had a big sign in the window saying, 'Hey Dudes. Bart Simpson shirts on sale here.'

Wherever I went, people were unfailingly polite; maybe not as excessively polite as in California – perhaps with just a hint of British reserve. They were also very accessible. Doing business is casual and relaxed. Sydney, I concluded, was the place for a conference.

'About Sydney, sir,' I said marching into the chairman's office on my return.

'Sydney? Sydney who?'

'Sydney, sir. Sydney, Australia. For the sales conference.'

'Oh that. Forget it. We're going to Scarborough, didn't I tell you? Nice place Scarborough. Whatever made you think we were going to Sydney?' His indecision was final.

'G'day,' I said, and left.

Boston

Wine books; six-feet-long telescopes weighing 4.5 cwt; teddy bears: businessmen take the wildest things on overseas trips. Especially their secretaries. One American I know always travels with his current secretary. 'Meet my latest single,' he always bawls at me across a crowded departure lounge. But somehow wives are different. Especially other men's wives.

I had it all worked out. Originally I was scheduled to fly out to Boston, or Bawhston, as they say, on Saturday. I was going to rest up at the Ritz-Carlton with its white-gloved 'elevator operators' and drive leisurely through New England on Sunday to see whether the fall foliage was really one of the seven wonders of the world or just the kind of thing that stops my train from Buxted arriving on time at Victoria between the end of summer and the beginning of winter.

I arrived at Boston as planned. From Logan International Airport I telephoned the Ritz-Carlton and asked to be put through. A gin-soaked cackle answers the 'phone.

'Hello, could I speak to your father, please?' I say automatically.

'Oh that's not my father,' squawks the three witches of Macbeth rolled into one. 'That's my husband.'

'Oh. I'm sorry,' I say, wishing I'd never said it. But before I could stop myself I was saying, 'But you sound so young.'

'Henry, Henry!' I could hear the cackle ricocheting across the empty Beefeaters. 'This nice man on the 'phone thinks you're my father.' Silence. 'He says I sound so young.' Even longer silence. I felt my bowels beginning to shrivel within me, as Charles Ryder would say. This was obviously a marriage made in hell.

'I guessed it was you,' said a voice I didn't recognise.

'Look, I'm sorry,' I whispered. 'How was I to know? You never told me. If you'd—'

'I know, I know,' said a more recognisable voice. 'It's just that. Oh. Never mind.'

'So, listen, are we still going to . . .?'

'I don't know. I'll call you back.'

'Okay. Any time. No problem.' I put the 'phone down. What could I do?

I tried all the hotels. Full. It was Columbus Weekend, and the Regatta, and Oktoberfest across the Charles River in Harvard Square, Cambridge. The only place that had a vacancy was the Guest Quarters, the big suite hotel, way past Back Bay. Except they had no suites, only one single. I took it.

Normally I take the airport water shuttle across the huhbah or harbour, which does not have quite the same charm as arriving at Venice and hopping on a boat to your hotel, but it's usually fast and cheap. This time, because I was going to the other end of town, I took a cab. As I got in I noticed that the driver was reading the Bible which he had strapped to the centre of the steering wheel. After about an hour crawling through the tunnel to the nowhere-near Express Way, I asked the driver, who by now must have finished the second Book of Kings, how much longer it was going to take.

'Hell,' he said, 'it's only another couple of miles. About seven hours.'

Reading about Elijah and his chariot of fire, I thought, was one thing. Couldn't he use his influence to get me there quicker? The city, he told me, recognised the problem. It was the only city in the States where people could triple-park without being towed away. They were building a five-lane tunnel beneath the city to get the traffic moving again. It was one of the biggest transportation projects in the States, costing around US$5 billion. If they didn't do something, they estimated that within five years it would take seven hours to cross the city.

'Fantastic,' I said. 'When is it going to be ready?'

'In ten years' time,' he said and went back to his Bible.

I got to the Guest Quarters in the middle of the night. They had let my room. They didn't think I was coming.

'But . . . But . . .' I began.

'No need to get toothache.' The girl in reception gave the standard 'no problem' smile. 'I sutton we can gittah nother one for yuh. It's even bettah.'

Even better! I've been in some hotels in my life, but never a room like this. It was, I swear, designed for a dwarf. Everything was low, and tiny with it. The bed was low. The bath was practically in the floor. The wardrobe? I hung my shirts in the wardrobe and they doubled up on the floor. Was it worth complaining? Was it worth asking for another room? Hell, this was Columbus Weekend, Regatta weekend, Oktoberfest weekend. And in any case we were going on a fall foliage tour . . .

I rang the Ritz-Carlton again. 'This is Harry's daughter,' rasped the cackle. 'I'm so looking forward to . . .' The 'phone sounded as if it had been dropped inside a cocktail shaker.

'I guessed it was you,' Harry's voice whispered down the line.

'Look, about—'

'Don't worry, we're still going,' he said quickly. 'I'll see you around eight.'

'Look forward to it.'

'Except she's coming as well.' What could I say? 'And she's insisting on driving.' The line went dead.

Bawhston is one of my favourite American cities. If I had to be bawn Amerikern, it would be a pleashaw to be bawn in Bawhston and speak propuh English. I like their approach to life; the way they describe the Bawhston Tee Potty; how Paul Revere, the patron saint of Bawhston, razed the alahm by screaming the British are coming, even though most of the

British army was already billeted in town. And I just adoah the way they apologise because there's no lift or air-conditioning inside the monument on Bunker Hill, which incidentally should have been built on Breed's Hill nearby where the battle actually took place and which was not a victory for the Americans but a defeat. But that's not impawtant now.

An Italian Bostonian once gave me the best explanation I've heard for the Great Fire of Boston. 'There were snipers on the roof, right? They had to get rid of the snipers, right?'

'Right,' I said.

'So what d'they do? They burn the town down. No roofs, no snipers, right?'

To me, Boston seems somehow more civilised than most US towns and cities. It is calm, quiet and safe. It's also the kind of town other Americans like because it gives them a chance to wear the new clothes they would never risk wearing at home. I mentioned this to a Bostonian.

'Sure,' he drawled. 'Half of Boston's built on land-fill from all ovah America. That's why they all feel at home here.'

Another thing is that the Boston Irish deliberately decided to use the Red Hand of Ulster on the traffic lights; not to keep the pedestrians in order – it doesn't – but to remind people how bad things could be if they weren't in charge.

I like Beacon Hill on the north side of Boston Common, with its narrow eighteenth-century streets where they keep the gas lights on day and night – presumably because they've heard that they're not dependent on the Arabs for the gas. Charles Street, at the bottom of the hill, is always fun. The bookshops are the only ones I've ever seen which have a special category for anonymous authors. I've still nevah bin to the Bull and Finch pub facing the public gardens which is the setting for *Cheers*, the late lamented television series which to Americans seemed more important than the Constitution.

Sunday afternoon, if I get the chance, I like strolling down Newbury Street, which looks to me like an up-market resi-dential street which has fallen on bad times and has opened up the ground floors of the houses as shops. Bostonians, however, insist on telling you it is one of the top three most expensive retail sharping areas in the States. It's so expensive that the dress shops are called wear-houses. None of them is allowed to sell secondhand, or as they say in Harvard, 'vintage' clothes. Instead they call them 'closet clothes' because they've just come out of the closet. What's more they don't have anything as common as litter bins. They have wine barrels instead. Even the Church of the Covenant on the corner of Berkeley Street boasts more Tiffany glass than anywhere else in the world.

There is a pet shop called A Fish on a Leash and, one of my favourites, Emak and Bolios, sell fabulous frozen yoghurts. Eat their whole range of thirty-five in one go and they give you a prize: another range of thirty-five.

'But why Emak and Bolios?' I once asked them.

'Everybody calls their shop after the owners. We thought the customers were more important, so we named it after our first two customers,' they told me.

I like popping across to Cambridge and wandering around Harvard Square, which is supposed to have the greatest concentration of bookshops in the whole US. Harvard itself always feels like an old school university built by a red-brick architect even though it was only built in the 1920s with a $2 million cheque written over lunch by George Eastwood, who founded Kodak.

During Oktoberfest, Harvard Square becomes a cross between a street market, a jumble sale, a music festival and an African market. Trouble is you can't tell whether the hustlers are illegal immigrants, genuine shopkeepers or Harvard professors of marketing in pursuit of excellence.

One year the hit of the show was a knockwurst. 'What's a knockwurst?' I asked the marketing expert serving out what looked like ordinary hot dogs. 'It's a brockwurst soaked in beer,' he said. 'Next.'

A Senegalese professor of marketing next to him, who I'm sure was one of the gang of sellers who chase me all over

Dakar whenever I go there, was doing a roaring trade selling secondhand, sorry, closet clothes. 'No obligations,' he kept shouting.

I retreated, not to Words Worth, but to the bookshop opposite which I somehow felt knew what it was like trying to sell books to students. 'Cambridge Booksmith', said its sign. 'Dedicated to the fine art of browsing.'

And I just love that accent.

Sunday morning I was at the Ritz-Carlton early with my old Everyman copy of Thoreau's *On Walden Pond*. Instead of going to Mass at the cathedral, I went to St Anthony's Shrine which turned out to be 'the Worker's Chapel' in the financial area. But it was not a shrine, or even a chapel. It was more like an ecclesiastical department store with wide open stairways leading to different Masses in different languages on different floors. I chose the English Mass on the ground floor, although for all I could tell it might have been the Spanish or the Italian. Or perhaps it was just the Mass in Boston English. All I could see was the priest waving his finger during the sermon, then pointing sharply to a door with a big red sign on top saying Exit.

I walked across Boston Common, where there is the most miserable statue I've ever seen of four broken-down knights on even more broken-down horses which Bostonians tell me is Dukakis' campaign committee preparing for another shot at the presidency. In the Botanical Gardens, crossing what was once the smallest suspension bridge in the world, I came across a bearded, no-good, down-at-heel tramp slumped against the wall whispering into a two-way radio. Which maybe explains a lot about the calm and quiet and safety of Boston.

As soon as I get to the Ritz-Carlton, which boasts that to date Bush is the only US president not to have stayed there, I call Henry. 'Be right down,' he snaps.

I go to the kiosk and buy the *Sunday Boston Globe* and the *New York Times*. Within five minutes, I've read them both from cover to cover; all 2,000 pages, all 400 supplements and colour magazines. And I still don't know what's happening in the world. US newspapers, I'm convinced, are designed to carry advertisements, not to report the news. In any case how Americans can even pretend that they have time to read beats me. They're always busy, even when they're taking it easy. I mean, Americans don't play tennis any more. They improve their backhand.

Nearly two hours later, when I've practically re-read Thoreau, Henry and wife arrive. The hired car is a large, gleaming red Cadillac. The wife jumps straight into the driving seat, switches on the engine and shoots away. Henry and I leap in. The doors are still open.

'The door,' gasps Henry.

'Well aren't you going to close it for me?' she snaps. 'If you saw it was open, why didn't you close it?'

'I couldn't close it because I was trying to get in.'

I slump down on the back seat and try to think of Henry David Thoreau, a Bostonian who fled to Walden Pond. Was it, I thought, as a result of a drive in the country with Henry and wife? Suddenly at the junction with Commonwealth Avenue – the inspiration, Bostonians will tell you, of Nat King Cole's song 'On the sunny side of the street' – she turns on a quarter, swings into Dartmouth Street and stops. I collect myself from the floor of the car. 'If you'd have passed me my camera quickly I wouldn't have had to stop,' she barks at poor Henry. Cars are hooting, sirens blaring all around us. 'That dog,' she says. 'I've never seen a dog like it before.'

'But don't you think . . .?' She thrusts the camera back at him. 'Thank you for putting the cap back on,' she hisses.

We shot forward, heading I thought west to Worcester and Springfield on the Massachusetts Turnpike, although all the best fall foliage tours – see the greatest FREE show on earth. Adults: $35.00. No admission, meals or driver's gratuity included – head north to the Crotched Mountains and New Hampshire. That's what the tour companies tell you. Bostonians tell you the only reason everybody goes to New Hampshire is because they don't have any tax on liquor. A trip looking at trees is one thing, but a trunk full of cheap booze is even bettah.

Thoreau claimed that he would tramp eight or ten miles through the snow just to look at beech trees, but today some Bostonians are saying he is a fake. Instead of being virtually the first Green, they say, he was a useless mummy's boy who lived on Beacon Hill with his mother until one day, frustrated because he couldn't get a job, he upped and fled to Walden Pond. What's more, they say, his hut wasn't so much a hut as a fully furnished, comfortable, well-appointed country cottage. And as for being a recluse and living a life of solitude in mystic communion with nature, he was in Concord at least once a week doing his shopping. And what's more they have the shopkeepers' diaries to prove it.

Paul Revere gets the opposite treatment. The now legendary Paul Revere wasn't famous at all until Henry Wordsworth Longfellow came along and wrote his poem in 1861 about his midnight ride 'On the eighteenth of April in Seventy-five'. Before that practically nobody had heard of him. He wasn't mentioned by historians of the time as being involved with the War of Independence. He wasn't even mentioned in any biographical dictionaries. Less than ten years after the poem was published, he had practically won the Waw singlehanded. He was hailed as the greatest miniaturist, artist, coppersmith, silversmith, blacksmith, architect, statesman, horseman and father of sixteen that ever lived: a kindah Minuteman, Clint Eastwood and Terminator all rolled into one. From then on no civil war history was complete unless Paul Revere's name was on every other page; no dictionary of national biography could publish without him. Even J.P. Morgan was prepared to blow $100,000 for one of his silver punchbowls.

'Help,' Henry suddenly screamed. 'You're on the wrong side of the road.'

'Well, if you gave me the correct directions I wouldn't be.'

'Okay, I'll drive then.'

'No. I'll drive. You're no good at navigating, I'm better than you. But I'll drive.'

I slipped further down the back seat. I could just about see some leaves, but whether Massachusetts leaves or New Hampshire leaves I couldn't tell.

'Which turning is it?' I grabbed the edge of the car. 'Left,' said Henry. The car swung right. 'I said left,' Henry said gently.

'Oh for God's sake get it right,' she screamed over the screech of brakes as we did an immediate 180° turn.

'I didn't say, turn round,' Henry said in a voice that was getting calmer and calmer. The lull before the storm, I was almost frightened to think to myself.

'Yes you did.'

'No I —'

'Well why should I turn round then? Answer me that.'

Oh for Walden Pond, I thought, and the beech trees and yellow birches. I wouldn't even care if a sparrow never sat on my shoulder.

'We're on Route 93,' she cackled.

'It's not possible. We're on Route 95,' whispered the man who in the office terrifies everyone, including the chairman. If you're five minutes late he rains down upon you every curse under the sun. But now? With his wife?

'I tell you it's Route 93. You've given me the wrong directions again.'

'Well I'll drive then.'

'No.'

We drove for I don't know how long in absolute silence. I was frightened to move in case the fires of hell were called down upon me. Then suddenly the brakes were slammed on again. I shot on to the floor. The car, I swear, almost stood on its bumper.

'Oh shut up,' she screamed.

'But I didn't say —'

'Trust you to be in one of your moods. It's always the same whenever I want to enjoy a day off.'

I eased myself slowly back on to the seat.

'Where are we?'

'We can't be.'

'Not according to the map.'

'Well the map is wrong.'

'The car shot forward again. Didn't Henry James say something about summer afternoons being the two most beautiful words in the English language?

'Shall I turn here?'

'Yes, if you want to ...'

'Well you've got the map.'

'Yes, but it depends where you want to ...'

'Give me the map.' For heaven's sake, I thought, give her the map. 'See, you're wrong. We're here, not there. You need a new pair of glasses.'

'No, I don't.'

'Look, you're squinting now. Why you won't go to see about your eyes I don't know. It's just because I ask you to, that's why.'

Wait till I tell everyone back at the office, I thought, especially the chairman; he won't have to feel so guilty about being late for meetings in future. Was the car slowing down? It was, and gently. Chances were I'd not be thrown on to the floor again. I looked up out of the window. I couldn't see the wood for the leaves. We were turning into what looked like a cross between a Tudor manor and a Scottish castle.

Inside it was sumptuous – the rooms enormous, the decorations luxurious. They even had, I was assured, 'working fireplaces'. The meal was fabulous. The company, however, was chilled. The conversation was zero. Apart from when the waitress asked if we were having wine. 'Yes, please,' Henry and I smiled at her.

'No you don't,' the wife barked. 'You know you always get a headache when you drink. Have a coffee instead.' No wine, I screamed silently to myself. I didn't dare look at Henry. A headache. This I must tell everybody.

A card on the table told me all about autumn. 'In the annual pattern of fall foliage the leaves of deciduous trees start to show vivid colouring when night temperatures drop to 40°F or lower. That starts a chemical process that halts the production of chlorophyll, the chemical that gives leaves their green colour, permitting other colours to become visible. As the chlorophyll disappears, yellow appears in poplars, birches, tulip trees and sycamore leaves, produced by carotene. The most brilliant colours of all, bright orange, red and crimson, appear in maples caused by another chemical, anthocyamin. A little later, the same chemical causes the oaks, the last trees of the fall to change colour, to appear brown, signalling the beginning of winter.' So that's why we came all this way.

I washed down my lunch with coffee, a gastronomic experience I'll never forget. I then excused myself and fled to the countryside. The leaves, in the circumstances, looked fantastic. Completely different from the ones that delay my train to London for hours every autumn.

The drive back to Boston was better than the drive coming. Because we were going back. I read Thoreau and looked at the trees. They really were a mass of colours; light browns, dark browns, red, yellow, gold. The Irish sing about a thousand shades of green. These leaves, whether I was in Massachusetts or New Hampshire, were truly spectacular.

I'm beginning to feel relaxed and happy. Maybe I won't tell everybody back at the office about . . .

'Whatd'yadothatfor?' Henry suddenly shrieks in blind terror.

I drop my book in panic.

'I can get petrol can't I?' sneers the wife in the nicest, slimiest tone I've heard her use all day. 'Or do I have to ask your permission?'

That does it. Now I am definitely going to tell everybody; I don't care what happens. Enough is enough. Even poor old Thoreau would have cracked under this strain. Wife gets out, stomps to the back of the car then stomps back again.

'How do you open the petrol cap?' he screams.

'I don't know,' Henry replies carefully. 'I thought when you hired the . . .'

'Well you could have been looking while I was waiting. Or have I got to do everything?'

'Are there any levers?'

'How do I know? I've been driving.'

Henry shuffles across into the driving seat and starts trying the switches and levers. He puts his hand on the brake. 'Goodness me,' he screams, 'it's red hot. The brake's boiling. Have you been driving all this time with the brake . . .?'

Now I am going to tell the whole world and nothing's going to stop me.

'How do I know?' she barks back at him. 'If you don't know where the petrol is, I'll have to ask.' She storms towards the pay kiosk. An attendant follows her back and flicks a switch on the car floor. 'Okay, shake it,' he says and wanders back to the kiosk.

'Why didn't you know that?' she barks at Henry. 'Maybe if you spent less time working and more time at home you'd know about things like that.'

Henry got out, fixed the petrol, went over to the pay kiosk, came back to the car, climbed in, put the money on top of the dashboard. 'Shall I leave the money there for you?' he whispered.

'I can't do everything,' she snapped crunching the car into gear and ostentatiously taking the brake off for all the world to see. 'You want me to put it in your pocket for you?' She swung straight on to the middle of the ten-lane highway without stopping, let alone looking to see if anything was coming. Then for the first time she actually acknowledged my presence. She turned round. 'Expects me to do everything,' she smiled.

I went cold. It wasn't the size of the ten-storey truck that was hurtling straight towards us at the regulation 55 mph. It wasn't because I was cursing other men's wives, especially on business trips. It was because I suddenly found myself praying in that Bawhston accent.